PALESTINE JEWRY AND THE ARAB QUESTION 1917–1925

Palestine Jewry
and the
Arab Question
1917–1925

Neil Caplan

FRANK CASS

First published 1978 in Great Britain by
FRANK CASS AND COMPANY LIMITED
Gainsborough House, Gainsborough Road,
London, E11 1RS, England

and in the United States of America by
FRANK CASS AND COMPANY LIMITED
c/o Biblio Distribution Centre
81 Adams Drive, P.O. Box 327, Totowa, N.J. 07511

ISBN 0 7146 3110 8

British Library Cataloguing in Publication Data
Caplan, Neil
  Palestine Jewry and the Arab question, 1917–1925.
  1. Palestine – History – 1917–1948
  2. Palestine – Politics and government
  3. Jewish–Arab relations – 1917–1949
  I. Title
  956.94'04   DS126

  ISBN 0–7146–3110–8

Printed in Great Britain by offset lithography by
Billing & Sons Ltd, Guildford, London and Worcester

For Mary and Nat
my loving parents

Contents

Acknowledgments

I feel privileged to have been under the guidance of Professor Elie Kedourie when preparing the academic dissertation on which this book is based, and wish to express my warmest appreciation to him. During my stay in Israel I was fortunate to have had the additional advice and encouragement of Dr Y. Porath. I also wish to express my appreciation to the following people for their generous advice and assistance: Dr Y. Bauer, Mr Y. Gil-har, Dr S. L. Hattis-Rolef, Dr Y. Heller, Dr M. Heymann, Dr I. Kollat, Dr N. J. Mandel-Lamdan, Mr E. Marmorstein, Mr E. Rubinstein and Professor M. Vereté.

I am grateful to Jennie and Emile Marmorstein, Miri Hexter and Tana Weiss for their translations of several German and Yiddish documents.

I owe a great deal to my good friends, Drs Bernard Wasserstein and Moshe Mossek, for their unselfish assistance on many fronts.

I am grateful to the Directors of the following archives for permission to consult material, and to their staffs for their kind personal attention: Central Zionist Archives (CZA) and Israel State Archives (ISA), both in Jerusalem; Weizmann Archive (WA), Rehovot; Private Papers Collection, Middle East Centre, St. Antony's College, Oxford; and Public Record Office (PRO). I would also like to record my appreciation for their special attention to: Mr I. Philip, CZA; Mr H.

Solomon and Ms Yosepha Tislitski, ISA; and Mrs Louisa Calef, WA.

The original research undertaken was made possible by the generous financial support of the Canada Council. I am also grateful to the Québec Government, the Truman Institute of the Hebrew University, and the Vanier College Professional Development Fund for grants which allowed me to undertake the revision of the original manuscript for publication in its present form.

In the later stages of preparing the manuscript, I was fortunate to have the prompt and generous assistance of Eli Shaaltiel and Nehama Chalom.

For her devotion and constant help throughout, my wife Marilyn merits the greatest acknowledgment of all.

Montreal, April, 1978   N.C.

List of Abbreviations

(* – see Bibliography)

AE	Arab Executive (Executive Committee of Palestine Arab Congress)
ACS	Assistant Chief Secretary, Palestine Government
APC	Anglo-Palestine [Banking] Co.
CO	Colonial Office
CPO	Chief Political Officer, EEF
CS	Chief (or Civil) Secretary, Palestine Government
CZA	Central Zionist Archives (*)
DG	District Governor
DMI	Director of Military Intelligence
EEF	Egyptian Expeditionary Force
EZF	English Zionist Federation
FO	Foreign Office
GSI	General Staff Intelligence
HC	High Commissioner for Palestine
ICA	Jewish Colonisation Association
ISA	Israel State Archives (*)
JA (E)	Jewish Agency for Palestine (Executive)
JNF	Jewish National Fund
LC	Legislative Council
LPCW	*Letters and Papers of Chaim Weizmann* (*)
MCA	Muslim-Christian Association

MG	Military Governor
MNA	Muslim National Association
OETA (S)	Occupied Enemy Territory Administration (South)
PLDC	Palestine Land Development Company
PRE XII ZC	*Political Report of the Executive to the XIIth Zionist Congress* (*)
PRO	Public Record Office (*)
PZE	Palestine Zionist Executive
SMC	Supreme Muslim Council
STH	*Sefer Toldot ha-Hagana* (*)
VL (E)	*Va'ad Leumi* (Executive)
VZ (E)	*Va'ad Zmani* (Executive)
WA	Weizmann Archive (*)
ZAC	Zionist Actions Committee
ZC	Zionist Commission to Palestine
ZE	Zionist Executive (London)
ZO	Zionist Organisation
Zst Cong	Zionist Congress

Preface

It is impossible to write about the early stages of the Arab-Zionist conflict without being conscious of the fact that the subject is still a delicate and controversial issue for many people. As a result, unfortunately, too much of the literature on the subject is given to justification and/or attempts at persuading the reader to support the cause of one side or another.

It is not my intention here to add to the list of works devoted to balancing 'right' against 'wrong' or 'justice' against 'injustice'. Neither is it my intention to present a history of missed opportunities in the noble search for solutions to the Arab-Zionist conflict. Perhaps out of too much respect for the maximalist positions of the parties involved, the present study makes no attempt to discern desirable solutions or to chastise any party for missing a peace settlement that might or should have been. My underlying assumption throughout is that there is no overall, rational solution to this dispute.

To many observers today, the continuing state of war between Israel and the Arab world is proof that the leaders of Zionism – by what they have done or, more often, failed to do in their relations with the Arabs over the years – are primarily responsible for creating or aggravating an 'Arab problem'. The present examination of the attitudes of members of the Palestinian Jewish community – the 'Yishuv' – would seem to

contradict this view of widespread Zionist ignorance or neglect. What does emerge, on the contrary, is a picture of
Palestine Jewry's acute awareness of a real *gap* already
separating the basic positions of Jews and Arabs in Palestine
during the period under review.

When dealing with so sensitive a subject, the researcher is
often faced with the problem of distinguishing between what
was 'really' believed and what was said or written for the
requirements of good public relations. To the extent that it is
at all possible to determine what Zionists 'really' thought
about the 'Arab question', we may be brought a little closer to
a balanced and accurate account by studying private correspondence, minutes of closed debates or secret meetings, etc.
In the case of studying the Yishuv, some other advantages
become apparent. Many Palestinian Jews displayed a refreshing lack of patience for circuitous 'politics' and public relations exercises, preferring to approach the 'Arab question'
with a minimum of self-delusion. Leading Yishuv personalities, in addition, were imbued with the feeling that they
were 'creating history' in the vanguard of modern Zionism,
and have taken pains to preserve their letters, diaries,
speeches and writings, many of which are now available in
published collections.

The present study is based primarily on archive materials of
the central bodies of the Yishuv, the Zionist offices in Palestine and in London, and the British authorities in those places.
I have supplemented these materials with several basic works
on the Palestinian Arabs, the Jewish community, and the
published letters and writings of several leading personalities.
(See also, 'Note on Archival Sources', page 252.)

I have tried to use commonsense and consistency in the
transliteration of Hebrew and Arabic words. The letter *'ain* is
denoted by a diacritical mark ('). An apostrophe (') is occasionally inserted for ease of pronunciation. The silent *he* at the
end of certain words is transliterated only when required for
pronunciation. I have not altered the commonly-accepted
English spelling of certain words (e.g., *Zion, Po'alei-Zion*).

Introduction

Although the intricacies of Middle Eastern politics and society have long been a popular subject in the West, recent interest of many Europeans and Americans has been generated and sustained largely by a single topic – the Arab-Israeli dispute. To outsiders this has become 'the' Middle East conflict. To Arabs, it is the 'Palestine question' or the question of 'Zionism' and 'imperialism'. And to most Jews and Israelis it is known as the 'Arab question'. This book is written primarily from the latter perspective.

The Zionist movement has, between 1882 and 1948, succeeded in changing the map of the Middle East to include the Jewish state of Israel. This change could not have been accomplished without political endorsement from the 'powers' of the day; the mobilisation of Jewish commitment, funds and immigrants; and the sacrifices and ingenuity required by land-reclamation, colonisation and economic development. But, above and beyond these challenges, which have been met with ultimate success, there was a further obstacle to overcome, the legacy of which still haunts today's Israelis. This was the alteration of the basic demographic, social and political facts of the area – in short, the change from 'Palestine' to 'Israel'.

The area known to the English-speaking world as Palestine at the turn of the present century has always been known to most Jews as *Eretz-Yisrael*, the land of Israel, the homeland of the Jews in biblical times. But it was an inconvenient fact for modern Zionism that this territory has been inhabited until recent decades by more non-Jews than Jews. When we add to this the further fact that the bulk of the resident Muslim and Christian population did not spontaneously welcome the new Jewish arrivals who claimed to be 'returning' to 'their' home-land, we have the makings of what has become known, to Zionists and Israelis, as the 'Arab question'.

The present study examines the confrontation of the Jewish community of Palestine – referred to in the following pages by its Hebrew name, 'the Yishuv' (lit., settlement) – with its Arab question in the period immediately following World War I. Our main focus will be on the different ways in which the men and women of the Yishuv perceived and defined the question of relations with the Arabs, and how they proposed to deal with the problems that arose.

The period begins (1917) with a situation of great excite-ment, expectation and uncertainty, which soon results in viol-ence perpetrated against the Jews of Palestine (1920, 1921). But gradually a sense of stability and security begins to be felt. By the end of our period (1925), a state of apparent calm and prosperity has been achieved, leading some – but not all – Zionists to the optimistic conclusion that most of their prob-lems, including the Arab question, have been effectively resolved.

Awareness of the Arab Question, 1917–1925

Although it is common to designate the Arab Revolt of 1936–39, or even the Wailing Wall riots of 1929, as a major turning-point for Yishuv attitudes on the Arab question, it is also possible to see different forms of 'awakening' to this problem during the period 1917–25, and even before 1914.[1] While the Arab question, as such, may not have been consis-tently in the forefront of popular concern or at the top of every meeting's agenda, the issue was nonetheless vitally interwoven into many aspects of Yishuv life after 1917: rela-tions with the new British rulers of Palestine; constitutional arrangements; Jewish immigration, land-purchase and settlement; education and cultural autonomy; diplomacy and relations with the Arab world outside of Palestine; and – most of all, in view of the uncertainty and insecurity of the years 1918–22 – defence from Arab attack.

Of course, the 'Arab question' meant different things to different people, but three main attitudes seem to be present during the period under discussion. An active minority saw it as a fundamental problem challenging the very moral foundations of Zionism; in this view, an accommodation with Arab opposition deserved priority consideration and 'peace' had to be obtained even at the cost of considerable concessions. A larger segment of Yishuv opinion took the question less seriously, regarding it as little more than a temporary obstruction, to be handled carefully and coaxed out of the way. A third, and perhaps the largest, segment of opinion viewed the Arab question as a real one, requiring effective counter-measures and defences which had to be developed in response to the serious demographic, political and/or physical threats posed by the Arabs.

In the following pages we shall find illustrations of all three tendencies, but it will be clear that most Yishuv circles were not as ignorant or unaware of the Arab question as some recent works have implied.[2] Studies of Jewish-Arab relations during the period 1882–1914 have suggested that 'the trend of subsequent developments in Palestine was already set' before 1914, and that the latent conflict had reached the stage where a number of people on each side were beginning to understand the aspirations and intentions of the other only too well.[3] The present examination of the years 1917–25 reveals a fairly widespread feeling in the Yishuv that there existed an almost unbridgeable gap between what the Zionists were committed to making out of Palestine, on the one hand, and what they believed their Arab 'neighbours' were insisting should *not* happen to the country, on the other. People who held this view quietly but firmly accepted the probability that the upbuilding of their national home, which they regarded as an historic necessity, would lead to an unfortunate, but unavoidable, clash with the Arabs.

For a variety of reasons, most Jews who came to believe that common consent would never resolve the conflict be-

tween Zionist and Arab interests did not publicise their
theories of a 'basic incompatibility'. For they realised that it
would have done little good to broadcast such a view for
outsiders to hear. After all, the support of their British protec-
tors, public opinion in England and abroad, and the sanction
of the League of Nations all rested on altogether different
assumptions. And were not the Arabs using the argument of
inevitable Zionist injustice to discredit the moral foundations
of the Palestine Mandate? Even for internal consumption,
such pessimistic analyses were not in order, for they ran the
risk of destroying the morale of all but the most committed
and hard-headed supporters of a movement which considered
its goals not only idealistic, historic and capable of realisation,
but also just in the absolute sense.

Yet, against the pessimists, there was also an active and
articulate minority of 'believers' – people driven by the overwhelming need to find a long-term solution to the Arab
question and by an undying optimism that a way to peace,
based on rational compromise and mutual concession, could
in fact be found. The most prominent among the optimists
during our period was Haim Margaliut Kalvaryski, the
Russian-born land-purchase agent who emigrated to Palestine in 1895. Kalvaryski cultivated many contacts and friends
among the Arab élites and became a controversial Yishuv
'specialist' on Arab affairs.[4] The 'bi-nationalist' thinkers who
became active after 1925 are another case in point,[5] while the
socialist-internationalist ideology of the Jewish labour
movement provided its own answers which prevented its followers from reaching despairing conclusions about relations
with the Arabs. The theory of a fundamental identity of
interests between the Jewish and Arab masses is of long
standing and may not yet be dead.[6]

In the end, despite their sincerity and conviction, individual
or small groups of 'peace-seekers' had little impact on the
majority, who continued after 1917 to find further confirma-
tion of their pessimism about the chances of arriving at an
agreement with the Arabs. Many drew on their experience
and practical wisdom to conclude that the Arab majority in
Palestine was unlikely to agree voluntarily to change places
with the Jews as majority and minority. One of the tacitly

accepted ways of dealing with the Arab question was *not* to think or talk about it unless it was absolutely necessary, and not to waste time and energy in making futile overtures or pursuing unreal negotiations.

There were, however, numerous occasions which required some form of outward response. When the situation demanded, Yishuv leaders made public statements reassuring the Arabs in a general way that Jewish intentions were peaceful, constructive, and would bring benefit to the Arabs. Frequent denials were issued to the accusation that the Zionists were contemplating the expropriation, expulsion or subjugation of the Arab population, or the desecration of its Holy Places. While Jewish progress and development in Palestine were thought to be bringing benefits to the Arabs in an automatic way, some concrete and visible efforts were also undertaken to assist the Arab 'neighbours', e.g. through easy or free access to Jewish medical services. At times, when the Arabs presented the Yishuv with a more immediate political or physical threat, various other means were used in the attempt to forestall or avert the anticipated danger. These latter responses are dealt with in this book under the headings *hagana* ('defence', or 'self-defence') and 'Arab work' (supporting 'moderates' against 'extremists', cultivating good press opinion, etc.) Even negotiations were sometimes considered a necessary expedient in such circumstances: if they succeeded in bringing about a certain 'peace', many felt, so much the better. Optimists, it is true, took a less cynical view and attached more importance to any talks with Arabs, but just as passionately as they believed that a rapprochement with the Arabs was essential, so would the majority grow progressively more sceptical that reconciliation was possible.

If most Yishuv leaders did not publicly express their concern for the Arab question by drafting peace plans which they hoped Arabs would sign, they did believe that they had an answer. This was to proceed as quickly as possible towards the creation of a strong and vibrant Jewish majority in Palestine – on the assumption that 'Arab psychology' understands and reacts appropriately to the fait accompli and to material prosperity. Many Zionist leaders explicitly defended large Jewish immigration and other forms of strengthening the Yishuv as the most effective response to the Arab question, and they steadfastly rejected the contention that these factors *aggravated* Arab hostility and that the key to 'peace' lay in the reduction or restriction of Zionist development.[7]

Jewish immigration was, of course, the basic business of Zionism, with or without any 'Arab question'. But, since the Arabs were there, immigration was also the specific tool by which the Jews were supposed to change places, by a peaceful process, with the Arabs as majority and minority. And, for those Zionists who stopped to do some calculations, it became obvious that, even without political opposition or a security threat, the numbers and the rate of natural increase of the Arabs presented the Yishuv with an 'Arab question' of considerable proportions. The first and second waves of Jewish immigration to Palestine (*aliyot* – singular, *aliya*, lit. 'ascent') had increased the local Jewish population (the 'Old Yishuv') from about 23–24,000 in 1882 to approximately 80–90,000 by 1914. Following the ravages of war and the Turkish expulsion of alien nationals and politically undesirables, the number of Jews in November 1918 was estimated by the British military authorities at 66,000, which represented 10 per cent of the population. By the end of the period we are discussing (June 1925), the number of Jews had nearly doubled to 122,000.[8] Yet, owing to the Arab natural increase and

POPULATION OF PALESTINE AND JEWISH IMMIGRATION
1918–1925

	1918 est.	*1922 census*	*1923 est.*	*1924 est.*	*1925 est.*
Arabs	572,883	660,641	681,421	701,754	717,006
Muslims	512,000	589,177	609,331	627,660	641,494
Christians	60,883	71,464	72,090	74,094	75,512
Jews	66,102	83,790	89,660	94,945	121,725
Others	153	7,617	7,908	8,263	8,507
Total	639,138	752,048	778,989	804,962	847,238
Jewish Immigration	?	7,844	7,421	12,856	33,801

Sources: See Note 8.

some Arab immigration, the Jewish proportion of the total population had risen to only 14 per cent (see table). Clearly, this race to outnumber the Arabs by a gradual process of immigration was going to take longer than most people had originally anticipated. This was a source of concern to Zionist leaders, and some of them doubted that the Arabs would be content to sit back and wait patiently while this slow process worked its way to its logical conclusion of a Jewish majority.[9]

Some Characteristics of the Palestinian Jewish Community

Before we enter into our discussion of Yishuv–Arab relations during 1917–25, a few general remarks about the Yishuv might be in order. In 1936 the Peel Commission found the Yishuv to be 'a highly educated, highly democratic, very politically-minded, and unusually young community'.[10] This perceptive observation is valid also for our period, 1917–25, with the addition of another trait: a pronounced heterogeneity, which for political purposes meant an embarrassing lack of unity. Indeed, the diversity and internal disunity of the Yishuv form a background feature which it is difficult to overlook. Successful relations of the Yishuv with the larger outside world – the Zionist movement, the British authorities and the Arab world – were hampered so long as the term, 'the Yishuv', denoted a disorganised, motley collection of sub-communities which for many years could not agree on a central communal organisation and leadership. This continually fluid and fast-growing society was made up of Jewish groups taken from diverse cultural backgrounds and espousing an assortment of religious, social and political ideals which were often in sharp conflict with one another. Today's Sephardi-Ashkenazi, secular-religious and other rifts in Israeli society were already present in the Yishuv of 1917–25, and the problem of internal disunity constituted something of an obsession, taking considerable energy away from other public issues.

Another dimension of the Yishuv which should be commented upon is its relationship to the Zionist world as a whole. To date, histories of Zionism have devoted little attention to the Yishuv as an independent factor. Instead, much has been written from the vantage-point of the great thinkers or leaders, the decision-making and internal ideological debates. Understandably, such studies have not felt it necessary to isolate the Palestinian Jewish community as a separate entity or to treat it as more than the secondary factor which it was, from these points of view, at least until the late 1930s. Despite the fact that the Yishuv was, in effect, the flesh-and-bones of the lofty ideal known as the 'Jewish National Home', the Palestinian Yishuv was for many years relegated to the back seat by the European Zionist leaders who were doing the driving.

The relations between Yishuv and 'outside' Zionist personalities were not always smooth and easy, and in matters affecting the Arab question difficulties came to the fore. Although the Yishuv was respected by Zionists abroad for its pioneering spirit and dedication, its local leaders were often considered to be difficult to get along with, unsophisticated, over-sensitive or obsessed with petty issues. For their part, Yishuv leaders came to look on the official Zionist leadership as overbearing, captive of diplomatic phrases, weak, inept and cut off from the realities in which *they* had to live in Palestine. Still, it was this team of 'outsiders' which controlled the Zionist Organisation and exercised, many in the Yishuv felt, too much power to decide the fate of the local people. The friction which developed between Yishuv and other Zionist leaders on the Arab question involved matters such as the need for Zionist funds for Yishuv-inspired projects and the proper role of Yishuv representatives in the consultative or decision-making processes.

Whatever the real power of the Yishuv vis-à-vis the Zionist leadership, it is nonetheless important to study the Yishuv as an independent factor for at least one reason. In the end it was the leadership and the spirit of the Yishuv – far more than the 'foreign' Zionist establishment – that came to provide the tone and direction of Israeli society today. In particular, the energetic and ideologically-motivated labour leaders of the second *aliya* (1904–14), who were in the ascendant during the period we are discussing, have become the overwhelming majority of the élite in modern Israeli society.[11]

Finally, a few remarks about some of the institutions and leading personalities who will be referred to in the pages that follow. Prior to October 1920, the *Va'ad Zmani l'Yhudai Eretz-Yisrael* (Provisional Council of the Jews of Palestine), or *Va'ad Zmani*, was the central body dealing with local matters. Its 'provisional' existence for almost three years before it finally convened a 'Constituent Assembly' testifies to the difficulty of achieving Yishuv consensus on organisational matters. The *Va'ad Zmani* had a membership of some thirty representatives and its principal organisers were Dr Ya'akov Thon and Bezalel Jaffe.

The Elected Assembly (*Assefat ha-Nivharim*) of October 1920 elected the first *Va'ad Leumi*, or National Council of the Jews of Palestine. The *Va'ad Leumi* consisted of thirty-six local leaders and was headed during the 1920s by a 'Praesidium' – Dr Thon, David Yellin (a Jerusalem notable) and Yitzhak Ben-Zvi (a labour leader; later second President of Israel) – and an Executive Council of fourteen. Both the *Va'ad Zmani* and *Va'ad Leumi* were the organs which embodied the Yishuv's slow and painful quest for a purposeful leadership which would transcend the particular loyalties of each sub-group to its own narrower goals and leaders. At the close of the period we are studying, the *Va'ad Leumi* had still not succeeded in making itself respected as the authoritative and supreme organ it was aspiring to become. Yet, even if it was incapable of unifying the entire Yishuv under its control and of presenting a single voice to the outside world, the *Va'ad Leumi* did provide a central forum for the exchange of the differing views on topics of concern, including the Arab question. Although this forum was frequently criticised and sometimes despised for its indecisiveness and powerlessness, it was nevertheless a valuable mirror of the various Yishuv opinions on the Arab question, and its debates are a major source of the material used in this study.

Mention should also be made of one other distinct Yishuv group which was becoming an important force in Yishuv politics at this time. The labour movement, with its own national and social orientation, consisted of several political parties united in the *Histadrut*, or General Federation of Jewish Workers in Palestine. Apart from running its own political and socio-economic organisations, the labour movement participated as a powerful bloc within the *Va'ad Leumi*, winning one-third of its seats in 1920. From the labour ranks came the dynamic leadership of men like David Ben-Gurion, Yitzhak Ben-Zvi, Moshe Shertok (Sharett) and Haim Arlosoroff. Their contribution to Yishuv politics increased from year to year.

Some of the personalities whose activities and ideas will be discussed below are better known than others whose political involvement was narrower or whose ideas made them marginal to the mainstream of public life. Biographical notes are appended for the benefit of the reader.

PART ONE

Under the Military Administration

1

In the Shadow of the Balfour Declaration, I: 1918

Jewish 'Exclusivism' in Palestine

Before the outbreak of the First World War, the Jews in Palestine had already provided themselves with a relatively sophisticated structure of regional and local associations and organisations, with social services and with an arbitration tribunal.[1] Most of those who arrived after 1882 (the 'New Yishuv') had immigrated with the conscious purpose of creating a new, self-contained Jewish society. Even Arthur Ruppin, a man known for his repeated warnings of the need to improve relations with the Arabs, insisted that the pattern of Jewish settlement had to avoid scattering Jews at random throughout the country, but had to concentrate on a few points. 'It is only in this fashion', he lectured the XIth Zionist Congress in 1913,

> that we can, within certain limits, achieve to-day the objective we have in view, namely the creation of a Jewish milieu and of a closed Jewish economy, in which producers, consumers and middlemen shall all be Jewish.[2]

Notwithstanding the occasional apologetics to the contrary, the Jews had not come to Palestine in order to combine with their 'semitic cousins' to form any sort of hybrid cultural, social or political unity.

It is not surprising to find that hostile critics of the new

Yishuv denounced it as 'exclusivist'.[3] The situation was to become even more awkward after 1918, when added to the resentment of suspicious native elements, Jews would meet with the further displeasure of the British, who instinctively saw the Jews offending their own good 'liberal' ideals. While some Jews were indeed sensitive to these charges of 'exclusivism', others insisted bluntly that there was nothing to be ashamed about, and that this was the natural way to fulfil the task of building a new life for Jews in a Jewish Palestine. Haim Margaliut Kalvaryski exemplified the former trend (see pp. 43 and 200 f., below), while Aaron Aaronsohn may be cited as an extreme exponent of the latter attitude. 'It is true', he wrote in an unsigned article prepared for the *Arab Bulletin* in 1917,

> that we have strictly avoided Arab infiltration in our villages, and we are glad of it. From national, cultural, educational, technical and mere hygienic points of view this policy has to be strictly adhered to . . .[4]

Whatever their stand on the question of 'exclusivism', the Palestinian Jews were, of course, aware that there were 'neighbours' in the country, and everyone agreed on the general principle that good neighbourly relations were preferable to bad relations. The Jews would learn from experience how best to 'get along' with their neighbours. But, beyond the avoidance of unnecessary friction and disputes, most Jewish settlers found it preferable and natural to have few, rather than many, contacts with the Arabs.

As 'exclusivist' as the Yishuv may have been, it had nevertheless had a good deal of experience with various forms of its 'Arab question' prior to the Balfour Declaration, the point at which we take up the story in late 1917. Other studies have described in detail the ways in which the Yishuv and the Arabs first came to know each other,[5] and after 1917 we are dealing in many cases with the continuation of developments which had their origins before the War. Jewish labour continued after 1917 to be faced with its particular 'Arab question' – i.e., the inability of 'expensive' Jewish workers to compete with 'cheap' Arab labourers on the Jewish plantations and colonies. Those concerned with land purchase would continue to find themselves in the intricate business-world of the 'effendis', while at the same time being forced to deal generously with the tenants whose land was being disposed of without their knowledge. Local security problems, which first arose as a result of the general lawlessness in a frontier setting, would become more serious and, on occasion, widespread and even 'political' in character. The original response to this latter problem – local watchmen who soon formed a professional, country-wide organisation known as *ha-Shomer* ('The Watchman') – would be superseded after 1917 by more elaborate preparations for self-defence. The decidedly unfriendly tone which the Arabic press had begun to display before the War would continue to require Zionist efforts to counteract the damage which was being done to the Yishuv's image.[6]

When we take up the story of the Palestinian Jews and the Arab question at the end of 1917, we find all these elements, with the addition of two new features of some importance. The first is the presence of the British as the ruling power in Palestine, a factor which was perhaps more decisive than the Ottoman factor had been and which makes it impossible to treat Yishuv–Arab relations in isolation. Secondly, we have the Balfour Declaration of 2nd November, by virtue of which the British Government was pledged to 'use their best endeavours to facilitate the achievement' of a 'national home for the Jewish people' in Palestine. While this declaration did little to alter the basic patterns of Jewish–Arab relations which had developed over the preceding generation, it certainly intensified the existing latent conflict. Above all, it had a profound effect on the mind and the expectations of the Yishuv:

> From a minority of no special standing in a few provinces of the Turkish Empire, the Jews of Palestine became the nucleus of a projected Jewish National Home, united by common political aspirations, with the ambition, at first greatly inflated, of sharing in the governance of the country, or at least maintaining wide autonomous rights within it.[7]

It was to take several difficult years for the Yishuv to learn to accept a state of affairs which did not match up to these inflated expectations. The euphoria which swept through the Zionist world in late 1917 and early 1918 was perhaps greatest among the nationalist elements of the Palestinian Jewish community. In December 1917 the Yishuv was reported to be 'elated at the recent declarations in favour of Zionism, which they [were] interpret[ing] as very liberal'.[8] While many recognised Zionist spokesmen were avoiding public expression of phrases such as 'Jewish state' or 'Jewish government', Yishuv leaders did not hide the fact that they were indeed hoping for 'a Jewish state in Palestine' as a result of the forthcoming peace settlement.[9]

The Va'ad Zmani and the Zionist Commission

During the twelve months following the publication of the Balfour Declaration and the arrival of British troops in Palestine, we can find little evidence of an integrated approach on the part of the Yishuv to any political aspects of the 'Arab question'. What did concern most nationalist-minded elements in the Yishuv during this time was the reconstruction of the exiled and impoverished Jewish community. For the greater part of 1918 only southern Palestine came under British military administration, and the issues facing this fragment of the Yishuv included: relief, Hebrew language and education, arbitration tribunals, internal discipline and consolidation, and relations with the Zionist Commission (see below). Three 'Preparatory Assemblies' were convened, and were attended by delegates from the various local and regional bodies and associations, with the *Va'ad Zmani* serving as the provisional authoritative council.

The local *Va'ad Zmani* was not the only Jewish body in Palestine during this period. On 4th April 1918 the more authoritative Zionist Commission (ZC), composed of leading Zionists from the Allied countries, arrived at Jaffa. The Commission had been conceived in London, following publication of the Balfour Declaration, to advise the British authorities in Palestine 'in all matters relating to the Jews, or which may affect the establishment of a National Home for the Jewish people in accordance with the Declaration of His Majesty's Government'. Ranking fifth among its seven enumerated tasks was: 'to help in establishing friendly relations with the Arabs and other non-Jewish communities'.[10]

Both before and after their arrival in the Middle East, members of the ZC were well aware of the British concern to minimise unrest in the area, and to calm the Arab anxieties resulting from the news of British promises to the Jews. While the *Va'ad Zmani* concerned itself with internal Jewish matters, the British enlisted the ZC in a campaign of 'explanation' and 'moderation'. The Commission met with 'representative' Arab leaders and sought to explain to them that the 'true aims' of Zionism did *not* include those things which the Arabs appeared to fear most: viz., (a) the immediate imposition of a minority Jewish government; (b) the expulsion of the Arab inhabitants to make room for massive Jewish immigration; or (c) Jewish desecration of Muslim or Christian Holy Places.[11]

In almost every sphere of their relations with local Yishuv leaders, the 'foreign dignitaries' of the ZC soon assumed a 'big-brother' attitude,[12] and enjoyed a monopoly of official status in British eyes. This was also true with regard to the Arab question. Without having to consult the local Jewish leaders, the Commission undertook its 'diplomatic' activities with Arab notables in Cairo, Jerusalem and Jaffa.[13] At the time, the *Va'ad Zmani* acquiesced in this ZC monopoly over 'external affairs' – i.e., relations with the British and with the Arabs – and contented itself with hearing periodic reports from members of the Commission. Only in mid-1919 do we find the first overt Yishuv grumbling about this ZC predominance, but there were few in the Yishuv who were prepared to demand greater local responsibility for the Arab question at this early stage.[14]

Dr Weizmann himself attached particular importance to one diplomatic enterprise: the creation of an entente between Zionists and the Amir Faisal, leader of the Hejazi forces. Even before his first meeting with the Amir, Weizmann had decided that it was necessary to treat the Palestine question as part of the larger Arab question. As he saw it, the former was 'an economic problem, not a political one', while it was with Faisal that the Zionists would establish a 'real political entente'.[15] The Zionist leader reached these clear-cut conclusions not only on the basis of his talks with British 'experts';

his own recent experience at negotiating with Arab representatives in Cairo and Jerusalem had no doubt strongly conditioned his positive preference for an agreement with Faisal.

In his relatively successful (if less important) Cairo talks,
Weizmann felt that he was dealing not so much with committed 'nationalist leaders' as with landowners whose interest in
Palestine and Zionism was 'merely financial'.[16] In Palestine
itself he had hoped that the patient removal of local 'miscon-
ceptions of our real aims' would have been enough, but he was
forced to back away from further talks with local notables
after being met with deep suspicion, obstinacy and 'a state of
mind' which made 'useful negotiations impossible'.[17] Indeed,
the Zionist leader had confronted the basic fact that talks with
Arabs of Palestine would always prove more difficult than
with Arabs from other countries.

It was by an agreement with Faisal that Weizmann hoped to
bypass local obstacles. After his first meeting with Faisal at
Uheida on 4th June 1918, Weizmann felt that he was at last
dealing with 'an honest and fearless man', not like 'all the
others' who were 'fluctuating people ... from whom we
could never expect any real co-operation'.[18] Weizmann proposed what we might call an 'exchange of services' between
the two movements which Faisal gave every indication of
understanding and appreciating, despite his stated inability to
make any firm commitments at the time. The meeting left
Weizmann very optimistic that Zionism would not clash with
'the real Arab movement' which was 'developing in Mecca
and Damascus', and he even envisaged his own movement
serving as a natural bridge between Great Britain and the
future Arab state, a bridge between the West and the
Orient.[19]

National-Communal Autonomy

When the Zionist leader informed the Yishuv's Second Preparatory Assembly (17th June 1918) of his recent meeting
with Faisal, he felt 'justified in stating that it [was now] possible to find a modus vivendi for the thorny political Arab
problem'.[20] The Assembly expressed its congratulation and
satisfaction, but to judge from later evidence the local leaders

could not have been genuinely enthusiastic (cf. pp. 33 f. and 169 f., below). They were far more concerned with the immediate local situation, and despite this and other 'diplomatic' efforts of the ZC, relations between the local Jewish and Arab communities continued to exhibit growing mutual suspicion and aggravation. A new era was dawning, precedents were being set under the new régime, and each community eyed jealously anything which could be regarded as a gain for the other. Controversies arose over such matters as the allocation of seats on mixed municipal councils and the use of Arabic and Hebrew for official business.[21]

In such an atmosphere the Yishuv's concern for its autonomy was not merely an internal organisational matter, but was becoming very much a 'national' question. Any trace of sovereignty which the overwhelming Arab majority might receive at the hands of the British régime would likely be at the expense of the political aspirations of the tiny Jewish minority. Nationalist-minded Yishuv leaders were therefore most unhappy to see the new European power in Palestine carelessly applying its own familiar assumptions of numerical democracy to the local situation. They would have much preferred the British to have understood the 'special' position of the Jewish minority and to have endorsed the principle of local communal autonomy for all groups (see below).

The Yishuv obsession for its national autonomy could not fail to touch upon the question of the Arabs in the country. During the preceding 25 years the Arab population of Palestine, without ever being considered a rival 'nation' by the Yishuv, had nevertheless presented a number of practical problems. As mentioned above, one such problem was the threat of cheap labour perceived by the Jewish labour movement. In the first debates following the British occupation, Jewish labour representatives continued to raise this issue, and pressed Jewish employers to recognise their 'national' duty to assist in the creation of a Jewish working class. Thus, when the agronomist Y. Wilkansky lectured on the five principles of Zionist colonisation work, he stressed two which were of a far more political than agricultural nature: namely, Jewish labour 'without exception', and the need to become a majority in the country.[22]

The installation of the British Military Administration offered several other practical issues which served to illustrate the Yishuv's jealousy for its national autonomy, and which also concerned relations with the Arabs. One might have expected the British suggestion for the formation of a local Jewish militia to assume responsibility for defence of outlying colonies to have appeared an eminently acceptable one to Yishuv minds. Yet several leaders raised strong reservations, and insisted on receiving firm assurances that there would be absolute Jewish control over its composition, training and functions. A resolution was passed, accepting the British suggestion in principle, but stipulating that any militia would have to conform to 'all our national demands', which in this case were defined to be: the training school should be for Jews only; the militia should be financed by Jewish funds; Hebrew and English should be the only official languages; and an organisational link should be established between the militia and the *Va'ad Zmani*.[23]

The idea of a Jewish militia and the very nationalistic thinking which prevailed in certain Yishuv quarters are both illustrated even more clearly in the creation of the local Jewish Battalion. Two Battalions of overseas Jews (38th and 39th Royal Fusiliers) had been formed in America and in England, and while they were on their way to the Middle East, a third (40th Royal Fusiliers) was enlisted from among Palestinian Jews in the recently liberated areas. The two aims of the Palestinian Jewish enlistment movement reveal the high level of political consciousness of the organisers:

(a) to participate in the War of Liberation of the Land of our Forefathers, which is about to return to being the Land of our Future in accordance with the Balfour Declaration;

(b) to create the nucleus of a future Jewish militia, which will be set up for the defence of the country after its conquest.

Beyond the concrete need for security against Arab attack, the initial inspiration for the Jewish Battalions was the idea that the Jews should become a weighty *political* factor, not to be ignored or lightly brushed aside in the imminent peace settlement.[24]

The British Factor

While not openly confronting an 'Arab question' as such during most of 1918, Jewish leaders were preoccupied with expressing their disappointment with the *British* attitude to the Yishuv. The correspondence, memoranda and reminiscences of this period show an almost total preoccupation with the British factor.[25] Disappointment with the British was, of course, directly proportional to the extensiveness of Zionist expectations; but even in terms of simple hopes – such as that for an enlightened and sympathetic European administration to replace the corrupt and arbitrary Turkish bureaucracy – there was cause for widespread disappointment.

The issue of Yishuv–British relations, more than any other single question, had very direct repercussions on Yishuv–relations. In July 1918, Dr Ya'akov Thon, head of the *Va'ad Zmani*, expressed Yishuv expectations and disappointments with regard to the British attitude. In a letter to Dr Weizmann, Thon complained that the embargo on land-purchase was being interpreted by the Arabs as a 'victory' which had been achieved by pressure on local officials. He enclosed excerpts from the Arabic press which, he felt, should have been stopped by a wise British censor. In the wider context of Jewish–Arab rivalry in Palestine, Thon saw the British as clearly encouraging, wittingly or unwittingly, the Arabs to take an aggressive stand, instead of 'preparing and accustoming' them to acquiesce in the 'future position'.[26] Thon's complaints were echoed by many others, producing an endless stream of complaints, pressure for the introduction of more Jews into administrative posts, and demands for direct control (*via* the Zionist Organisation) over major appointments.[27]

The liberation of Samaria and Galilee, the fall of Damascus and the cessation of hostilities in autumn 1918 should all have contributed to an improvement in the Zionist position in Palestine. In particular, Faisal's entry into Damascus on 3rd October 1918 evoked official Zionist joy and congratulation, and Zionists now felt justified in considering that this amounted to the final fulfilment of 'Arab national aspirations'.[28] The stage was now set for a second meeting between Weizmann and Faisal in London. The two leaders elaborated more clearly an 'exchange of services' and prepared to harmonise their respective stands at the Peace Conference.[29]

While the situation appeared somewhat encouraging in Europe, the same could not be said for Palestine. Far from satisfying, once and for all, 'Arab national aspirations', the establishment of an 'independent' Arab régime at Damascus in October 1918 was regarded by the Palestinian leaders as a means of better resisting Zionism. For the next two years the Arab claim was that Palestine was really 'Southern Syria', and entitled as such to partake in the 'independence' of greater Syria.[30] In vain did Jerusalem Jewish leader David Yellin protest that the local Arab movement was 'only artificial, the Arabs of Palestine never having got mixed up in this movement which had its centres in Beirut, Damascus and in Egypt'.[31] Artificial or not, the 'aggressive' side of the pan-Arab movement was immediately visible to Yishuv leaders. Local observers were forced to witness Damascus becoming the centre of propaganda and organisational activity directed against Zionist plans for Palestine. Sir Mark Sykes, then visiting the area, even had to admonish Syrian leaders that 'Damascus cannot and must not busy itself with Palestinian problems', and he tried to convince them in their own interests to 'come to an understanding with the Jews'.[32]

In Palestine itself, the first anniversary of the Balfour Declaration was the occasion for a proliferation of Arab protests demanding its withdrawal.[33] Some Arab youths assaulted a Jewish school procession which marked 'Balfour Day' in Jerusalem, and the incident required a Government-sponsored reconciliation between Jewish and Arab notables of the city.[34] Jewish observers could not fail to notice the formation of Muslim-Christian committees – 'always agitating against us'[35] – and some even felt that a 'pogrom movement' was afoot.[36]

Although they did not fail to *notice* the increase in Arab agitation in late 1918, Jewish observers were divided on how to react to it. There were a few who thought that this restlessness had to be confronted by a show of Jewish 'strength'. For Jabotinsky, there was 'not the slightest doubt that had the Jerusalem ruffians [of 2nd November] known that there [was] a Jewish garrison in the City there would never have been any disturbances'.[37] To those most intimately involved with the Battalions, it appeared that GHQ was deliberately and 'skilfully' keeping Jewish soldiers in the background. Even worse for general Yishuv morale, British plans for the Northern Palestine campaign denied the Palestinian-Jewish Battalion the passionately-awaited honour of participating in the liberation of part of 'its' country.[38] 'Samaria and Galilee', wrote Jabotinsky, 'were not given the privilege of seeing one Jewish soldier ... This absence of Jewish soldiers [was] a strong coefficient in making Jews feel depressed and Arabs bold.'[39] Among the Jewish legionnaires themselves there followed a period of intense frustration and rebelliousness; neither in 1918, nor later, would GHQ share the Jewish soldiers' view of their 'national-political' role and importance.

The dominant tendency in most Jewish circles was not, however, to look to the Jewish Battalions, but rather to the authorities, to keep the situation in check, while hoping that the forthcoming peace conference in Paris would soon pronounce its verdict, bringing calm to the country. In an isolated local initiative, some Jerusalem Jews felt it important to form a committee whose object was to engage Arab notables in friendly dialogue. No results of any importance were achieved.[40]

The 'Eretz-Yisrael' Conference and the 'National Demands' to the Peace Conference

If the *de facto* division of powers in Palestine was keeping political responsibility for the 'Arab question' in the hands of the ZC, this did not result in total Yishuv deference and abdication on this issue. With the Peace Conference now the centre of attention, the 'Eretz-Yisrael Conference' – the first post-War meeting to be attended by representatives of the entire Yishuv – was convened in late December 1918.[41]

One of the major items discussed at the five-day Conference was the political future of the Yishuv. Much of the debate centred around a draft outline, composed by Akiva Ettinger, Yitzhak Wilkansky and Vladimir Jabotinsky (the latter on behalf of the ZC), of a 'Plan for the Provisional Government of Palestine'.[42] The Plan embodied the 'National

Demands' which the Yishuv would present to the Peace Conference and asked that the international community endorse
two fundamental assumptions: (a) 'the claim of the Jewish
People that Palestine should become its National Home
... and that in all matters of the Government and administration of Palestine a decisive voice belongs to the Jewish
people throughout the world'; and (b) the choice of Great
Britain as the Trustee Power for the League of Nations, 'with
the task of assisting the Jewish people in the upbuilding of its
National Home'.

According to the Plan, Palestine was to be ruled by a
'Governor-General' and an appointed 'Executive Council'. A
representative of the Zionist Organisation would serve in the
Home Government of the Trustee Power as 'Permanent
Under-Secretary for Palestine', and appointments to the
Executive Council would be made by the Trustee Power from
a list submitted by him. A 'Colonisation Association' would
be created and endowed with extensive rights and privileges
with regard to the disposal of State lands and the distribution
of public-works contracts and concessions. 'National-
communal Autonomy' – affecting matters of religion, education, courts and social welfare – would be granted to all
groups, and there would be complete equality between Hebrew and Arabic as official languages.

The principal Yishuv demands, as reflected both in the
body of the Plan and in the Conference debates, echoed the
same aspiration for internal autonomy which had characterised the earlier debates of 1918. The Yishuv now sought
international endorsement of a pro-Zionist régime in Palestine which would permit the maximum growth and development of the Jewish community until such time as the Jews
became the majority. The realisation of such a programme
was, necessarily, greatly dependent on the Trustee Power;
after nearly a year of disturbing evidence of the Military
Administration's imperfect sympathies towards the Balfour
Declaration and Jewish national aspirations, the drafters of
the Plan laid heavy emphasis on the need for Zionist control
over administrative appointments, and for a strong and truly
'partisan' Trustee to govern the country during the transition
to a Jewish majority. At the end of the transition, a Jewish

state was implicit: a constitutional democracy in which the Arabs would be granted the appropriate minority rights.

There was no doubt in anybody's mind that the Arabs actually constituted the vast majority of the population of Palestine, and that the period of transition would present great difficulties. Indeed, it was on this key question that many speakers focused during the debates over the Plan. How could the promises of a 'Jewish National Home in Palestine' be implemented in the fullest and most meaningful way while the Arabs possessed the country by virtue of their numbers, and were very likely to obstruct any Zionist plans? It was evident to participants at the Conference that the 'normal' application of the principles of 'democracy' or 'national self-determination' could result in disaster for the Jewish claim to Palestine. Although Jewish people throughout the world may have *focused their hopes* on Palestine, the Jewish population *actually resident* there formed only a tiny minority (perhaps 10 per cent) of the inhabitants. Thus, Jabotinsky was forced to confess to the Conference that it was

> impossible to express our demands in brief, but only in a complex form. If we had been settled on the land, then we could have said 'INDEPENDENT', and with this we would have expressed everything. Since this is not the situation at present, we must enter into details . . .

Somehow, the nations of the world would have to be convinced that Palestine did not constitute a 'normal' case for national self-determination.

A number of suggestions were made for overcoming the problems posed by the existence of a large Arab majority in Palestine. Several speakers pointed to the obvious 'solution' of creating, as quickly as possible, a Jewish majority through mass immigration. For some speakers, hope lay in the possibility of convincing the international community to allow a generous interpretation of the principle of the Jewish 'historic connection', to the point of enfranchising all the Jews of the world as 'citizens *in potentia*' of Palestine; this approach was, however, criticised as endangering the position of Jewish nationals in their countries of residence. One speaker was shouted down by the chairman when he tried to suggest a franchise based on a literacy test, which would have had the effect of disqualifying enough Arabs to make a Jewish constitutional majority possible immediately. Another speaker even raised the question of the possible transfer of the Arab population to Mesopotamia or across the Jordan River; but the few who did bring up this last delicate subject had to confess that such a suggestion, coming from the Jews, was ultimately impracticable and would only arouse harmful controversy.

Alongside all these suggestions, various arguments were adduced to show how little hardship the Arabs would suffer should the Peace Conference in fact satisfy the Yishuv's 'National Demands'. General declarations were made to the effect that, although the Jews did hope to become a majority in Palestine, they had no intention of 'dominating' the Arabs. Constitutionally, the framers of the Plan felt that they were being sufficiently generous to Arab interests by according one seat on the proposed six-man Executive Council to an Arab, who would be designated the 'Minister for Arab Affairs'. Furthermore, it was argued, the provisions for 'National-Communal autonomy' would apply equally to all groups, thereby allowing the Arabs the same internal freedom as the Jews themselves were seeking.

Yishuv representatives felt the strongest justification of all for their demand for a Jewish Palestine by pointing out that legitimate Arab national-political demands would be amply satisfied in an independent Arab state (Hejaz, united with Syria) – in other words, *outside* the boundaries of Palestine. Thus, they felt that it was not at all unreasonable that Palestine – which was but a 'small corner' of all the Arab lands, but which had strong associations for the Jewish people – should be set aside to become a Jewish country. Jabotinsky made a dual appeal to the magnanimity of the 'Arab people' and to post-War millenial justice:

> ... we must pose this matter not as a 'question' between the Jewish people and the Arab inhabitants of Palestine, but between the Jewish people and the Arab people. The latter, numbering 35 million, has half of Europe, while the Jewish people, numbering ten million and wandering the earth, hasn't got a stone ... Will the Arab people stand opposed? Will it resist?

[Will it insist] that . . . he who has a piece of land bigger than England, France and Italy combined shall have it [all] for ever and ever, while he who has nothing shall forever have nothing? We should stress the perspective of the 'Jubilee Year': He who has nothing, give to him; he who has too much, take from him . . .

In the event that the Arabs who would find themselves inside the Jewish Palestine should feel any cause for concern, one speaker pointed to the existence of Jewish minorities in the Arab world as a strong 'moral guarantee' for the continued safety and well-being of the future Palestinian Arab minority.

The 'National Demands' which were the product of the 'Eretz-Yisrael Conference' of December 1918 represent the first comprehensive statement of the Yishuv's post-War political aspirations. While the Demands were subsequently criticised by 'outsiders' as unrealistic or too far-reaching (see below), during the Conference itself criticism was in the opposite direction. Why had the original drafters of the Plan not asked for a Jewish state outright, demanded David Ben-Gurion and Yosef Sprinzak. In fact, it was this body of opinion which guided the revision committee (Ben-Gurion, Ettinger and Jabotinsky) to produce the final draft which was approved by a 55–1 vote. The revised Plan contained a number of small alterations, all of which toughened up its original tone. Most notably, the phrase 'National Home' (*bayt leumi*) was changed to read: 'Jewish Commonwealth' (*medina 'ivrit*).

The text of the Plan submitted by the Yishuv to the Peace Conference was, thus, a 'maximalist' one which did not, on the face of it, seem to take into account the possibility of Arab objections. But, from what we have seen of the debates on the Plan, it is clear that this glossing-over the 'Arab question' was deliberate and tactical, and not based on simple ignorance. The facts of a very large Arab majority in Palestine and Arab opposition to Zionist aims were well known to participants at the Conference. How to bypass the problem of Arab opposition – this was a central issue in the discussions, evidenced equally by those who preached the overriding need to 'come to terms' with the Arabs (e.g., Ya'akov Thon, David Remez) as by those who denounced any suggestion which appeared to be inspired by 'the Arab scare' (e.g. Ludvipol, Schiller). Yet, as the Plan shows, realisation of the fact of Arab opposition did not automatically entail deferring to it, and most Yishuv representatives seemed to be assuming and hoping that, in the end, the Arabs would not actively oppose a fait accompli properly imposed by the European Powers and faithfully implemented by a sympathetic Trustee.

The Conference also had the benefit of hearing hard-headed and pessimistic analyses of the 'Arab question' from the original drafters of the 'National Demands'. While expressing himself as 'in favour of an agreement with the Arabs', Jabotinsky felt the need to warn his listeners that there were contradictions which might not easily be over-come. The one thing, in his view, which the Jews could not concede on any account was 'that the Government should be entirely ours'; but, he asked, could the Arabs, who had been 'living in the country for 2,000 [sic] years', be expected to agree 'that another people [i.e. the Jews] should come and multiply in it'? He further warned the Jews not to fool them-selves into believing that the Arab majority would be easily dislodged from its predominant position by any Jewish offers of a constitution based on parity. He respected the shrewd-ness of the anti-Zionist agitators who focused their opposition not so much against a 'Jewish Government' as against Jewish immigration, which they correctly recognised as the effective instrument by which a Jewish majority, and a Jewish govern-ment, would eventually come into being.

In the course of his opening address to the Conference, Dr Thon had included a brief but optimistic reference to the Arab situation, basing his optimism on the news he had received about the agreement which Dr Weizmann and the Amir Faisal were currently discussing in London. But Jabotinsky and Wilkansky both showed a greater concern for the real and imminent dangers of aggressive pan-Arab nationalism which were then being felt 'on the spot' in Pales-tine. While expressing the hope that 'in the course of time *we* shall become the power in Palestine', Wilkansky stressed that the Jews 'must not forget that, for the time being, we are a minority here' and that 'our neighbours are no "quantité négligeable" '. He graphically portrayed Palestine as lying in the midst of an Arab world which was in the throes of reorganisation and consolidation; the Yishuv would require 'real strength' to withstand a triple pressure – viz., from Egypt, Damascus, and the Arabs of Palestine. 'This [Arab] nation is now weaving its web: either this web will embrace [i.e., and assimilate] us, not allowing us to develop at all, or it will turn us "out".'

Wilkansky's reaction to the 'transfer-of-population' suggestion also indicates that he was at an advanced stage in recognising the difficulties which the 'Arab question' posed for the implementation of Zionist aspirations. Unfortunately, he confessed, it was 'impossible to evict the fellahin, even if we wanted to':

> Nevertheless, if it were *possible*, I would commit an injustice towards the Arabs... There are those among us who are opposed to this from the point of view of supreme righteousness and morality. Gentlemen, ... if one wants to be a 'preventer of cruelty to animals', one must be an extremist in the matter. When you enter into the midst of the Arab nation and do not allow it to unite, here too you are taking its life. The Arabs are not salt-fish; they have blood, they live, and they feel pain with the entry of a 'foreign body' into their midst. Why don't our moralists dwell on *this* point? We must be either complete vegetarians or meat-eaters: not one-half, one-third, or one-quarter vegetarians.

In closing, he rejected the Herzlian optimism which had regarded Palestine as 'a country without a people'. Zionists, he argued, had to face and cope with the inconvenient fact that they would be entering a country which was already inhabited.

2

In the Shadow of the Balfour Declaration, II: 1919

The Yishuv Delegation to Europe

Armed with the revised version of the 'National Demands', a five-man Yishuv delegation headed by David Yellin left Palestine for Europe in late January 1919. In Paris and London the delegation participated in numerous Zionist meetings and held interviews with several British and other world leaders. A few of the delegates returned to Palestine at the end of May, bearing reports which were far from encouraging.[1]

The Yishuv delegation suffered its first major disappointment immediately on its arrival in London. An official set of Zionist Organisation (ZO) Proposals had already been submitted to the Peace Conference, rendering superfluous the National Demands which had been worked out at the 'Eretz-Yisrael Conference'. Even worse, the contents of the official Proposals were not at all in the spirit of the Yishuv's Demands. The former were considered weak on at least six points,[2] and the Yishuv delegation tried in vain to have revisions made. On the other hand, the extensive National Demands of the Yishuv were an embarrassment to official Zionist spokesmen, who wondered whether it was unsurpassed nerve – 'hutzpa' – or simply a lack of political realism which had led the tiny Palestinian Jewish community to expect international endorsement for such an unashamedly 'Zionist régime' as envisaged in its National Demands.[3]

The Palestinian Jews met with further disappointment in the British attitude. While the delegates clearly knew 'in advance' that 'the Arabs would be against us', they did not expect that ('and could not understand how') the British would 'take this opposition into account'. The adverse comments made by several British statesmen to Zionist leaders about the 'situation between Jews and Arabs in Palestine' were interpreted by the Yishuv delegates as a 'new tactic' against Zionist interests and a 'very great hindrance'.

As it had indeed been anticipated that the Arabs would be 'the main stumbling-block', the Yishuv delegates were prepared to contact Arab leaders while in Europe. On Dr Weizmann's suggestion, a formal audience with the Amir Faisal was arranged on 15th April, and this encounter gave the appearance of being a source of mutual reassurance. The Amir began with the customary greetings, and added some flattering words about how much happier and more comfortable it was for him to meet with his 'semitic brothers' than with British and French politicians, 'upon whom it is impossible for us to rely'. He then raised the issue of Israel Zangwill's latest suggestion for the removal of the Arab population of Palestine by massive camel-trek.[4] In an effort to relieve Faisal's apprehensions, the Yishuv representatives protested that Zangwill was 'completely outside the [Zionist] camp'. Apparently reassured at these words, the Amir proceeded to give the Jews a pledge of his continued good faith and loyalty to the kind of Zionism espoused by Dr Weizmann. On his return to Syria he expected to pass through Palestine and promised to do his best to influence his 'Arab brothers in favour of Zionism'.

The Yishuv delegates were not really overwhelmed by the 'nice things' Faisal had said. After the Amir withdrew, the Jews exchanged more sober words with 'Auni 'Abd al-Hadi, Faisal's personal secretary and a Palestinian. 'Auni remarked that it was 'obvious why the Amir said these nice things … It doesn't hurt to say nice things.' And, as Yellin noted afterwards, Faisal had spoken as though he regarded Palestine as *his* country to dispose of (cf. below). Yellin and Meir Dizengoff met privately with Auni a few days later, and the three drew up plans for a joint committee to begin working towards improving Jewish–Arab relations in Palestine, but nothing seems to have come of these plans.[5]

In the weeks following their audience with Faisal, the Yishuv delegates began to realise that there was little more for them to do in Europe, except to await the final results of the overall Zionist effort. All-in-all, their experience in Europe had been a sad and humiliating one. They would have to return to Palestine with the realisation that the Yishuv would not be receiving all that it expected from the peace settlement. At best, sufficient opportunities would be granted for immigration and development; but it seemed very unlikely that the government itself would be given to the Jews.

When he returned to address Yishuv audiences, David Yellin could not bring himself to disclose the full extent of the delegation's disappointment with their European trip. But before leaving Paris Yellin had given full and frank expression of his feelings in a letter addressed to the Zionist Actions Committee.[6] On the whole, the Yishuv delegation had ended its mission having played a far less important role than it had expected to play. Yellin was bitter, in particular, that European Zionist leaders had forgotten the central importance of the Yishuv when it came to dealing with the Arab question. The working out of an agreement with Faisal and the diplomatic activity surrounding the Zionist and Arab appearances at the Peace Conference had all been the personal prerogative of Dr Weizmann. When Faisal appeared to be reneging on his support for Zionism, it was with Weizmann, Frankfurter, Lawrence and Meinertzhagen that the appropriate counter-statement was drawn up.[7] With specific reference to the latter document, Yellin complained that, had Faisal's letter been addressed not to Frankfurter, but to the Jews of Palestine, 'it would have had among the Arabs of Palestine a far greater value to our interests'.

But, with Faisal and an Inter-Allied Commission about to embark for the Near East, it appeared that the political uncertainty would be prolonged. This was a source of much Zionist and Yishuv concern. In spite of Faisal's 'nice words', Yellin

believed that the Amir was 'really opposed to the Jewish
political idea in Palestine'. With the political focus shifting
back to the Middle East, Yellin felt that there was a special
need for Zionist leaders in Paris to issue instructions and
entrust full responsibility for relations with the Arabs to local
Yishuv leaders.[8]

Tension in Palestine: Spring 1919

During the time that the Yishuv delegation and Zionist leaders were attempting to finalise important political gains in
Europe, the situation in Palestine had been steadily
deteriorating. A conference of delegates from a number of
new Muslim-Christian Associations met in Jerusalem at the
beginning of February, and further evidence indicated that
Arabs in other parts of the country were voicing strong
opinions and organising opposition to the advent of Zionism.
In addition, practical questions affecting relations with 'the
neighbours' (e.g., labour on Jewish colonies) continued to
trouble the *Va'ad Zmani* and its Executive.[9]

But a new and more compelling item had forced its way
onto the agenda of the *Va'ad Zmani* and the ZC – security.
The tension which began to be felt in November 1918 continued to mount, notwithstanding Sir Mark Sykes' energetic
attempts to put an end to Arab 'agitation' (cf. p. 22, above).
A ZC report on the Jerusalem situation at the end of March
1919 noted 'real and increased unrest among the Arabs', and
commented that conditions were 'far more serious' than they
had been 'a few years ago, or even a few months ago'; the
smallest incident of friction would easily 'take on a definite
nationalistic color'.[10]

If, at this time, the 'European' Faisal was saying 'nice
things' to Zionist and Yishuv representatives in Paris, Jews on
the spot in Palestine were impressed only by the local facts,
which told an altogether different story. It became difficult to
imagine that Damascus – which was now seriously suspected
as the origin of definite preparations for anti-Jewish riots in
Palestine[11] – had recently figured as the 'key' to a satisfactory
Zionist-Arab agreement. Alexander Aaronsohn (brother of
Aaron, quoted above) regarded the British act of 'handing

over' that town to the Arabs – a thing which 'in their wildest dreams' they had never imagined possible – as a stimulus to new heights of 'arrogance and fanatical ambitions'. He was not alone in interpreting this as a direct cause of the deterioration of the local situation.[12] Yishuv leaders were beginning to doubt the possibility of an amicable settlement with Arabs who were now claiming 'a pan-Arab state *which also includes Palestine*'.[13] The Faisal who returned to Damascus in May was seen to be swept along by anti-Zionist 'extremists' and guided only by a 'policy' which consisted of giving elusive and contradictory assurances to different people at different times. Akiva Ettinger publicly denounced the whole idea of a grand Jewish-Arab 'agreement' negotiated by the 'big men', and he warned of the political dangers. Pan-Arab 'extremists', he feared, would easily deduce from the diplomatic to-and-fro that Zionists were flattering Faisal and in fact accepting his concept of a Greater Syria.[14]

The distinct possibility of an Arab outbreak in Palestine threatened the Zionist position not merely with physical losses in the country, but also with important political setbacks in Europe. Responsible Jewish leaders began impressing the Yishuv with the need for patience and tact, and for not allowing the slightest provocation to the Arabs. While nominally acceding to such entreaties, many people in the Yishuv tired quickly of hearing this 'refrain'. As local elements saw it, the real provocation was coming not from themselves, but from the Arabs, while the British were encouraging Arab boldness by leaning openly to the Arab side.[15]

As one alternative to greater 'tact' in the face of mounting tension, some Jews argued for the 'deterrent' effect which could be had from the Jewish Battalions. Eliahu Golomb, who had organised the enlistment movement and who was soon to become a founder and guiding spirit of the '*Hagana*', attached great practical and symbolic importance to the Jewish military force:[16]

> The Legion accustoms the Arabs to the idea that we are destined to rule this country and puts a fear among them which prevents them from doing anything against us. Perhaps a foreign army can also prevent disturbances, but if we are here there won't be even a chance of their making a try. The Arabs know and understand

that if they do we shall not only defend [ourselves] and pacify [them], but we shall also retaliate.

Motivated by such beliefs in the beneficial application of Jewish troops, several Yishuv leaders pressed for the 'moral protection' which would result from the stationing of the Battalions close to Jewish population centres.

The King-Crane Commission in Palestine

It was in this uncertain and insecure atmosphere that the Yishuv soon had to cope with the additional burden of preparing to greet a commission, coming in the name of the Peace Conference to ascertain the preferences of the local population on the subject of its political future. The hopes which had been expressed at the 'Eretz-Yisrael Conference' that Palestine would not be treated as a 'normal' case for national self-determination were now seriously shaken by the decision to send a commission out to Palestine. In the following pages we shall see how the coming of the 'King-Crane' Commission (as it was subsequently called) gradually forced the Yishuv to confront the 'Arab question' in the open, as a legitimate item for discussion and debate.

At first the Arabs did not seem to cause very much worry in *Va'ad Zmani* councils. At the first meeting of its Executive, following the news that a Commission would be coming to Palestine, discussion on preparations included no mention of anticipated Arab representations, but only of the feared harm that might be done to the Zionist cause by *Jewish* anti-Zionist elements in Palestine.[17] Two weeks later, at a full meeting of the *Va'ad Zmani*, discussion centred round an outline of a memorandum which was to be submitted to the Commission on behalf of the Yishuv. The main theme of the document was the economic achievements of the Yishuv during the previous generation and the already-existing internal autonomy of the Jewish community. Only incidentally was the 'Arab question' to be touched upon, namely, in references to the salutary economic and cultural influence of Jewish settlements on their neighbouring Arab milieu.[18]

If this was a side-stepping tactic similar to the one behind the 'National Demands' formulated for the Peace Conference, there was one voice at this meeting who spoke out against it. Haim Margaliut Kalvaryski found the draft outline curiously defective:

> According to the impression I had, the Commission is not going to ask about the condition of the vineyards and the winecellars at Rishon le-Zion, Zikhron Ya'akov or Rosh Pina. It is going to look into the existing relations among the various elements in the country and their political maturity. We must be prepared for opposition to our desires and our demands from the Arab side. Perhaps we should get in touch with them so that their opposition won't be so great.

The effect of Kalvaryski's intervention was merely the passing of a resolution asking the Executive to prepare 'special material on the political situation' and appointing a committee. Three weeks later, the *Va'ad Zmani* Executive was still planning to base its appearance before the Commission on its past achievements, and to invoke the same fundamental principles upon which the 'National Demands' had been built.[19]

Yet the energetic preparations which the Arabs were making in anticipation of the arrival of the Commission were bound, sooner or later, to attract the notice and the concern of Yishuv leaders. At a meeting of the *Va'ad Zmani* Executive on 19th May Dr Thon – in the three-fold hope of increasing Jewish awareness of the need for Arab friendship, of 'softening the antagonism between us and the Arabs a little', and of 'creating a certain impression for external consumption' – suggested including in the submission to the Commission a declaration to the effect that the Jews 'desired to live in friendship with the Arab people and to erect the National Home of both peoples by mutual assistance'.[20] But this was going too far, and the motion failed to gain support at the meeting.

On 11th June 1919, the long-awaited interview took place between a *Va'ad Zmani* delegation and the Commission.[21] The protracted internal debates on whether to mention the Arab question ended with the last-minute decision – 'following doubts' – to 'bring the discussion round to this item by ourselves if they [the Commissioners] did not do so'. But all the tactical discussions had been so much wasted breath; for,

during the course of the interview, the delegation found that
'the key question, as far as they [the Commissioners] were
concerned, was the Arab question'.The expected question on
the Yishuv's choice for the Mandatory Power was not even
asked, and, apart from a general question on the definition of
Zionism, all the questions directly or indirectly sought the
respondents' opinions of Arab fears of imminent oppression
if Palestine were to be 'given' to the Jews.

In their replies members of the Yishuv delegation were
candid enough. They did not deny that the Jews indeed hoped
to become a majority through mass immigration, and that the
government would one day be a Jewish one. But, they argued,
there was plenty of room for both the expected Jewish immigrants and the Arabs already living in the country. The future
Arab minority would be well treated. Replying to a question
on the 'exclusivism' of the Jews, the Yishuv delegates
described from their local experience the great benefit which
the Arabs were deriving from neighbouring Jewish settlements, the very satisfactory commercial relations between
Arab villages and Jewish colonies, and the successful experimental Jewish-Arab school in Rosh Pina. While admitting
that there did exist a 'kind' of exclusivism in Palestine, Kalvaryski gave his opinion that this was a natural pattern of
inter-communal relations in the Middle East; 'the rest', he
argued, was 'the fruit of the imagination and the exaggeration
of the agitators.'

A separate audience was given by the Commission to Rabbi
Bension Uziel, *Hakham Bashi* (Chief Rabbi) of Jaffa, who
was accompanied by Sigfried Hoofien, a leading Yishuv
banker. The Commissioners asked similar questions relating
to Arab fears of Jewish domination or interference with the
Holy Places. Both in his opening statement and in reply to
specific questions, Rabbi Uziel stressed that no injustice, but
only benefit, would be reaped by the Arabs as a result of
Jewish progress and developments in Palestine. The Rabbi
ingenuously pointed out that whereas the Arabs were currently agitating against the Jews, the Yishuv strove only for
peace.

Of all the Yishuv representatives to appear before the
Commission on 11th June, only Hoofien squarely confronted

the political angle of the Arab question. He invoked the wide panorama of lands which the 'Arab nation' would be receiving from the peace settlement, and asked: How could this 'Arab nation', thus endowed, begrudge the 'Hebrew nation' its rightful claim to this tiny 'corner', Palestine?

> If [he argued] the thesis were that the non-Jewish inhabitants of Palestine are a Palestinian nation against which stands the Hebrew nation, only then would it be possible to 'create difficulties'. But, since the heart of their claims is that they are bound together with the greater Arab nation, therefore they have no special national claim to Palestine.

If any guarantee of Jewish 'good behaviour' towards the Arabs inside the future Jewish Palestine were required, Hoofien pointed out that 'we here are, at best, only a drop in the Arab sea'.

Following the Jaffa audiences with the Commission, most *Va'ad Zmani* leaders felt a sense of relief, and were under the impression that the questions posed had been rather superficial and had been successfully handled. From Jaffa the King-Crane Commission proceeded to Jerusalem, where the ZC had been preparing the Jewish representations. In contrast to the *Va'ad Zmani's* doubts and hesitations, the ZC had planned from the start to discuss the Arab question, and to invoke the ZO's 'friendly' relations with the Amir Faisal.[22] After the Jerusalem interviews, Harry Friedenwald of the ZC reported his hope that the visit of the Commission had afforded a harmless 'safety-valve' for the expression of local opinion. But, reflecting the mood of the Yishuv, he now confidently expected that

> when the Peace Treaty is published announcing the Jewish Homeland, the task of carrying it into effect will not be a difficult one for a wise and strong trustee.[23]

Political Work Among the Arabs

Anticipation of the arrival of the King-Crane Commission in 1919 had stimulated not only Yishuv debates on whether to *mention* the Arab question, but also some heated discussion on whether the Jews should attempt to *do* anything in the direction of improving relations with the Arabs. With all hopes pinned on the British 'promises' and the expected verdict of the Peace Conference, Zionist and Yishuv leaders in Palestine did not consider the removal of Arab antagonism a top priority. Even the intense excitement among the Arabs in anticipation of the King-Crane Commission did not really stir many people out of the prevailing mood of passivity and caution.

When Dr Weizmann began negotiating seriously with Faisal in late 1918, it became a matter of ZC policy to avoid any semblance of 'official' talks with Arabs in Syria and Palestine.[24] Local Yishuv leaders seemed to follow the ZC's lead, and direct negotiations with local Arabs were not considered either promised or politically desirable.[25] Even David Yellin, who had sought Zionist authorisation while in Paris for a more active role for Yishuv leaders in 'Arab work', found that he had to readjust his 'activist' intentions to fit the local realities of May 1919. Shortly before the arrival of the King-Crane Commission, anti-Zionist agitation was creating such tension that Yellin cancelled his plan to collect signatures from 'friendly' Arab villages.[26] When an American member of the ZC suggested 'the possibility of discussing discreetly the current political problems with leading Arabs', it was the disparaging advice of Yellin and Hoofien that 'the results of such meetings would be meagre'.[27]

Against this dominant tendency to abstain from political contact with Arabs there were several individuals who nevertheless favoured a Jewish initiative in improving relations with the Arabs. Addressing the Fourth Meeting of the *Va'ad Zmani* (24.4.1919), Harry Friedenwald, an American then serving as Chairman of the ZC, stressed the dual need for internal Yishuv unity and for 'bringing about a change in the attitude of the Arabs towards us and our hopes'. Friedenwald was critical that the attitude of the local Jews to the Arabs had not always been a wholesome and praiseworthy one:[28]

> It is evident [he lectured] that it is a problem which must be solved in time, and that we have already lost valuable time in the past. We dare not delay longer ... it is we who must take the initiative and who must guide the course of altering the relations which have [existed]: noblesse oblige.

H. M. Kalvaryski, who entirely shared these views, was already active, approaching Arab notables with the aim of softening their attitude towards Zionism before the arrival of the King-Crane Commission. At one point he had caused a scandal in official Jewish circles by trying to organise a *mixed* deputation of Arabs and Jews to appear before the Commission.[29] He presented Arabs with his own 'Programme for a Jewish-Arab Entente' (see below), established Jewish-Arab 'Palestinian Union' clubs in Safed and Haifa (to combat the Muslim-Christian Clubs), and everywhere preached passionately that Jews and Arabs had to find a basis for co-operation.

Supplementing his arguments based on moral conviction, Kalvaryski sought to give a living example of the oft-expounded Zionist argument that Jewish immigration would bring concrete benefit to the Arabs. Entirely on his own initiative, he became an ambassador of Zionist 'largesse', visiting Arab charitable institutions, promising to establish Jewish-Arab schools, and generally attempting to illustrate the advantages which the Arabs could expect to reap from a Zionist programme.[30]

But neither the ZC nor the *Va'ad Zmani* appeared willing to approve Kalvaryski's work, which would have entailed accepting some responsibility for fulfilling the economic and political expectations which he was arousing among the Arabs. In early May 1919, the ZC discussed the need to draft a letter asking Kalvaryski not to associate it with his private work.[31] Soon afterwards the *Va'ad Zmani* Executive also discussed the step of formally requesting Kalvaryski to cease his 'Arab work' activities.[32] Unable to receive full authorisation from either of the two recognised Jewish bodies in Palestine, Kalvaryski nevertheless persisted on his own responsibility, because (as he later explained) he found it impossible to sit idly by and watch the 'animosity against us growing and growing', even to the point of preparations for a 'pogrom'.

It was this persistent and unauthorised political activity which provoked the Yishuv's first major post-war debate openly devoted to relations with 'our neighbours'. At the Fifth Meeting of the *Va'ad Zmani* (convened on 9th–11th June, to coincide with the visit of the King-Crane Commission) Kalvaryski lectured on his experience with the 'Arab question' and gave an account of his recent activities.[33] In the course of his address he recalled the abortive Jewish-Arab meeting of 1914, and the advice which the disappointed Nassif Bey al-Khalidi had given to Dr Thon: 'Gardez-vous bien, messieurs les sionistes: un gouvernement passe, mais un peuple reste.'[34] This, in Kalvaryski's view, was exactly what had happened during the past five years. The Turks had gone, but the Arabs stood, more determined than before, in the way of Jewish national development. It was dangerous, he warned, for the Yishuv to belittle the importance of his opposition. Stressing throughout his passionate conviction that Arab sympathy had to be won as a prior condition for the success of Zionism, he asked the *Va'ad Zmani's* forgiveness for not having been able to restrain himself during the previous months of mounting anti-Zionist agitation.

The debate which followed Kalvaryski's lecture revealed two basic tendencies within the Yishuv.[35] The two were united on only one point: the fact that relations with 'the neighbours' were *not* good. A minority (represented by Blumenfeld, Gordon, Thon and Yellin) agreed with Kalvaryski that Arab hostility to Zionist aims had to be considered, and approached, as a serious obstacle. Yet only two speakers openly supported Kalvaryski's call for an undisguised Jewish initiative in the direction of removing Arab suspicion and winning Arab sympathy.

The majority of those attending the meeting did not arrive at the same conclusions. For them, good relations, however desirable, could never be a *prior* condition for Zionist work, but rather just the opposite: good relations would either follow as a 'natural' result of the 'real' (colonisation, economic development) work of Zionism, or else they would not; but to divert valuable Zionist energies at this early stage to the business of courting Arab favour was considered wasteful or even dangerous.

One frequently cited argument against Kalvaryski's approach was that relations with the Arabs would 'improve [only] with our becoming stronger in the country'; the smallness and weakness of the Yishuv was, in this analysis, the defect to be corrected. One speaker considered the 'Arab question' as just one of many Zionist 'questions': 'if we solve all our colonisation problems, then we shall also resolve the question of relations between us and the Arabs, or it will resolve itself.' Similarly, socialist analyses focused on the prior need to resolve the 'Jewish labour' problem – a solution which implied the *reduction* of Arab-Jewish contact – before the broader question of 'relations' could be solved on the basis of separate 'national' autonomies.

A number of speakers expressed their strong doubts about the chances of *ever* being on really friendly terms with the Arabs. For them, it was dangerous for the Yishuv to expose its weakness by making overtures to the Arabs, who (they felt) would never be reconciled to Zionism simply by dialogue or diplomacy. 'Why', asked Yosef Sprinzak, 'should we, at this critical time, start with such things [peace overtures] when, after reverences and curtsies between Mr Kalvaryski and the Arabs, an attack takes place on Merhavia?' The most extreme and the most eloquent expression of this pessimism was expressed by David Ben-Gurion:

> Everybody sees a difficulty in the question of relations between Arabs and Jews. But not everybody sees that there is no solution to this question. No solution! There is a gulf, and nothing can fill this gulf. It is possible to resolve the conflict between Jewish and Arab interests [only] by sophistry. I do not know what Arab will agree that Palestine should belong to the Jews – even if the Jews learn Arabic. And we must recognise this situation. If we do not acknowledge this and try to come up with 'remedies', then we risk demoralisation. ... We, as a nation, want this country to be *ours*; the Arabs, as a nation, want this country to be *theirs*. The decision has been referred to the Peace Conference.

The practical conclusion to be drawn from the majority analyses was that very little political work should be undertaken among the Arabs, as this would only hinder or limit the fullest and fastest realisation of the 'real' Zionist work of building up the Jewish National Home. Only 'intelligence' or harmless 'public-relations' work might be permissible.

Linking the perceived dangers in Kalvaryski's work with the broader issue of Yishuv unity and discipline, Akiva Ettinger called upon the *Va'ad Zmani* formally to 'request' (and, failing that, to 'demand') a cessation of 'Arab work'. In his defence, Kalvaryski protested several times that *he* would be willing to cease his own activities, so long as the Yishuv did not abandon altogether the important work of trying to win over the Arabs. In the end, his work was neither condemned nor endorsed; a compromise resolution took note of Kalvaryski's lecture on the subject of relations with the Arabs, added that the *Va'ad Zmani* 'recognised the importance of the matter', and referred the issue to a committee.

Retreat from the 'National Demands'?

In spite of the Yishuv delegation's discouraging reports about the prospects in Europe (above, pp. 30 f.), it is interesting to note that far-reaching hopes such as those embodied in the 'National Demands' of December 1918 continued to be entertained by Yishuv leaders throughout 1919.[36] During the course of the *Va'ad Zmani* debate discussed above, H. M. Kalvaryski presented his 'Programme for a Jewish-Arab Entente', and by examining Yishuv reactions to this programme we may be able to appreciate how sacred were the 'National Demands' to the majority of Yishuv leaders.[37]

Kalvaryski's seven-point Programme began by defining Palestine as the homeland of all its inhabitants, whether Muslim, Christian or Jewish. The constitution would be secular and would recognise and encourage Arabic and Hebrew as official languages. All forms of 'exclusivism' were to be abolished; in particular, this meant new obligations on the Jews – in exchange for Arab recognition of the status of their National Home – to make their welfare and banking institutions available to all. In view of the undeniable benefits which would accrue to the entire population, there would be complete freedom of Jewish immigration.

Several *Va'ad Zmani* members were quick to pounce upon the obvious contradictions between this programme and the 'National Demands'. Yosef Sprinzak, who defined himself as 'one of the admirers of a Jewish-Arab "alliance" ', nevertheless termed Kalvaryski's programme 'absurd and dangerous' at the present moment; in his view, it was 'a programme for the future – when we become a community of two million in the country'. Among the specific 'absurdities' commented upon was the requirement that Jews, for the sake of an understanding of the Arabs, should teach Arabic as a compulsory language at a time when the Yishuv itself was not yet united around Hebrew as the 'national language'. The invitation which Kalvaryski extended to the Arabs to expect considerable material gain from Jewish development also appeared 'absurd' to some; few seemed willing to offer to 'purchase' from the Arabs the recognition of what they considered was their precious and inalienable right to immigrate. In any case, it was asked how Kalvaryski could promise the Arabs agricultural loan banks 'at a time when we haven't the ability to establish such banks for ourselves'.

Even more than its specific details, the whole *tone* of Kalvaryski's programme provoked strong reaction at the meeting. Defending himself against the nationalist resentment which he had aroused, Kalvaryski protested that, both in the Programme and in his personal conversations with Arabs, he had told them 'explicitly that we are demanding that Palestine become a Jewish National Home' and had 'given them to understand that we are indeed "stealing" Palestine from them ...' While one speaker felt that it would be all to the good if Kalvaryski succeeded with his programme to 'sugar-coat' the Balfour Declaration pill for the Arabs to swallow, others felt uncomfortably aware of a contradiction between Kalvaryski's liberal ideas and the Yishuv's basically nationalist outlook. Even while they insisted on the fullest realisation of Jewish national aspirations, many firmly held that the legitimate civil, religious and economic rights of the Arabs of Palestine would not suffer. Some reacted sharply to the criticism expressed or implied by Kalvaryski that the Jews were treating, or might treat, the Arabs unjustly in the pursuit of Zionist goals. Several speakers saw in this exaggerated concern for Arab interests a weakening of the Jewish national position, and they stressed very forcefully the prime importance of 'letting the Arabs know' the situation clearly. As one labour spokesman put it, 'The Arabs should know that we are progressing towards the creation of a majority, and that they will become a minority ... It is necessary to emphasise this at all times.'

The majority of the *Va'ad Zmani* members who opposed any departure from the 'National Demands' and rejected Kalvaryski's Programme nevertheless had to justify their 'do-nothing' philosophy by pointing to some other solution. One such 'solution' was the expected beneficial effects of practical Zionist work. Another was the decision which was awaited from the 'governments', i.e., the Peace Conference.

Kalvaryski's activities were based on the dictum ' . . . un peuple reste'. Although he never denied the importance of support from outside 'Powers', he nonetheless insisted that 'if the road to immigration is not prepared' by securing Arab assent, 'then we shall achieve nothing in spite of the promises of the governments.' But, once again, Kalvaryski's views were not those of the majority, which advocated clinging with single-minded tenacity to the 'National Demands' and to 'what we should be receiving from the governments'. Many were indeed hoping that, once the excitement of the war years and the peace settlement had subsided, the Arabs would settle down to live with the fait accompli.

Waiting for the 'Fait Accompli'

As it happened, the fait accompli for which the Yishuv was so keenly waiting came neither quickly nor all at once. It came only in small doses: the first, ten months later at San Remo (April 1920); then the ratification of the Mandate (July 1922); and finally the coming into effect of the Mandate (September 1923). Even then, none of these historic steps fixing the international political status of Palestine was followed by the hoped-for response on the part of the Arabs. None of these external 'facts' created a situation which matched the expectations expressed during the 1918–19 Yishuv debates on the 'National Demands' and relations with the Arabs.

During the first waiting period (1919–1920), the ZC continued to enjoy its monopoly over the 'external affairs' of the Yishuv. Local bodies left the initiative to this official Zionist body, which began, in the second half of 1919, to put great stress on the argument that practical economic activity, quite apart from its obvious value to Zionism, would also bring in its wake benefits and pacification to the Arab population. Zionist representatives in London and in Palestine mounted heavy pressure for British permission to begin such work.[38]

At the same time, the Yishuv saw no evidence to cause it to cease its struggle for a more favourable overall attitude on the part of the local authorities. This factor was still regarded by many as *the* essential precondition for a satisfactory 'solution' to the 'Arab problem'.[39] When the American Justice and Zionist leader, Louis D. Brandeis, visited Palestine in July 1919, Yishuv leaders took advantage of his presence to express the true extent of their despair on this and other pressing matters. On the question of Yishuv–British relations, Dr Thon explained that, whereas it had been possible for the Jews (with outside help) to do battle against an inefficient Turkish bureaucracy, it would not be so easy for them to oppose a British administration which deliberately chose to be hostile.[40] Thon realised that people on the 'outside' were in the habit of discounting Yishuv grievances as exaggerated, and he was at great pains to convince Brandeis that there really was something fundamentally disturbing about the British attitude, and that what the Yishuv was reacting to was not merely 'incidental' signs of British hostility, but the basic problem that 'even in the future, the Mandatory Power will find it right to reckon with the Arabs more than with us'.

Dr Thon therefore recommended that Brandeis should urge other Zionist leaders to concentrate all their energies on a single task – viz., to convince the British Government of the following principle:

> no political Arab question could be raised in Palestine. Here, in Eretz-Israel, there is only one political problem: – to erect the Jewish Commonwealth at the earliest possible date. Let them please the Arabs to their hearts' content in the vast Arabistanic lands, but not on our account here. We do not wish to interfere with the general and civil rights of the Arabs here, but it should be clearly understood that they have no right whatever to hinder, in the least, our development in the direction of the promises given to us.

This principle may be taken as a fair summary of the political outlook of the Yishuv in the shadow of the Balfour Declaration.

3

Arab Violence and the End of the Military Administration

Continuing Uncertainty

Towards the end of 1919, many months of uncomfortable uncertainty about the political future of Palestine were having their effect on the population. The mounting tension waited, from month to month, to be broken by the 'word' from the Peace Conference. During this period the 'National Demands' continued to serve as the optimal expectation of many Yishuv leaders, while many Arabs clung to the hope of Syrian-Palestinian union and independence,[1] with an end to any plans for Jewish immigration or a national home. The Arabs, in Col. R. Meinertzhagen's view, 'certainly [did] not realise' and were 'not in a fit state to be told openly' at the time that the Powers were committed to a Zionist programme for Palestine.[2]

A vivid indication of this persisting uncertainty may be gained from the following extract of a conversation between Musa Kazim Pasha al-Husaini (then Mayor of Jerusalem) and Menahem Ussishkin on 8th October 1919. Ussishkin had just arrived in Palestine to serve as acting Chairman of the ZC, and was asked about the latest news from Paris:

> *Ussishkin*: ... With regard to our country one thing is clear, and that is that Palestine is separated from Syria; [Syria to be under French, and Palestine under British protection].

Musa Kazim: – But we do not agree to this. We asked for American protection, and England only enters the second degree of our considerations. We demand no division from Syria, and no changes in the internal situation, with no [special] rights for anybody.

U:– I have already told Your Honour that there is no doubt on this question. Palestine is separated from Syria, and this has become a fact ... There is no going back now. With regard to the rights to which you hinted, you refer of course to the Jews. I can say that we have already spoken to the Emir Faisal on this matter and we have come to an agreement. You have read of this in the newspapers, I suppose?

M.K.:– Indeed, we have read the newspapers. But we do not submit to the Emir Faisal with regard to our political demands. Nor do we depend on him in this matter. We are opposed to any rights for Jews ... I speak not only for myself but also for all my brothers, the Arabs, and we have already issued a protest against the concessions of the Emir.

U:– But the English Government has also promised Rights to the Jews, and they have issued a special declaration on this matter, the famous Balfour Declaration about which you have heard, no doubt; and if England gave a promise, she knew what she was promising and without doubt she will know how to keep her promise.

M.K.:– Yes! We heard that the English Government has given a promise, but that this promise was given *for the present only* to the Jews, *and not to us*. It is therefore impossible for us to agree with their exaggerated and premature demands which follow one upon the other. Wait until the official announcement is made by the English Government, and then ...[3]

When Dr Weizmann arrived in Palestine later that month, he delivered a political report to the *Va'ad Zmani* and was questioned sharply on the fate of the Yishuv's 'National Demands'. Ben-Gurion also wanted to know why the official Zionist position before the Peace Conference had not been a demand for a Jewish state. He received the famous reply: 'We did not ask for a Jewish state because we would not have received it.'[4] But, on another subject Dr Weizmann's outlook was quickly modified to resemble that of the Yishuv. The Zionist leader soon reduced his hopes of resolving local difficulties in Palestine by means of a deal with leaders of the pan-Arab movement. While Weizmann's 'friendly' relations with Faisal in Europe were already considered to have resulted in frustration and disappointment, the Zionist leader was now able to see for himself the ominous face which the pan-Arab movement presented to Jews and Zionists in Palestine. He soon reported back to London that Damascus was 'full of agitators who preach massacre of everybody who is not Arab', and he sought (without success) to correct the situation by urging Faisal that he was 'morally responsible for [the] serious consequences which may arise from' the violent Damascus propaganda.[5] During the next six months it would indeed be Damascus (rather than the elusive friendship of Faisal) which would preoccupy Zionist and Yishuv leaders.

Tel Hai

Following a visit to the Galilee in late autumn 1919, Dr Weizmann described a 'deplorable' situation which might become 'threatening at any moment'.[6] Once British troops began to evacuate southwards in accordance with the Anglo-French agreement on Syria,[7] the Jewish settlements of Metula, Kfar Giladi, Tel Hai and Hamara found themselves in a no-man's land. The French were slow to establish their authority over the area, and during the next four months the Jewish outposts were left exposed to increased harassment, searches and attacks by Beduin raiders.

While continuing to stress the 'law-and-order' aspect of the situation in the North, many Jews were beginning to regard an adequate response to the challenge as a 'national-political' necessity. Defence of the besieged settlements was seen as a critical test of the Yishuv's determination and strength; the British, the French and the Arabs all had to be shown that this territory was considered an inviolable part of the 'national home', and that Jews would fight to hold on to every inch of Galilee. 'Abandon and retreat', wrote labour thinker Berl Katznelson, 'would be decisive proof of our weakness and insignificance. The only proof of our right to our land', he continued, 'lies in a stiff-necked and desperate stand with no looking back.'[8]

In Tel Hai and Kfar Giladi, settlers voted in favour of

holding their positions at any cost, and the *Va'ad Zmani* met in Jaffa (23–25.2.1920) to consider what help could be arranged.[9] At the latter meeting opinion was virtually unanimous in favour of sending men and arms quickly to fortify the northern outposts. Many viewed the situation in terms of the general principle that no Jewish settlement, once founded, should be abandoned in the face of danger. To flee, even from these 'bandits', would be to set a dangerous precedent from which there might be no turning back. Any demonstration of Jewish weakness at this time would, many agreed, be fatal. 'If we ourselves are not a force', declared one speaker,

> then we shall not accomplish anything here ... And if we fear the force which is stronger than ourselves, then we must abandon Metula today, Tiberias tomorrow, and other places afterwards. Our strength now lies only in the fact that they [the Arabs] still think that we are strong.

Only one speaker during this debate, V. Jabotinsky, preached the 'unheroic' and unpopular line that the *Va'ad Zmani* had a duty to inform the young defenders of the 'bitter truth' that it would be impossible to hold their positions and that they should return temporarily to the safety of British-held territory. In his opinion, the strength of the Arabs and the cost of putting up an effective defence dictated a policy of withdrawal and consolidation.[10]

Despite the near-unanimity on the principle of holding ground at almost any cost, there were nevertheless internal disputes over tactics. The main question was in what form the reinforcements would be sent to the North. Menahem Ussishkin, attending the meeting on behalf of the ZC, opened the debate by stressing the gravity of the issue, and by urging Yishuv representatives to 'apply clearheadedness ... and not only enthusiasm' to the discussion which would ensue. In his opinion, there was a great danger of sparking off a larger Arab-Jewish war. He appreciated, and claimed to share, the dilemma which faced the Yishuv leaders. As Ussishkin phrased it: 'emotionally', an assessment of 'Arab psychology' – viz., 'the Arabs respect only force' – dictated a course of action which would prove to the Arabs that the Yishuv would not sit idly and allow its settlements to be attacked with impunity; yet, 'rationally', the Yishuv had to realise that the likely effect on the Arabs of the appearance of a large number of armed Jews would not be so beneficial. The Arabs would conclude that the Jews were coming to side with the French: 'This is what the Arabs will say ... Without, and even against, our wishing it, we will be drawn into a war between Europeans and Arabs.' What Ussishkin was suggesting to the *Va'ad Zmani* was to employ the stratagem (as he himself had done several days earlier) of quickly and discreetly 'increasing the labour force' in the region: not 'soldiers', but '*halutzim*' (pioneer settlers).

Several speakers expressed similar fears and endorsed a cautious approach. But labour spokesmen were instinctively opposed to making any special efforts in order not to 'provoke' the Arabs. Ben-Gurion could not see why the Yishuv's decision had to be dictated by a fear of what the Arabs would think or say. For him and several others, the objective situation was clear enough. Notwithstanding the promises of Arab Amirs, bandits continued to attack Jewish settlements; Jews had to defend themselves; and the national honour of the whole Yishuv was at stake. Y. Tabenkin, who attended the meeting as a delegate of the besieged settlers, urged the *Va'ad Zmani* to view the Beduin attacks not as an isolated issue, but as something to be considered in the larger context of general Arab animosity towards the Yishuv. If Kfar Giladi, Metula and Tel Hai were not strengthened and held, he argued, the news of 'bandit' successes would only stimulate the 'murderous instincts' of the Arabs in the rest of the country, and 'they will attack us without restraint. This', he added, 'we knew before the Balfour Declaration, and we have not forgotten it since the Declaration.'

Notwithstanding the internal debates, there was no doubt in anybody's mind that efforts would have to be made to send as many men and arms as could be found. The meeting ended with a resolution which was worded in the 'responsible' spirit of Ussishkin's remarks: the settlements would be defended 'by means of an expansion of the labour force'; donations and volunteers would be enlisted from the whole Yishuv in the hour of crisis.

A few days later a special Yishuv mission set out to examine the situation at close hand. But it was already too late. The mission arrived in the North in time to witness the retreat of the evacuees of the fallen colonies. Several days earlier, on 1st March, a scuffle resulted when the Arabs who were being allowed to search Tel Hai (to ascertain that no French soldiers were hidden there) had attempted to disarm one of the girl settlers. Shots were fired, triggering off a day-long battle at the end of which the settlement was abandoned with the loss of six killed and five wounded. Notwithstanding the heroic decisions to defend Kfar Giladi and Metula to the last man, the evacuation of these remaining posts followed two days later.

The fall of Tel Hai provided the Yishuv not only with its first modern legend and martyrs, but also with a practical illustration of the need for developing effective self-defence: *hagana*. When placed in the context of the situation prevailing in the rest of Palestine, Tel Hai was also an omen of what the Jews of Palestine might expect if expressions of Arab hostility were not kept in check.

Arab Demonstrations and Yishuv Proclamation

While the fall of Tel Hai – the first major armed victory of Arabs over the Jews in post-war Palestine – was the outcome of the peculiar local security situation and the entanglement in an Arab-French struggle, tension in the rest of the country mounted over political questions directly affecting Zionism and the Arabs. The population awaited the decisions of the Peace Conference, which had recently adjourned into smaller conferences to finalise the terms of the post-war settlement.

As in 1919, one type of Jewish response to the growing feeling of insecurity was to demand the deployment of more Jewish troops. Under these circumstances, M. Ussishkin sought to obtain permission for a re-enlistment of the Jewish Battalions, suggesting to military headquarters in Cairo that Jewish troops 'might be properly employed in the Jewish colonies for the purpose of inhibiting [Arab] raids'. But the military authorities rejected this suggestion, seeing in it the danger of 'inflam[ing] ... inter-racial feeling'.[11]

In late February, after almost two years of Zionist pressure, the Administration gave the first hint to the Arab public that the Allies were, in fact, contemplating certain rights for the Jewish people in Palestine.[12] While, for the Jews, General Bols' press interview on the subject represented 'the one bright feature of the past few weeks', the Jerusalem paper *Suriyya al-Junubiyya* ('Southern Syria') called upon the population to show its displeasure in a peaceful and orderly fashion on 27th February. The Authorities granted permission for the demonstrations on the grounds that this would provide a welcome 'safety-valve' to relieve the tense atmosphere.[13]

But Yishuv leaders – who were at that very moment considering how best to send reinforcements to the troubled North – could hardly appreciate such reasoning. Eleven months earlier, during a period of similar tension, the previous Chief Administrator had earned Yishuv gratitude for having taken firm measures, including the cancellation of a scheduled Arab demonstration in Jerusalem.[14] Now, as soon as Jerusalem Jewish leader Yosef Meyuhas learned the names of the organisers of the demonstration, he expected the ZC to ask the Government to 'detain these men for a few days, and thus put an end to all this business and frighten the rest'.[15] But Dr Eder of the ZC does not appear to have taken such a serious view of the situation, and no strong protests were lodged officially with the Administration.

The demonstrations of 27th February 1920 were, by all Zionist accounts, small and had failed to arouse any genuine popular enthusiasm.[16] But this hardly proved to be a source of much relief to the Jews. Only three days later came the news of the fall of Tel Hai, adding (as Tabenkin had predicted) to the sense of insecurity in other Jewish centres. The excitement in Jerusalem may be gauged from the rumour, current among the Arabs, that the Beduin had killed 1600 (!) Jews in the North.[17] In several towns Arabs began declaring boycotts on contacts with Jews; the Arabic press grew steadily bolder, and the Jews failed to notice any effective censorship.[18] While the Yishuv had considered the *official permission* as the only possible success of the 27th February demonstrations, it soon had to accept the distressing fact that the Government would be authorising another day of Arab demonstrations on 8th

March. Stronger Zionist warnings and protests preceded this second series of demonstrations.[19]

Much of the Arab agitation of these weeks centred on the continuing claim that Palestine was 'Southern Syria' and was aspiring to become an independent Arab state free from any trace of Zionism. Zionist intelligence was well aware that, in addition to the propaganda and inspiration, instructions and envoys from Damascus were behind the organisation of the 'peaceful protest' demonstrations.[20] On 7th March 1920, the Syrian-Palestinian movement for independence and union reached its climax at the meeting of the Syrian Congress which declared Faisal 'King Faisal I' of the United Arab Kingdom of Syria. The Congress unilaterally proclaimed

> The full and absolute independence of our country Syria, including Palestine, within her natural boundaries, based on a civil, representative form of government, protection of the rights of minorities, and rejection of the claims of the Zionists to Palestine as a national homeland or place of immigration for the Jews.[21]

Apart from the embarrassment which this defiant move was designed to cause France and Great Britain, it underlined the already obvious failure of Dr Weizmann's studied attempt, since early 1918, to establish Zionism *inside* Palestine, while supporting the 'Arab national movement' and keeping it *outside* that country.

The second series of demonstrations in Palestinian towns on 8th March 1920, coincided with the public announcement that Faisal had been proclaimed King of Syria *and* Palestine. This resulted in a vast improvement in Arab participation and enthusiasm. Waving portraits and banners in honour of their new 'King', the Jerusalem demonstrators expressed their excitement in speeches and behaviour which was, in the words of the subsequent British military enquiry, 'decidedly nasty', 'seditious' and 'extremely threatening' to the Jews.[22] Several Jews were hurt in scuffles, the signboard of the Rothschild Hospital was damaged, and the local Jewish Council lodged a strong complaint with the Military Governor. If the Authorities were really interested in inter-communal harmony, it was argued, then they should not grant permission – which the Arabs would interpret as encouragement and approval – for demonstrations which gave rise to a 'venomous atmosphere' and the popularisation of vulgar anti-Jewish slogans and chants. It was further pointed out that the Authorities were, by their leniency, lending their hand to demagogues who wished to poison the minds of the peace-loving masses. Following this second series of Arab demonstrations, the Chief Administrator seems to have been impressed with the limitations of the 'safety-valve' logic, and he prohibited all further demonstrations.[23]

After 8th March there was no doubt within the Yishuv that a real crisis was at hand, and that something had to be done. Zionist intelligence reported that the Arabs of Palestine had 'heard openly that FEISAL is their King, ... [had] insulted and humiliated the Jews ... without meeting any opposition ... This success [has] made the situation very serious.'[24]

The main thrust of Yishuv reaction to the increasing insecurity continued to be the demand for a British 'firm hand' in dealing with 'agitators' and the press. But the Jews had little confidence in relying only on the Authorities. Jabotinsky felt that the present situation could be reduced to 'one problem – the problem of the immediacy of a Jewish military contingent'.[25] Yet, realising the slim chances of British approval for this 'ideal' solution, and in the face of a danger which was growing from day to day, Jabotinsky opted for a second-best solution: independent Jewish self-defence. He formed a *hagana* committee and began the strenuous activity which was to earn him the esteem of the Yishuv, and the epithet '*Magen Yirushalayim*' – 'Defender of Jerusalem'.[26]

While there is little evidence that the 'venomous atmosphere' in Palestine permitted any useful personal meetings between Jewish and Arab leaders, the Executive of the *Va'ad Zmani* decided that it was essential to address a proclamation to the Arab people.[27] This decision was indeed a 'bold' step, especially when we recall the previous unsuccessful attempts of Kalvaryski, Thon and Yellin to force the Yishuv to react openly to the Arab agitation of 1919. Now, with a distinct physical threat in the air, more Yishuv leaders were coming round to the view that to remain silent was more dangerous than to acknowledge publicly that there were some 'problems' with the Arabs. Nevertheless, there were still some who opposed the idea of a proclamation to the Arabs on the grounds that this would 'arouse unnecessary debate'. Even though the official word of the Peace Conference had yet to be handed down, David Ben-Gurion felt that 'the debate on Palestine [had] already ended at the Peace Conference, and we should not provoke discussion all over again'. But this time Ben-Gurion was in a minority, as most Yishuv leaders felt compelled to reply to a 'debate' which had already been aroused by the Arabs.

The themes expressed in this first Proclamation to the Arabs were to become familiar ones in future appeals.[28] The Yishuv urged the Arabs to pay no heed to those who were whispering lies about Jewish intentions, which, in truth, did not include the suppression of Arab rights or the expulsion of Arabs from their lands. The Jews were coming to Palestine to work the available land and to live in peace with their neighbours. Jews and Arabs had shared a common history, and the two semitic nations also shared a common fate. It was stressed that 'no power' could prevent Jewish development in Palestine; the Jews were determined to return to and rebuild Palestine – 'our only homeland, the land of our past and our future'. To offset this tough language, the Proclamation pointed to the economic benefits which all the inhabitants would enjoy as a result of the continued application of Jewish 'energy', 'knowledge' and 'material and spiritual forces' to the development of the country. Those Arabs who were not inclined to quarrel and strife – 'the masses of farmers, labourers and workers' – were invited to participate in a joint and peaceful effort for the 'revival and uplifting' of Palestine – for 'our good, for yours, and for the good of the whole country'.

The most delicate problem concerning this Proclamation was not the formulation of its contents, but the actual situation in the country at the time of its issue. The Proclamation began with a reference to 'this serious moment in the history of the Jewish people and the Arab people'; but there was little doubt in Palestine that the moment was a serious one, in a *physical* sense, only for the Jews. The Yishuv was visibly on the defensive, calling out to the Arabs from a position of weakness in the hope of forestalling further setbacks. The only real value of the proclamation may have been its 'public-relations' effect abroad, demonstrating the Jews' desire for peace through the world's press. As we shall see, it certainly had no effect in 'pacifying' the Arabs of Palestine.

Jerusalem Riots, April 1920

The last days of March 1920 were, for the Yishuv, days of extreme anxiety and tension. Isolated incidents of Jews being bullied or beaten by Arabs became more frequent. During these days, Jews and Zionists in the country – including Dr Weizmann himself – experienced an almost total disillusionment with the good faith of the Military Administration.[29] Even before the outbreak of any riots, there were Jews advocating the provocation of an open confrontation which would expose the anti-Zionist 'scheming' of the local authorities.[30]

There seemed little doubt to many in the Yishuv that the British Administration was either unable or unwilling to keep the mounting Arab agitation in check. In the weeks following the second day of Arab demonstrations, the *hagana* committee attracted some 500 or more volunteers, who began drilling and training each morning in Jerusalem. Except for the illegal possession of a few arms, the *hagana* group ('Jabotinsky's army') made – as the Palin Report confirms – 'no attempt at secrecy'.[31] On 27th March, exercises were held below the Mount of Olives for all to behold, and the *hagana* 'boys' marched back through Jerusalem streets in formation. It is clear that Jabotinsky expressly wanted the Arabs to know that the Jews were preparing to defend themselves, and he hoped that this knowledge would deter any attacks which were in contemplation. At the same time, both he and industrialist Pinhas Rutenberg made frequent approaches to the local authorities, warning of the looming danger and requesting legal recognition and arms for their group. Storrs, the Military Governor of Jerusalem, replied formally to the 'Representatives of the Jewish Self-Defence League' that their proposals had 'not been found acceptable', but that the authorities were fully conscious of the danger and that 'every precaution' would be taken 'to ensure public safety during this, as during the last two, festivals of Nebi Moussa'.[32]

Events soon proved that the measures taken by the authorities were wholly ineffective in preventing the outbreak of violence and in restoring order once it had erupted. Friday, 2nd April, was the first day of the Nebi Musa pilgrimage and a day of anticipated trouble, but it passed without incident. On Sunday 4th April, however, a procession of Hebron pilgrims was 'gradually worked up into a highly inflammable condition' by speeches of 'a flagrantly political character' and by the exhibition of portraits of Faisal, 'King of Syria and Palestine'. Shortly afterwards the mob broke loose, attacking Jews, who suffered at least 118 casualties in the first few hours, despite attempts at retaliation. The local (Arab) police 'at an early hour' became accomplice to the attacks and looting, and 'ceased to have any value as a force'. When order was temporarily restored later that day, Jabotinsky and Rutenberg approached Storrs with various suggestions for joint security operations, but none of these was put into execution. After an all-night vigil, British troops were pulled out of the walled city at 6:00 a.m. to permit 'business as usual'. But the 'business' which resumed a few hours later was violence. Martial law was proclaimed that afternoon (5th April) and the Arab police were removed. Notwithstanding these steps, Tuesday (6th April) was a day of still more looting and attacks, including two cases of rape. Total casualties after three days amounted to five Jews killed and 211 wounded, with four Arabs killed and twenty-five wounded.

The Palin Report concluded its account of the riots with the observation that it was clear to the Commission that

> the incidence of the attack was against the Jews, and . . . was made in customary mob fashion with sticks, stones and knives. All the evidence goes to show that these attacks were of a cowardly and treacherous description, mostly against old men, women and children, and frequently in the back.

Pointing to this, and to its finding that the 'retaliatory efforts' of the Jews had resulted in very few of the Arab casualties, the Report criticised the Authorities for having entertained the view 'that the Jews were in some way concerned as aggressors'. Yet, as soon as censorship was lifted (14th April), the Arabic press was free to present the masses with a different version, in which the Jews had been the attackers, assisted by arms supplied by the Administration. For weeks the threat of Arab 'revenge' hung over the Jewish communities of Palestine and Syria.[33]

Aftermath of the Riots

Immediately after the first day of horror in Jerusalem there was little doubt in Jewish minds that they had 'lived to be eyewitnesses to an actual pogrom in Jerusalem, the like of which we did not see during hundreds of years of Turkish rule'.[34] Consistent with this description – 'an actual pogrom in Jerusalem' – the Yishuv singled out two elements for blame: 'a few Arab agitators', and 'the hostility towards the Jews evinced by a large number of local authorities'.[35]

In the wake of the riots, the Hebrew press urged the Yishuv not to hold the entire 'Arab people' responsible for the work of a few journalists and agitators. Indeed, Yishuv anger was directed not so much against its 'cowardly and treacherous' assailants and not even against the 'agitators', as against the British authorities. Eighteen months earlier (November 1918), when Jews were sensing the first danger-signs of Arab aggressive intentions, Jabotinsky had remarked:

> If the Arabs try a pogrom I will not hold them responsible; responsible are those whose policy leads, nay – forces savage minds to believe that such acts will be tolerated and even welcomed . . .[36]

Now, in April 1920, this was exactly how Yishuv leaders reacted to the 'pogrom' which had taken place. Ben-Gurion told a meeting of the *Va'ad Zmani* that direct guilt lay 'not even on the inciters, but on Bols and Allenby'; Ben-Zvi, Berligne and Ussishkin echoed the identical view.[37]

All the previous suspicions that the local authorities had been actively encouraging the Arabs to oppose (even physically) the Zionists now seemed totally justified. For the Yishuv, more shocking than the outbreak itself were:– the participation of the Arab police, the tardy appearance of British troops, British interference with *hagana* bands trying to enter the walled city, and the harassment and detention of

Jewish Legionnaires who were in the Jerusalem region at that time.[38] Despite the strict censorship, Jews sought to use the word 'pogrom' frequently and deliberately to indicate their conviction that the authorities were guilty of direct complicity.

The official and unofficial anger of the Jews was expressed in a flood of demands to both Jerusalem and London. Common to many lists were the following demands:– replacement of the Arab police by British and/or Jewish forces; recognition and arms for the embryonic *hagana*; the re-enlistment and expansion of the Jewish Battalions; calling the military chiefs to account, or to trial, for their actions of the previous months; severe punishment of the organisers of the Nebi Musa processions, dismissal of the Mayor of Jerusalem and closure of the Arab clubs; the immediate opening of the country to unrestricted Jewish immigration; and the establishment of an impartial public enquiry, with the participation of Jewish representatives.[39] On 26th April, the *Va'ad Zmani* organised a day of public protest and fasting in all Jewish centres. Petitions were signed and forwarded to London, repeating the undisguised direct accusation that the local Administration was 'aim[ing] at the destruction of the hope of the promise of a National Home for the Jewish people in Palestine'. The methods of this hostile Administration were 'the cause of stirring up the Arabs, encouraging them to threaten the Jews with pogroms, and to actually carry out such threats'.[40] A delegation of Jerusalem Jews was sent to London to convince the British Government of the need to change the régime in Palestine. The Jerusalem Jews brought with them a voluminous and detailed report on the riots which they presented to the War Office.[41]

The reaction of the principal 'accused' to all this was equally angry and bitter. Immediately after order was restored in Jerusalem, the military authorities arrested Jabotinsky and nineteen others for illegal possession of weapons. The men were quickly tried by a 'special' military court and were given exemplary sentences of hard labour: fifteen years for Jabotinsky, and three years for the others.[42] A war of nerves escalated, with minor provocations ultimately leading General Bols to submit a comprehensive report in which he requested the abolition of the ZC and its replacement by 'an Advisory Jewish Council attached to my Administration and under my orders'.[43]

This 'counter-attack' by the Administration left the Yishuv in no doubt – as though the 'pogrom' had not been enough – that local officials were now 'out for vengeance', doing everything in their power to further humiliate the Jews and weaken their position in the country. The prosecution of the *hagana* group was generally interpreted as an attempt to portray the Jews as aggressors in the riots, and to snuff out the movement for self-defence at the very moment when it seemed impossible to rely on British protection. As a mark of its lack of confidence in the Administration, the ZC stopped its former practice of providing copies of its intelligence reports on the grounds that the British had shown little inclination to act on them.[44] From the tone of the correspondence of the period, there is little doubt that Yishuv–British relations had sunk to a low level of mutual recrimination and mutual distrust:

> It was felt on both sides that the last stage of the conflict had been reached, and that the question was now reduced to its crudest and simplest form: either the Jews or the Military Administration would have to go.[45]

Hagana and 'Arab Work' after April 1920

We may be struck by the fact that the Yishuv reacted to the Jerusalem 'pogrom' almost exclusively in terms of the British factor. To understand this better we may recall that in 1918 and 1919 there were many in the Yishuv who entertained the belief that a 'strong and wise' Trustee Power would be able to implement the will of the Peace Conference, even in the face of some 'temporary' or 'ungenuine' Arab opposition. In this light, the British in spring 1920 were seen to have failed to play the part of the 'wise', 'strong' and 'sympathetic' Trustee. By focusing their anger on the European Power, many Jewish leaders were also relieved of the necessity of asking themselves whether the Jerusalem 'pogrom' had been the product of genuine and popular nationalist hostility, which, if it existed, might have to be considered a serious obstruction to the successful implementation of the Zionist programme.

Notwithstanding this focus on the British factor, it had now become painfully evident to everyone in the Yishuv that, whatever its nature, there did exist a real, physical Arab threat which had to be reckoned with. Zionists in London would work on obtaining a better British attitude, but there was also much local work to be done. On the Yishuv's 'home front', the weakness of the *hagana* (quite apart from the question of interference by the British police during the riots) was a source of worry to Jews both before and after 4th April. Following the outbreak and the vivid lesson of the ineffectiveness of British protection there was an even greater determination to strengthen the 'underground' side of Jewish self-defence. The disbandment of the veteran Jewish watchmen's association ('*ha-Shomer*') in May 1920 was followed in June by the decision of the labour group, *Ahdut ha-'Avoda* ('Unity of Labour'), to take over broad responsibility for defence matters and to re-organise the *hagana* on a new, populist (rather than the former élitist) model.[46] Public agitation also continued for a legal method of defence which would be recognised by the authorities. Many Jews now felt that the experience of the Jerusalem riots entitled them to demand the right to organise their own self-defence and to resume recruitment for the dwindling Jewish Battalions.[47]

That the rioting had not spread beyond the walls of Jerusalem may have been due, in part, to the 'Arab work' which had been undertaken by the ZC during the preceding months. This work had included the collection of signatures for pro-Zionist petitions to show the Peace Conference and the British public that the mounting tension did not reflect the 'true' feelings of the Arab masses. Petition-gathering was often combined with the fostering of good relations with individual rural shaikhs, with the practical aim of ensuring the safety of neighbouring Jewish colonies.[48] The effect of the Jerusalem riots was to underline the importance of continuing and improving this kind of public-relations work.

In May the ZC set up a committee of local Jews and gave it the task of finding ways of improving relations with the Arabs.[49] The committee discussed the various needs of the day: to counteract the influence of the Muslim-Christian

Association by a Muslim-Jewish alliance; to approach notables, like 'Arif Pasha ad-Dajani and Sa'id al-Husaini, for
support; to coordinate similar activities by Jewish committees
throughout the country; to improve the political position of
the Jews within the Jerusalem municipality. The chairman, H.
M. Kalvaryski, sought the committee's endorsement of his
'Programme' (p. 43 above) to serve as a basis for talks with
Arabs, but does not appear to have been any more successful
than he had been in convincing the *Va'ad Zmani* in June
1919. In the course of its meetings the committee heard
reports of regional initiatives, such as that of the Federation of
the Jewish Colonies of Judaea, which recommended the
importance of finding the money to purchase land from eager
Arabs, especially the ones who wielded some political
influence.[50] But, mainly because of differences with the ZC,
the committee was dissolved before converting any of its ideas
into practical action. The task of seeking ways to improve
relations with the Arabs then devolved to a three-man committee: Kalvaryski, Tel Aviv mayor Meir Dizengoff, and Jaffa
citrus-owner S. Tolkowsky. They were to be responsible to
the ZC and the *Va'ad Zmani* (later *Va'ad Leumi*) jointly (cf.
pp. 75 f., below).

If the April riots had led to the unanimous feeling that
'preventive' Arab work had to be improved, Yishuv opinion
was divided on the larger question of negotiating a positive
'agreement' with Arab leaders. In the first place, many evalu-
ated the chances of any serious attempt at Arab-Jewish
negotiations in the light of what was still seen to be the
anti-Zionist intriguing of British officials; with the negative
'encouragement' offered to the Arabs by these officials, few
Jews saw much point in entering into negotiations. And, once
the Arabs had demonstrated the physical vulnerability of the
Jews in the North and in Jerusalem, the whole question of an
'understanding' was further set back.

The success of Arab violence had indeed proved the pressing need for some sort of 'peace': but, many wondered, did
this mean that the Jews now had to approach their assailants,
cap in hand, suing for peace? This was the painful dilemma
which faced Yishuv leaders in the first weeks of April 1920,
and which was to confront them again in May 1921, in fall

1929, and during the years 1936–39. The choice which presented itself was not an easy one. At a meeting of the *Va'ad Zmani* Executive,[51] two opposing tendencies were represented. First, there were those who felt that the need to reach an agreement with the Arabs was now so pressing that the Jews were obliged to take the initiative in contacting Arab leaders without delay. Then there were others who felt equally strongly that, although it would indeed be necessary to get in touch with Arab leaders, 'on no account should we do it now; after we are able to show the Arabs our strength – then we shall negotiate with them.' Opinion within the Executive was so sharply divided that the result seems to have been inaction.

A strong factor in this absence of activity may well have been the moral repulsion felt by the victims of the 'pogrom' at the thought of making peace overtures to those 'whose hands had spilled Jewish blood'. The story is told by Judge Gad Frumkin of Menahem Ussishkin's deliberate rebuff to the Jerusalem Mufti, Kamil al-Husaini, in refusing to shake the latter's hand at a Government House reception at the close of the military régime. 'How could I extend my hand in peace to a religious leader whose followers raped Jewish women?' he explained to Frumkin afterwards. Even Frumkin himself, a native Jerusalemite who had daily contact with Arabs in the government service, noted that in the wake of the riots he and his Arab colleagues found it difficult to look each other in the eye.[52]

Thus, from a combination of rational calculation and emotional factors, the Yishuv tendency was not to make any advances from a position of weakness. Renewed hope was placed in the British to maintain order and to implement the decisions of the Peace Conference.

San Remo and the End of the Military Administration

Following the 'pogrom' of 4th–6th April 1920, it seems that the only possible source of encouragement for the Yishuv was the hope that outside help was on the way. And on 25th April, the San Remo decision concerning the allocation of mandates was announced; shortly afterwards it became known that the days of the military régime were numbered and that Herbert Samuel would become the first Civil Governor of Palestine. In a way, all this could be seen as a 'Zionist victory' – i.e., an 'answer' to those who might have been hoping that the April outbreak would have deterred the Powers from going ahead with an unpopular policy.

The news was made official in General Bols' address to the 'Heads of All Sects' on 28th April.[53] He announced that the Supreme Council of the League of Nations had decided to allocate the Mandate for Palestine to Great Britain, and that the terms of the Mandate included the Balfour Declaration, the text of which he then read for the first time in Palestine. This was followed by a list of British assurances that the minority would never be allowed to rule the majority, that there would be no interference with religious rights or Holy Places, and that immigration would be tightly controlled to suit the economic capacity and needs of the country. Bols concluded his address by pointing to the prospect of 'constantly increasing prosperity' to which all the inhabitants could look forward, and henceforth demanded 'an end to political strife and unrest':

> All true Palestinians must now strive with one another in healthy rivalry for the good of Palestine and for the welfare of future generations.
> Politics are the enemy of industry, and hard work is the only remedy to repair the waste of the last few years, and to build up a strong, healthy and contented Palestine.

The Yishuv wanted very much to believe that this long-awaited announcement would begin an era of stability and tranquillity. But the effect of the San Remo news in Palestine was not as decisive as many Zionists hoped; the 'new era' did not begin overnight. Observers in Palestine noted that much 'manoeuvring' was still going on in British and Arab circles. For a full two months after the Chief Administrator's address, Dr Eder was reporting that the Arabs were still hoping to bring about a change in British policy; that the country remained in a 'disturbed state' (owing mainly to Beduin raids in the North); that, in various spots, 'every day [brought] forth rumours of Arab attacks'; and that 'fermentation' was continuing, thus 'prevent[ing] those who are inclined to accept the new order of things from [coming to] an accord with us'.[54] Zionist intelligence and other reports were providing ample evidence that the Arabs had not yet settled down to the fait accompli as expected.

For the Jews, the good news of San Remo lost much of its impact when placed in the context of the bitter feeling which still lingered in the Yishuv. The continued imprisonment of the *hagana* members, notwithstanding a reduction of their sentences, served as a constant reminder of the British attitude which had made the 'pogrom' possible. Ironically, the San Remo news reached Palestine on the very day (26th April) of the country-wide fast which was called to protest against the local Administration. The Yishuv was caught between the two conflicting forces of mourning and jubilation. On the one hand, the 'militants' insisted that struggle and protest must not cease until the Jewish prisoners were released, and those who were really responsible for the 'pogrom' punished instead. On the other hand, 'official' Zionists called for quiet and dignity, now that a great political victory had been won and it was only a matter of time until a new régime was installed.

The news that Herbert Samuel had been chosen to be the first High Commissioner for Palestine seemed to have a more beneficial effect than San Remo on the temper of the Yishuv. 'Could there be anything better,' asked Haifa Jewish leaders, 'than to have one of our own at the head of the Palestine Government? A Nehemiah! A liberator!' At the beginning of May, Eder reported that the appointment was sure to be 'enthusiastically welcomed' by the Yishuv.[55] But apparently even this news was not enough to put an end to the excitement and bitterness which was, for some, still focused on the Jewish prisoners. When, amid the generally increasing optimism, no visible progress seemed to have been made in annulling their sentences, the prisoners decided on a hunger strike, and there was even some talk of an armed Jewish attack on Acre jail.[56] With the imminent arrival of Herbert Samuel and rumours that *all* prisoners might be released under a general amnesty, the *hagana* detainees proclaimed their categorical refusal to accept release on such terms, seeing personal and national insult in an amnesty which placed 'pogrom instigation' on the same level as self-defence.[57]

Weizmann was seriously worried that the Yishuv attitude would damage the new beginnings of the Civil Administration:

> If when Mr Samuel arrives they [i.e., Yishuv leaders] are going to besiege him with all their 'demands, protestations and requests', Mr Samuel will become utterly disgusted and will turn his back on the Jewish community just as the others did, and our best chance will have gone . . .[58]

Weizmann feared very much that on his arrival Samuel would encounter not only 'difficulties with the Arabs' and the 'legacy' of the old régime, but also 'the bad spirit amongst our own people, and that would be fatal . . .' It was only during the last week before Samuel's arrival that Dr Eder was able to report an increase of 'good sense' and calm among the Jewish population.[59]

PART TWO

Transition and Turbulence

4

The Calm Before the Storm: July 1920 – March 1921

The 'Honeymoon Period'

The coming of Sir Herbert Samuel seemed to bring about a near-miraculous change in the 'bad spirit' and uneasiness which had been noticeable in the Yishuv even two weeks before his arrival. The 'ceremonial' beginnings of the new régime were particularly effective in winning the heart of the Jews, and the Yishuv soon hailed Herbert Samuel as 'their' High Commissioner ('*netzivenu*'), almost forgetting that he was, first and foremost, a servant of HM the King.[1] On 7th July the new High Commissioner received a deputation of the *Va'ad Zmani* headed by Dr Ya'akov Thon, who expressed his appreciation of the 'difficulties' of Samuel's task, and pledged that the Yishuv was 'ready, as one man, to help him to the utmost'. At the same time, the *Va'ad Zmani* also declared its desire for 'peace with the Arab people and co-operation in the reconstruction of the country'.[2]

In his first week of office Samuel set about cleaning up part of the legacy of the former Administration. He decreed an amnesty for all those convicted of crimes during the Jerusalem riots and also informed the War Office of his view that the results of the inquiry would best be buried. The *hagana* prisoners at Acre accepted their amnesty, but not without registering a warning about the likely effect this *general* amnesty would have on the Arab mind.[3]

Nevertheless, even Jabotinsky began encouraging Jewish audiences to place 'great hopes' in Samuel, and that an appropriate '*situation nette*' was at last being created in Palestine.[4] During his first months of office Samuel consolidated the good impression which he had created on the Jewish community, to the extent that in late November Dr Thon felt as though he were dealing with 'a brother' at Government House. Even though local Jews still saw room for improvement in the attitude of Government officials, there was a noticeable change for the better in the spirit of Yishuv–British relations and in the tranquillity which returned to the country in the second half of 1920.[5]

As far as the Yishuv was concerned, one of the most welcome changes which occurred during Samuel's 'honeymoon period' was the apparent improvement in the Arab attitude towards the Jews. Following the French-Arab confrontation in Syria and Faisal's flight from Damascus, there was a temporary lull in the anti-Zionist propaganda emanating from this outside base.[6] From July until November 1920 the Zionist press pointed enthusiastically to the decline in Arab agitation. In many reports destined for external consumption, this happy state of affairs was attributed directly to the respect which Samuel had earned for himself and his Administration among all sections of the population.[7] This improvement was accompanied, in the same analyses, by repeated references to previous Arab opposition as having been artificial. While it was admitted that there were some 'extremists' who stubbornly refused to accept the fait accompli of San Remo, it was pointed out that there were also many 'moderates' who were now prepared to co-operate with the new régime and the Zionist programme it implied. Indeed, several instances of superficial intercourse between Arab and Jewish notables on ceremonial occasions seemed to justify this impression.[8]

But, was this optimism really warranted? Perhaps it is more accurate to attribute the decline in overt expressions of Arab hostility not so much to a new spirit of 'co-operation' as to 'bewilderment' during a period of 'watchful waiting'.[9] And, if we examine the available evidence more closely, we are forced to the conclusion that, even during these months – perhaps under the most favourable conditions since the coming of the British – there was little conspicuous activity on the Yishuv's Arab front.

Revival of Arab Agitation

In the new atmosphere of Yishuv-Samuel confidence, Jewish leaders were anxious to begin the 'real' work of Zionism: immigration, land acquisition, settlement, and economic development. 'Our neighbours', wrote Katznelson, 'judge us only by our deeds, and the sole act which changes our position for the better in the country is *immigration*.'[10] From the outset Samuel showed himself to be truly sympathetic in assisting practical Zionist work. He approved the first immigration schedule of 16,500 certificates, and (unwittingly) prevented a serious unemployment crisis by granting a generous share of the new public-works projects to organised Jewish labour.[11] Samuel also granted one of the Yishuv's basic 'national' demands by making Hebrew an official working language of his Administration.

But, as hinted publicly in his first Proclamation to the people of Palestine,[12] Samuel's approach was to be a 'gradualist' one. Sir Wyndham Deedes, Samuel's first Chief Secretary, explained quite frankly in a letter to Dr Weizmann in November.[13]

> We go slowly perhaps but I think surely – and good foundations are being laid.
> *Secure* – particularly because I think I can say that, so far, no susceptibilities have been hurt among those very elements, the gaining of whose confidence is so essential to our success ...
> H. E. himself has gone further than anyone to allay [exaggerated, etc.] fears, and we shall go further still ...

The practical effects of this philosophy were readily felt by the Yishuv. When, for example, the ZC was eager to begin negotiations for the purchase of Trans-Jordanian lands from willing shaikhs, the HC recommended postponing any action until such time as public security in that region was improved. Similarly, when Jewish attempts to open a school for Samaritans in Nablus met with hostility and intimidation on the part of the Mayor and other notables, Samuel rejected Zionist requests for strong Government intervention, preferring 'tact and patience in the matter of Jewish infiltration into that city'.[14] While Yishuv leaders were disappointed – especially about Nablus – they were not bitter against Samuel.

Samuel's approach, which attempted to keep the confidence of Arabs and Jews simultaneously, was already showing its first signs of strain at the close of 1920. For Berl Katznelson, who was less enthusiastic than most people about symbolic victories, the good effects of the Samuel appointment had already worn off by late November.[15] Despite the 'new era', he felt, the Jews were 'still living in a country atop a volcano. True, it is in a quiet state at the moment, but the political intrigue around us will not sleep nor slumber.' Following several months of relative quiet, Damascus once again became a centre for anti-Zionist propaganda, and by spring 1921 both British and Zionist observers looked with apprehension at a wider 'pan-Islamic revival' in the surrounding countries.[16]

In Palestine itself, Arab jealousy had been aroused by alleged Government favouritism to Zionist practical work.[17] Such complaints were bound to have their effect on Samuel and Deedes, who were sensitive to the accusation that the Government was 'all Jewish'. Both men were anxious to minimise the spread of such accusations, and in late December 1920 the HC expressed to Dr Weizmann his reluctance to proceed with any further practical steps until after the ratification of the Mandate.[18]

The central event marking the revival of Arab unrest in Palestine was the Third Palestine Arab Congress, which met at Haifa on 13th–18th December, 1920 (the 'Haifa Congress').[19] The Congress passed resolutions calling for, inter alia:– rejection of the Balfour Declaration as contrary to the 'Laws of God and Man'; the establishment of national parliamentary self-government (but without explicitly rejecting the British presence in Palestine); and a revocation of the visible signs of favour which the Administration had already conferred on the Jews. The Congress elected Musa Kazim Pasha al-Husaini and 'Arif Pasha ad-Dajani to head the 'Executive Committee of the Palestine Arab Congress' (or, 'Arab Executive') to continue the struggle on behalf of the Arabs of Palestine. Perhaps as a demonstration of the strength of the new Arab Executive, the first organised protest demonstration under the Civil Administration took place in Nablus in January 1921, and the standing boycott against the Jews there was tightened. By the end of February the League of Nations was receiving a flood of Arab protests challenging the validity of the Balfour Declaration.[20]

At first this renewal of anti-Zionist cries caused only mild concern in British circles. In order to disarm this potentially hostile segment of the population, Sir Herbert Samuel affirmed his readiness to apply a wise, firm, but not aggressive policy.[21] But the Yishuv reacted with relatively more concern to the recent change in the outward attitude of the Arabs. On the eve of the Haifa Congress, Dizengoff considered the Arab question as one which was 'still unpleasant and still unresolved': a 'movement against us and against the High Commissioner' had been aroused, and it was 'very important for us to do something about it'.[22] For its part, the committee of which Dizengoff was a member continued its work of seeking 'an understanding with the Palestinian Arabs'. Its efforts seemed to be rewarded when several leaders of the Haifa Congress approached the committee 'with the intention to come to a definite understanding between Arabs and Jews'. While the exact terms of the Arab proposals remain a mystery, the Yishuv committee urgently requested the London Executive to grant it £5,000 for expenses, and to arrange facilities with the Anglo-Palestine Bank (APC) for granting loans up to a total of £10,000, 'which may be in part lost'.[23]

But this opportunity of coming to an 'understanding' with the Haifa Congress leaders, described at the time as 'a new situation ... rich in the greatest possibilities', came to nothing, because (as Dizengoff complained bitterly after the May riots) the committee's urgent request had received no reply from London.[24] All along, members of the committee had been working almost entirely at their 'own private expense', and the 'scope and effectiveness' of their work had been 'greatly restricted', 'owing partly to the fact that ... conditions [had] not been favourable for important political work, but chiefly owing to the lack of financial resources'. Apart from the larger question of reaching an 'understanding' with the Arabs, even the less ambitious forms of 'Arab work' ground to a halt owing to a shortage of funds.[25]

Plans for Jewish Defence

In the months following the Haifa Congress, Jews in Jerusalem and elsewhere began to fear a repetition of Arab attacks. 'Arab work' was not the only form of Yishuv response during what Jerusalem leader Yosef Meyuhas termed 'these days of crisis'.[26] The new Arab 'awakening' in Palestine also provoked strong reaction on the Yishuv's 'home front'. In December 1920, the founding convention of the *Histadrut* ('General Federation of Jewish Labour in Palestine') resolved to accept responsibility for setting up a country-wide, clandestine and independent defence organisation: 'the' *Hagana*.[27]

This decision came after several months of confusion among *hagana* enthusiasts themselves. Owing to the apparent tranquillity achieved since the start of the Civil Administration, opinion was divided over the extent to which 'trust' might be placed in the Samuel régime. Perhaps the strongest testimony of Jewish confidence in Samuel during his 'honeymoon period' was the fact that several devoted *hagana* activists were prepared to leave the 'sword' to the British, so that Jews might finally begin to apply their full energies to the 'ploughshare'.[28]

But a distrustful core-group remained relatively unaffected by the transition to Civil Administration. Jabotinsky, although not personally connected with clandestine preparations during this period, provided an eloquent expression of the kind of spirit which no doubt motivated this group. 'The Jew is inclined to optimism', he lectured before the *Va'ad Zmani* in July 1920,[29] and there were perhaps good reasons for this:

> There is peace between us and the English, and we have a High Commissioner in whom we can trust ... We see that the most dangerous element – Damascus – seems to be leaving the stage ... Then Jewish optimism, which invented the famous theory that the Arabs are not capable of anything, that there is no national movement among them, etc., and that therefore there is no need for defence, etc., [is liable] to be revived.

I believe that it is not good for people to devote even one minute of debate to such optimism. We have learned much here: we have settled among a people which understands, a people which is not to be despised, a people which has good sense. Therefore, I say that the question of *hagana* remains, and will remain, before us ...

The atmosphere of renewed Arab agitation in December 1920 served to refresh the memory of delegates to the *Histadrut* convention, if any reminders were needed of the 'lessons' of Tel Hai and Jerusalem. Few delegates could challenge the importance of and the need for a secret and independent defence organisation. 'Even if the country is quiet for a while', declared Eliahu Golomb, 'we cannot be certain about tomorrow.'[30] The decision of the workers to assume responsibility for the organisation of *hagana* and *shmira* (guard-duty) was opposed by only a minority of the delegates present, mainly committed pacifists and those who felt confident relying on British police and the existing system of local *shomrim* (watchmen).[31]

Among the general (and even the workers') public, however, the necessity for an independent and clandestine *hagana* was not yet so acutely felt. By mid-March 1921, the *Histadrut's* decision remained largely on paper and without concrete results. Golomb was worried about the lack of public interest, and pointed to lurking security dangers, especially in the North.[32] Ben-Zvi was equally concerned about the absence of tangible organisational results, and felt the need to warn the *Histadrut* Council against the illusion of believing that a great change in the security position had come about since the installation of the Civil Administration:

> ... despite the apparent quiet in the country, we are well aware how complicated and dangerous the situation actually is ... If the danger is not as great as it was last year, nevertheless the balance of forces in the country and along the frontiers obliges us to be on guard constantly. We are not prepared ...[33]

But it would require the shock of May 1921 to arouse sufficient popular concern for, and commitment to, the proper organisation of the *Hagana*.

Parallel to the plans for a clandestine self-defence organisation, Jewish leaders also took a strong interest in the *legal* defence arrangements which were being worked out by the new Administration. After Tel Hai and Jerusalem, the question of converting the Jewish Battalions into a permanent Jewish militia was not simply a symbolic one of pursuing 'national honour'. Very practical security needs gave a new reality to the campaign for the continuation of the Battalions. In June, the *Va'ad Zmani* appointed a committee to travel to London to argue for the retention of the Jewish Battalion, 'in which the Yishuv [saw] an indispensable need in general, but particularly in the wake of the situation now created in the country.'[34] Other Yishuv bodies joined in the public demands for the rejuvenation of the Battalions.[35]

Vladimir Jabotinsky, in particular, made a point of discouraging the creation of any Arab military units. In arguing this with the British, he urged that such units 'would never become a docile instrument in the hands of the Government', but would serve as the focal-point for aggressive Arab nationalism, with a 'natural drift' towards 'disaffection directed against both the Mandatory Power and the Zionist clauses of the Mandate'.[36] Jewish units, on the other hand, would become 'a magnetic centre of pro-British feeling among the Jews throughout the world'.[37] In arguing the case for Jewish, but no Arab, Battalions before Yishuv audiences, Jabotinsky was presenting a self-evident truth:

> Can we agree [he asked], to the extent that we have any say in the matter, that there should be any Arab army in the country, large or small? ... An army is a political institution, which only a political nation [*uma medinit*] has. It enhances our political status. The status of the Arabs [if given an army] would take on a different form and this would complicate our relations ... A great danger hangs over us from a mixed army.[38]

And the only way, in Jabotinsky's analysis, that the Jews would be able to demand the *unique* right to a military unit would be for the ZO itself to provide the enormous sums needed to finance new Battalions.

For a brief moment in late fall 1920 it appeared as though the creation of a permanent Jewish Battalion was at hand. On 7th October the War Office sanctioned new recruitment of up to 500 men, and Jews quickly set up regional enlistment committees. But, before long Government House in Jerusalem was gripped with second thoughts, owing mainly to budgetary considerations and Arab feeling.[39] Indeed, it appears that Allenby's fears of June 1919 – that a Jewish military unit 'would be interpreted as a preparation to enforce the claim of the Jewish minority on [the] rest of [the] population' – were equally compelling in military circles during 1920–1921.[40]

The Administration finally came up with its own preferred arrangements for creating a mixed force, and in March 1921 it appeared that the Zionist campaign for the Jewish Battalions had ended in failure. Although Deedes and Samuel had done their best to satisfy reasonable Jewish demands, the Yishuv accepted the official scheme for a 'Home Force' with great disappointment.[41] For some, the unsatisfactory character of this new legal arrangement gave added importance to the task of improving clandestine defence capabilities.[42] In any event, the implementation of the scheme was overtaken by the events of May, and a new series of discussions and proposals would be required in the second half of 1921 (cf. below, pp. 111 f.).

Mr Churchill's Visit to Palestine, March 1921

In an effort aimed at 'tidying-up' some of the outstanding problems of British rule in Iraq and Trans-Jordan, a top-level conference was held in Cairo in March 1921, attended by Winston Churchill, Colonial Secretary, and various senior policy advisers. While in the Middle East, Mr Churchill included a visit to Palestine, and both Jews and Arabs sought to take advantage of the Minister's presence to demonstrate their respective cases.[43]

To mark Mr Churchill's arrival in Palestine, the Haifa Congress leaders called for protest demonstrations to be held. But, except for Jerusalem, where a 'large but orderly' protest took place with Government permission, the Authorities were strict in forbidding such gatherings. In Jaffa this prohibition resulted in the closure of Arab shops in silent protest, but in Haifa the ban was defied, with the result that two Arabs were killed by police in the suppression of disorders.[44]

Zionists saw in the visit of the new Colonial Secretary an opportunity to play up to (what Dr Weizmann called) Mr Churchill's 'highly impressionable temperament'[45] from two angles. On the positive side, they sought to impress him with the practical achievements of Zionist settlement-work and the pioneering spirit of the *halutzim* (pioneers), and to show that the latter were not, as hostile propaganda was claiming, 'bolsheviks'. The complementary objective of Jewish preparations was to show Mr Churchill that Arab opposition to Zionism had no real basis in fact or in public opinion.

In preparing for the visit, Yishuv leaders were immediately sensitive to the great natural advantage which the Arabs would enjoy owing to their superior numbers. If the Secretary of State were to see only huge *Arab* crowds while in the country, this, it was feared, might lend some credibility to the politicians' demands to keep the country Arab in the 'national' sense. Therefore, special efforts were made to have Mr Churchill come into contact with as many Jews as possible and to make the Jewish minority disproportionately visible.[46]

Besides the numerical advantage, Yishuv leaders were also concerned that the only recognisable Arab 'voice' in Palestine seemed to be that of the hostile Haifa Congress. Some discussion was devoted to the idea of assisting rival notables to mount a second Arab deputation to inform Mr Churchill that most Arabs – in contrast to the 'unrepresentative' Haifa Congress group – in fact supported the Government and its Jewish National Home policy.[47] Thus, the appearance of a deputation of Beduin shaikhs from Beersheba which offered 'an expression of loyalty to HMG and to the British Administration of Palestine, as well as their repudiation of the right of the Haifa Congress to speak in their name' may not have been wholly spontaneous. In any case, the impact of this deputation was negligible, and the same shaikhs declared their allegiance to the Haifa Congress shortly after the May riots.[48]

On 28th March Mr Churchill received Arab and Jewish deputations at Government House in Jerusalem. The memorandum read by the Haifa Congress deputation[49] was a lengthy document, dotted with scurrilous warnings against the 'Jewish Peril' and obviously inspired by a recent edition of the 'Protocols of the Elders of Zion'. The Arabs presented detailed illustrations of how this 'Peril' menaced all the Nations, but especially Great Britain and Palestine. The Balfour Declaration was 'an act of modern Bolshevism, pure and simple'. From the legal, historical, moral and economic points of view, the Jews had absolutely no rights to Palestine, and the Arabs 'resent[ed] and [were] fight[ing] against . . . the idea of transforming Palestine into a home for the Jewish people'. The memorandum concluded with five demands: (1) abolition of the Jewish National Home policy; (2) establishment of a 'National Government'; (3) a stoppage of Jewish immigration; (4) return to the legal status quo prior to the British occupation; and (5) an end to the enforced separation between Palestine and her 'sister states'.

If the Arab memorandum was an hysterical warning, the submission of the *Va'ad Leumi* was a joyous vote of gratitude and confidence.[50] The Jews of Palestine thanked Great Britain for having been the first Power to recognise and support Jewish aspirations to return to and rebuild the ancient homeland. The appointment of Sir Herbert Samuel, 'a brother Jew', as first HC was hailed as 'the first concrete step' towards the implementation of the Balfour Declaration and the San Remo decision. Very kind words were said about Samuel's first eight months as HC, both in his capacity as governor of the country and also as one who appreciated his historic task in relation to the Jewish people. 'In safeguarding the rights of all the inhabitants, and in caring for their interests', the memorandum stated, 'the HC is fulfilling the Balfour Declaration in its full meaning.' The Yishuv also used this opportunity to reaffirm its earlier pledges 'to assist the HC in establishing cordial relations between all sections of the population.'

A prominent place in the *Va'ad Leumi* memorandum was accorded to the 'Arab question', indicating a departure from the 'glossing-over' tactics of 1918–1919. We can see in the submission to Churchill several similarities to the *Va'ad Zmani* proclamation to the Arabs of March 1920, with the accent for the Colonial Secretary somewhat shifted to reduce the 1920 stress on Jewish determination to 'return', and to strengthen the 'economic benefits' argument. The March

1921 memorandum was overflowing with optimism about the prospects for Jewish-Arab understanding, for the cultural and economic revival of the East as a whole, and for the increasing benefits which the Arab population of Palestine – and the British Administration as well – would enjoy as a result of Zionist prosperity and development.

The *Va'ad Leumi* memorandum was more specific than previous Yishuv declarations in mentioning the 'national-political' side of the Arab question. Even though the Arab world in March 1921 may have been far from satisfied with the results of the peace settlement, the *Va'ad Leumi* nevertheless felt justified in invoking the fulfilment of Arab national aspirations outside Palestine:

> · *The Jewish people treat the national aspirations of the Arabs with complete understanding* [the memorandum underlined]. But we know that by our efforts to rebuild the Jewish national home in Palestine – which is but a small area in comparison with all the Arab lands – we do not deprive them of their legitimate rights. On the contrary, we are convinced that a Jewish renaissance in this country can only have a strong and invigorating effect on the Arab nation [*Ie'um*].

The memorandum ended optimistically:

> Under the guidance of Great Britain, the Jewish and the Arab peoples will work hand in hand to establish a country of a glorious past and an ever-promising future.

The Colonial Secretary spent six days in Palestine, paying visits and receiving deputations. Wherever he went in the Yishuv Mr Churchill was royally received, and he responded with apparently genuine enthusiasm and warm sympathy. On several occasions he uttered words of congratulation and encouragement, and appeared especially impressed with the Zionists' practical achievements, which had, as he put it, 'changed desolate places into smiling orchards and initiated progress instead of stagnation'.[51]

But the real political victory for the Yishuv came with Mr Churchill's reply to the Haifa Congress memorandum. Regarding the principal Arab demand for a repudiation of the Balfour Declaration, the Secretary of State said: 'It is not in my power to do so, nor, if it were in my power, would it be my wish.'[52] He told the Arabs plainly that the creation of a Jewish National Home was 'manifestly right':

> We think it will be good for the world, good for the Jews and good for the British Empire. But we also think it will be good for the Arabs, and we intend that it shall be good for them ...

Drawing attention to the exact wording of the Balfour Declaration, Mr Churchill stressed that what was spoken of was 'the establishment in Palestine of *a* National Home' and not the making of Palestine into '*the* National Home' – a distinction which was (for him at least) of 'great importance'. Churchill himself was convinced that Zionism meant progress and prosperity, and not ruin, for the Arabs, and he urged the Arab leaders, in the interests of their own people, to take 'a wise and tolerant view' of Zionism and to give it a 'fair chance'. If they did so, they would see for themselves how the success of Zionism would be 'accompanied by a general diffusion of wealth and well being ... and by an advance in the social, scientific and cultural life of the people as a whole'. Sir Herbert Samuel supplemented Mr Churchill's remarks with a brief statement conveying his sincere conviction that the fears expressed in the Arab memorandum were 'unfounded', and reaffirmed his faith in a policy which sought to promote 'good-will among the three sections of the community'.

In spite of the paternal advice which Churchill gave to the Jews on the absolute importance of patience, moderation, tact, and practical economic achievements to relieve the Arabs of their fears, and even in spite of some less satisfactory phrases in his explanations of the meaning of the Balfour Declaration to the Arabs,[53] the net results of his visit left the Yishuv elated. Not since 2nd November 1917 had the hopes for a Jewish National Home in Palestine received such firm and unambiguous official endorsement. As one enthusiastic Jerusalem journalist reported:[54]

> In a sense, the Colonial Secretary's visit marks a turning point in our movement; it indicates the passing from discussion to real practical work. He has detailed our difficulties in no uncertain manner, but with the sympathy and understanding of a friend ...
>
> As for the clique of anti-Zionist Arabs, they will continue their intrigues, supported by certain interested parties, and we may

expect them to create trouble – but so long as we remain true to our ideal we have nothing to fear from them, discounted as they are by the best minds both here and in Great Britain.

We might have expected this firm backing of the Zionist position by a leading British statesman to have given an important boost to the Yishuv's self-assurance in approaching its 'Arab question'. At first it appeared to do so. During a secret meeting between *Va'ad Leumi* leaders and representatives of the Hebrew press, Dr Thon suggested that the time was ripe for 'a certain activism' in seeking an agreement with Arab leaders.[55] Y. H. Castel and Ascher Saphir supported this idea, but a third journalist familiar with the Arabs had his doubts. Even though he felt certain that Churchill's 'strong words' of only a few days ago had 'convinced' the Arab leaders, A. Almaliah was worried that 'activism' might prove dangerous: 'Whenever they see our peace-overtures, the Arabs think that they are the stronger ones.'

Notwithstanding isolated discussions of this kind, there is no record of any fruitful activity towards a Jewish-Arab 'understanding' in the aftermath of Mr Churchill's visit. This was less due to any reluctance on the part of Yishuv leaders than to external causes. In practical terms, there was 'no money at all' available for 'Arab work'.[56] More important, as we shall see in the following chapter, the Jews were unduly optimistic in their first assessments of the effect of Mr Churchill's 'plain words' on the Arabs.

The Yishuv would soon look back on the rhetoric and hopes surrounding the Churchill visit with bitter disillusionment.

5

Crisis and Turning-Point: May 1921

Riots and Attacks of May 1921

If the appointment of Sir Herbert Samuel and his first ten months in office had given the Yishuv as a whole the luxury of believing that Arab attacks and 'pogroms' were a thing of the past, then the events of May and June 1921 came as a profound shock. Sharp disillusionment replaced the optimism which had been bound up in the Yishuv's reliance on 'its' HC. In the wake of May and June, the 'security-obsession' of the few zealots spread to a wider circle, and the paramount importance of greater self-reliance became obvious to all.

Although the actual rioting which broke out in Jaffa on 1st May was almost totally unexpected, it is possible to see signs of a build-up in tension during the month of April. From the tone of the Arabic press during that month, as from subsequent events, Mr Churchill's outspoken affirmation of the Zionist policy seems to have angered, rather than pacified, Arab spirits.[1] Another irritant was the aftermath of the March 28th Haifa demonstration. For the Jews, the stern police action had been a source of relief and satisfaction: one eyewitness felt that had the police not acted, as it did, with 'extreme force', 'then the riots would have broken out in a much more serious form than in Jerusalem last *Pesah*'.[2] But the application of the 'firm hand' did not have the intended pacifying effect on the Arabs. Following the police action Arabs were left nursing a sense of injury, which the press readily exploited by denouncing British brutality.

After the uneventful passing of the Nebi Musa festival (the occasion of tension in 1919 and riots in 1920), the outbreak in Jaffa came as a shock and surprise to both Jews and British.[3] On May-Day, after several months of internal Jewish labour rivalry, clashes occurred between an authorised (*Ahdut ha-'Avoda*) and an unauthorised (communist, *Mifleget Po'alim Sotzialistim*) procession. This took place on the outskirts of Tel Aviv, within view of Arab crowds which had gathered on the edge of neighbouring Jaffa. Police fired in the air to disperse Arab and Jewish crowds, but shortly afterwards looting and a 'general hunting of Jews' broke out in the Menshieh quarter of Jaffa. In another quarter, the ZC's hostel for new immigrants was beseiged and attacked by an angry mob, which succeeded – with the passive or active co-operation of the Arab police – in killing thirteen Jews and wounding twenty-four, with a loss of one dead and four wounded. Troops began arriving during the afternoon, but rioting continued on 2nd May, bringing total Jewish casualties to forty killed and one hundred and thirty wounded, while the Arabs suffered thirteen killed and forty-five wounded. Perhaps as a result of the proclamation of martial law, 3rd May was a relatively quiet day.

At a meeting at the Jaffa Governate on 4th May, Arab and Jewish leaders undertook to calm their aroused people.[4] On 5th May, a larger assembly of Arab and Jewish notables of Jaffa was convened under the chairmanship of Sir Wyndham Deedes, and a proposal for a jointly-signed proclamation to pacify the public was entertained. This move was, however, opposed by several of the Arabs present, with the result that leaders remained individually responsible for keeping calm in their respective communities.[5]

But, even after acts of violence had ceased, excitement and false rumours persisted in Jaffa and spread to Kfar Saba, Ain Hai, Rehovot and other outlying areas. A massive Arab attack was mounted against the colony of Petah Tikva, but was thwarted by the timely arrival of Indian cavalry which happened to be in the area. The battle resulted in four Jews and at least twenty-eight Arabs dead, twelve Jews and at least fifteen Arabs wounded, and extensive damage to the colony's holdings. Another serious attack was directed against Hadera, but the Arab assailants were driven off by the sorties of a British aeroplane before any Jewish lives were lost; nevertheless, Hadera suffered heavy damage and losses through pillaging.

Samuel's Statement of Policy: 3rd June 1921

At the end of six days, Arab attacks had resulted in almost fifty Jewish deaths and one hundred and fifty wounded, with thousands of pounds of property damaged or stolen. The general picture left in the Yishuv mind after 6th May was that the infant *Hagana* had been caught by surprise and that the British had again been ineffective, on the whole, in protecting Jewish life and property. Once order had been restored Yishuv leaders waited in vain for direct responsibility to be cast upon Arab politicians and police, and the guilt of the Muslim-Christian Association (MCA) was, for some Jews, obvious enough to merit immediate Government closure and prohibition.[6]

But, instead of the expected punitive action against Arab 'criminals', Yishuv leaders grew increasingly frustrated at what they considered the Administration's demonstrated weakness and conciliatory attitude towards the Arabs. Only an imposed self-restraint prevented the Yishuv from giving loud public expression to its true feelings of bitterness against Sir Herbert Samuel and his Administration.

As far as the Yishuv was concerned, the most depressing sequel to the actual rioting was Samuel's announcement of a temporary stoppage of Jewish immigration. For the Jews, immigration was sacred. As Dr Thon declared during an interview with the Chief Secretary, 'If we had to choose between an important political declaration with restrictions on immigration, and no declaration – but complete freedom to immigrate – we would choose the latter.'[7] The dangers of conceding, even temporarily, to the forces of violence what they considered an elementary Zionist right haunted Yishuv leaders. If control over immigration were not left enshrined as an 'untouchable' right of Zionists, and Zionists alone – then, given the present tendencies of the Arabs and of the Administration, the net result of 'British' control would be that 'a visa from the British Government would be of no use' to the Jewish immigrant 'unless he also had a visa from Musa Kazim Pasha'.[8] This long-term possibility that the Arabs would, in practice, have the ultimate say in controlling Jewish immigration was one of the most dreaded consequences of Samuel's reactions to the May riots. It was at this point that some labour leaders began to contemplate illegal immigration as a necessary answer to the Administration's power to turn immigration on and off at will.[9]

Towards the end of May all sections of the population anxiously awaited a Statement which the HC was scheduled to deliver on the King's Birthday, 3rd June. The Jews, in particular, were awaiting that Statement with some apprehension, but also

> with the expectation that it would guarantee security of Jewish life and property, that it would resolutely assert the authority of the Government against violence and crime, and that it would maintain and proclaim the rights of the Jewish people to their National Home in Palestine.[10]

But – as the Yishuv could not fail to notice – the main thrust of the Statement of 3rd June was in another direction altogether – viz., to reassure an anxious *Arab* population that HMG would take all necessary steps to ensure that the realisation of the National Home would result in no injustice to the non-Jewish inhabitants. Arab fears, which only two months earlier Samuel had lightly dismissed as 'unfounded', now received the HC's primary attention.[11]

> If any measures are needed to convince the Moslem and Christian population . . . that their rights are really safe, such measures will be taken. For the British Government, the trustee under the Mandate for the happiness of the people of Palestine, would never impose upon them a policy which the people had reason to think was contrary to their religious, their political, and their economic interests.

On the delicate question of immigration, Samuel laid down new guide-lines and affirmed that 'it must be definitely recognised that the conditions of Palestine are such as do not permit anything in the nature of a mass immigration'. He followed this with a vigorous denunciation of bolshevik infiltrators, who would never be allowed to undermine the economic and political integrity of Palestine. Samuel also held out the prospect that the people of Palestine would be 'associated more closely with the Administration', and announced that London was presently studying the 'question of securing a free and authoritative expression of popular opinion' – i.e., although carefully avoiding the words, some form of 'representative institution'.

On the immediate question of the Jaffa riots, Samuel wished to reserve his opinion until after the report of the commission of inquiry. Nevertheless, he felt that 'the thoughtful men of all sections' of the population would share his view that the 'flagrant crimes' of murder, assault and looting which had been committed should be 'deplored and condemned'. Those found guilty of criminal offences would 'receive their due punishment', and to the families of the killed and wounded the HC offered his 'heart-felt sympathy'.

It is not difficult to imagine the alarm and despondency which this Statement caused in Zionist and Yishuv circles. As he sat in the assembly and listened to Samuel's address, the word 'Judas' came to Dr Eder's lips, and he reported to London that the Zionists had just 'gone through the gravest crisis in our movement since the declaration of war in 1914'.[12] In his diary entry of 4th June 1921, Arthur Ruppin wrote: 'Herbert Samuel, who was sort of a god to the Jews in Palestine only yesterday, has now become a traitor to the Jewish cause in their eyes.'[13] Samuel's 're-definition' of the Balfour Declaration –

> that the Jews, a people that are scattered throughout the world but whose hearts are always turned to Palestine, should be enabled to found here their home, and that some among them, within the limits that are fixed by the numbers and interests of the present population, should come to Palestine in order to help by their resources and efforts to develop the country, to the advantage of all the inhabitants

– was wholly at variance with Yishuv interpretations of the

extent of British promises (see below). As Dr Weizmann phrased it, 'the Jewish National Home of the war-promise has now in peacetime been transformed into an Arab National Home'.[14] Samuel's stress on the duty of Zionists to improve the lot of the Arabs led one Jerusalem correspondent to re-word the HC's interpretation as follows: 'only on the condition that whatever we do is to enrich all the inhabitants are we to be tolerated at all'.[15] Finally, Samuel's allusions to the establishment of representative institutions came as a severe shock and disappointment to the Yishuv, and set the stage for a future phase of Arab–Jewish relations in Palestine – the 'constitutional struggle' (cf. chapter 8, below).

Worse than any specific injury to the Jews was the whole tone of the Statement, which left the impression that the Administration was giving in to 'mob violence'. On 8th June, the *Va'ad Leumi* formally replied to the Statement of Policy and deplored that, in 'form and spirit', the speech was

> an indictment not of those who have committed crimes and organised disorder, but of those who have been the victims of those crimes and that disorder ... The general impression made by the statement is that it is an endeavour to protect the Arabs from the "Jewish Peril" ...[16]

While the stoppage of immigration, which 'follow[ed] promptly upon the crimes' in May, had appeared to all sections of the population 'as the sequel to and the reward of violence and outrage', Samuel's references to immigration in the 3rd June Statement were seen to 'confirm the victory of crime'. As Eliahu Golomb wrote at the time, 'not even in the Ukraine or in Russia was such remuneration given to rioters'.[17]

Yishuv Reaction: The British Factor

Events of May and June 1921 were of such an import as to bring about an abrupt end to many comforting assumptions which had been previously entertained in various Yishuv quarters. The optimism and complacency reigning in some circles at the time of Mr Churchill's visit were swept away overnight, and in this and in subsequent chapters we shall be dealing with the attempts at self-criticism and re-appraisal on all fronts: British, Arab and 'home'. Beginning with the British, Yishuv reaction after May 1921 appeared, on the face of it, to be not-so-radically revised from its reaction after April 1920.

Throughout May and June Yishuv leaders were overworked with daily meetings or with interviews at Government House. At the end of June many differences still separated the Yishuv from 'its' HC, and a *Va'ad Leumi* memorandum attempted to summarise these in a 'simple and undisguised manner' for Samuel's benefit.[18] After dealing with the questions of labour immigration and Zionist investment in Palestine, the memorandum went straight to the heart of the political question. Whereas, only two months earlier the *Va'ad Leumi* had warmly praised Samuel (in its memorandum to Churchill) for 'fulfilling the Balfour Declaration in its full meaning' (p. 81, above), now, at the end of June, it rejected his recent definition of that Declaration and clung firmly to the 'true contents of the promise of the British Government'. These 'true contents', as the Yishuv saw them, did

> not allow for any numbers or incidental interests of the present population of the country to affect the life and the historic aspirations of the Jewish people, whose return to the land of its fathers had been decided by historic justice and by the decision of the Nations.

As it had done before Mr Churchill, the *Va'ad Leumi* again protested that the Jews had no wish 'to encroach upon the Arab people', which possessed 'the right and the opportunity to revive its homeland in its extensive historic lands'. But, the memorandum repeated, these lands did *not* include Palestine, that small 'corner' which had been reserved by History, the League of Nations and the British Government as the homeland of the Jewish people. In no way would the 'individual rights' of the Arab people in Palestine be denied, 'but the *political* [my emphasis, NC] right to erect a National Home should be given [only] to the Jewish people'. Before reaching its pessimistic general conclusion, the memorandum presented complaints about the continuing lack of public security and levelled basic criticisms of the methods of the Administration. The Government had, on the one hand, 'rejected Turkish methods, which in certain cases are suited to local conditions', while on the other hand it had failed to set up a truly 'European' administrative system.

Thus, in mid-1921, we find that many Jews continued to assign an elementary and heavy responsibility to the British for having tolerated conditions which had made the outbreak of violence possible. Many were convinced that they had been the victims of another 'pogrom' – but this time worse than Jerusalem and (in Sokolow's words) even worse than Kishinov.[19] What made Jaffa, 1921, tragically worse was the fact that 'this time it took place in the Jewish National Home in Palestine and under the rule of a British High Commissioner who is a son of the Jewish people.'[20]

While Samuel's good faith was only rarely called into question, many in the Yishuv believed that the lower ranks of the Administration were staffed by enemies of the Jewish National Home policy, especially officials of the previous Military régime who should have been removed in July 1920. Some went further, stating that Samuel was 'a prisoner' of these officials.[21] To many Yishuv leaders, the riots were the inevitable outcome of Samuel's inopportune gentleness and misplaced liberalism in the face of mounting Arab arrogance.[22] When considering the amnesty granted to Hajj Amin al-Husaini (convicted for incitement in the April 1920 riots) and his subsequent appointment as 'Grand Mufti', and when considering the de facto prominence enjoyed by Musa Kazim and the Haifa Congress leaders, it was not difficult for Jews to conclude that 'their' HC had 'elevated to the highest rank the lowest of our enemies', thereby dealing a cruel blow to Jewish prestige among the Arab population.[23]

Even though many Jewish leaders were convinced that 'their' HC had thus undermined the Yishuv's political position – perhaps even more than the rioting had undermined its security position – it is noteworthy that almost every word of the despairing criticism thus far described was kept behind closed doors or was directed to Samuel privately. Instinctive first reactions to Samuel's stoppage of immigration in May and to his Statement of 3rd June had been to demand redress on the threat of mass resignations from all Jewish public bodies in Palestine. Yet, after sober reflection, most leaders were forced to realise that such a show-down would be either ineffective or harmful.[24] Only Yitzhak Ben-Zvi gave up his seat on the Government's Advisory Council on 11th May as a sign of protest against Samuel's handling of, and reaction to, the riots.[25]

Although the *Va'ad Leumi* decided to keep its frankest and most vigorous criticism of the Administration out of the public domain, it was nevertheless forced – as the recognised spokesman for the organised Yishuv – to adopt some form of public stand on the riots. Even in the public proclamation issued on 23rd May[26] we are able to see self-imposed restraint operating between the lines. Despite the conviction that a 'pogrom' had indeed taken place in Jaffa, the emotive word did not appear in the proclamation. Instead, the guilt of Arab agitators was violently denounced, and in place of direct criticism of Samuel's leniency and weakness we find the following:

> The Jewish population of Palestine affirms that the irresponsible haughtiness of the politicians of Oriental countries is not capable of appreciating either the humane and easy-going policy of the Jewish High Commissioner or the seasoned moderation of Western politics ...

The proclamation called for a speedy ratification of the Mandate, lodged a protest against the temporary stoppage of immigration, and summoned world Jewry to unite in contributing the men and the means for sustained immigration and development of the Jewish National Home. In a paragraph reminiscent of the March 1920 proclamation to the Arabs (p. 56, above), the *Va'ad Leumi* solemnly reaffirmed that the Jews were determined never to abandon the peaceful and constructive enterprise of building their National Home:

> Even now, after the bitter experiences which recent days have bequeathed to us, we proclaim that a spirit of peace motivates us, and that it is our desire to live together with the Arab people in fraternal peace on this land which is in such need of work and energy.

The Arabs: A 'National Movement'?

If, in its public utterances, the Yishuv tended to play down the British factor in the aftermath of the May disorders, it correspondingly played up the Arab factor. (This balance was precisely the inverse of the Yishuv's response to the April 1920 'pogrom'.) The picture painted for external consumption in the wake of May 1921 stressed the malevolent role played by Arab demagogues, agitators and 'effendis', by French agents, and by other 'interested parties'. Jewish testimony before the Haycraft Commission of Inquiry was one of the main channels used to convey this picture, and the Commission's *Report* gives a fair summary of these views:[27]

> It has been said to us by Jewish witnesses that there was no essentially anti-Jewish question at that time, but that a movement against the Jews was engineered by persons who, anxious to discredit the British Government, promoted discontent and disturbance of the peace by stirring up the common people against the Jews. It is argued by them that all the trouble is due to the propaganda of a small class whose members regret the departure of the old régime, because British administration has put an end to privileges and opportunities of profit formerly enjoyed by them; that in co-operation with them are certain foreigners, principally French agents, who are ready to make mischief for political reasons, and to encourage any sort of disturbance calculated to embarrass the British Government. These witnesses asserverate that Zionism has nothing to do with the anti-Jewish feeling manifested in the Jaffa disturbances.

The *Report* immediately rejected this analysis, noting that 'the feeling against the Jews was too genuine, too widespread and too intense to be accounted for in the above superficial manner'.[28]

While there were many Jews who did genuinely subscribe to analyses similar to the above, it would be wrong to assume that they all did. In fact, the extensiveness and the degree of organisation of the Arab attacks of May forced a number of Yishuv leaders to ask – although only behind closed doors – whether the time had come to 'call a spade a spade',[29] i.e., to acknowledge that there *did* exist a genuine, widespread or intense Arab hostility. This was a touchy question, even for internal discussion. While there had always been, in the past, isolated voices who preached that Jewish immigration and settlement were arousing the opposition of an awakening Arab 'people' or 'nation',[30] those who chose to raise this point in May and June of 1921 were testing the patience of many people who were still smarting from the recent 'pogrom'.

At a major *Va'ad Leumi* debate in mid-May, H. M. Kalvaryski linked this question to his familiar theme of Yishuv neglect of the 'Arab question', declaring that the Yishuv was involved in a 'struggle between two peoples (*'amim*)', and that the Jews had little hope of 'triumphing over the [Arab] people, dwelling in its land, by force of the [Balfour Declaration] alone'.[31] At the same meeting Ya'akov Thon also spoke of a 'struggle between two peoples' when replying to those who persistently called for British repressive measures. The 'strong hand', he affirmed, would never succeed in keeping the Arabs down, 'just as it will not suppress Zionism and immigration'.

> It is pointless [he went on] to consider this a question only of effendis. This may be fine as a tactic, but, between ourselves, we should realise that we have to reckon with an Arab national movement. We ourselves – our own [movement] – we are speeding up the development of the Arab national movement. All this we don't see. Yet there are several here among us who speak of 'hangings', thinking that this will resolve the question ... In future we shall have to deal with tens of millions of Arabs; this people will be united ...

In an article written after the riots, Haim Arlosoroff, a recent arrival in Palestine (and, ten years later, the head of the Political Department of the Jewish Agency), likewise called for a more rigorous self-appraisal and denounced the Yishuv's obsession with external factors, such as the 'strong hand' policy or the theory of the intriguing 'hidden hand'.[32] These, he claimed, may have been incidental to the present crisis, but the more fundamental issue to be tackled was to understand the nature of the 'Arab movement' in Palestine and to determine what attitude the Yishuv should take towards that movement and the 'Arab people'.

Arlosoroff admitted that, when comparing the Palestinian

phenomenon to recognised European national movements and when considering its social and economic underpinnings, it was possible

> to pass judgment that we have no Arab national movement here, and that, on the basis of the conditions prevailing in Arab society, neither is there any possibility for such a movement to exist.

'But', he asked, 'what have we gained by pointing out this fact?'

> It is like the doctor who stands at the bedside of a patient wallowing in malarial fever and denies the existence of the disease, simply because the microbes which he found in the patient's blood do not resemble those he is used to seeing under his microscope.

The important thing for the Yishuv, he argued, was neither the agitators, nor the artificiality of the 'movement', but the glaring fact that agitators had *succeeded* admirably in arousing popular hostility against the Jews.

On the question of definitions, he believed that the Yishuv was obliged to admit that there was a 'political force' in the country which generally went under the name 'Arab movement':

> An Arab movement – whatever its type – really exists, and in my opinion it would be a calamity for us to belittle its importance or to rely on bayonets, whether Jewish or British. This reliance can only be a temporary prop and cannot go on for decades.

The 'wisdom of the "strong hand"', he felt, would never bring Zionism to its final goal; what was needed instead was a 'policy of mutual understanding'.

It is interesting to note that even so keen a supporter of the 'strong hand' as Eliahu Golomb was able to reach identical conclusions as to the reality and power of an 'Arab movement' in Palestine.[33] It was in the further conclusions which he drew from this recognition that he differed from Thon and Arlosoroff. For Golomb, the existence of such a movement in no way altered the need to take a tough stand against it. In a letter to Moshe Shertok he insisted that the Jews had to realise that the course of this 'Arab movement' was 'undoubtedly very dependent on our own strength and on the course which the Government takes'. He even saw some hope in winning the Arab masses away from the current MCA leadership, replacing it with 'friendly' Arabs. But what was required for this 'transplant operation' was the proper policy and activity on the part of both Jews and British, with the aim of 'implanting the idea among the Arabs that we constitute a force with which they will have to reckon and to live'.

There were other Yishuv personalities who – while not going so far as to bestow the title 'national movement' on the Arabs – nevertheless acknowledged that the Yishuv was confronting popular hostility among the Arabs. But, for most of those who were prepared to admit this much, the *genuineness* of such hostility remained the decisive criterion (cf. Arlosoroff). Meir Dizengoff was convinced from his experience that the broad Arab public recognised the economic benefits of Jewish immigration and therefore could not be *truly* hostile:

> If the whole Arab people were against us [he declared before the *Va'ad Leumi*], then ten thousand troops would be of no use to us . . . It would be impossible for us to stand against the whole Arab people.

Fortunately, in Dizengoff's view, it had not come to that; antagonism stemmed 'not from the Arab people as a whole, but from the leaders, and', he added, no doubt remembering his own personal contacts, 'with the leaders it is possible to come to terms.'[34]

Other participants at the same *Va'ad Leumi* meeting simply denounced as a 'lie' or a dangerous 'hypnosis' the view that here was a 'struggle between two peoples'. While some were prepared to admit that such a struggle *might* develop sometime in the future, the present crisis was merely a 'pogrom' executed by gullible masses under the influence of 'gangs of agitators'. Why, they asked irritably, complicate matters by raising the question of a 'national movement'? Was it so difficult to 'arouse half-savage masses to attacks'?[35]

The debates over the existence of an 'Arab national movement' were, in a sense, the most abstract of all those stimulated by the events of May and June. While they give an indication of the new levels of awareness in the Yishuv of the seriousness of the 'Arab question', there were very few *practical* consequences attached to the outcome of such debates. For those who did believe in the existence of an 'Arab national movement' in Palestine, their belief did not result in any dramatic, practical suggestions for an effective 'Arab policy'; nor did it necessarily propel them headlong to the conference table with Musa Kazim al-Husaini. On the question of negotiating with Arab leaders, Yishuv reaction was quite similar to what we have noted in 1920 (above, pp. 63 f.). 'Believers' and 'non-believers' in the Arab national idea were equally conscious of what Sokolow called the 'tragic necessity' of reaching an accord with the Arabs. Yet, amid the despair, they saw the need to wait for the 'proper psychological moment' – i.e., not while Arab hands were freshly 'stained with blood', but perhaps after the Mandate was ratified.[36]

But ratification did not follow as soon as expected, and the whole notion of the 'proper psychological moment' was a most elusive phenomenon. In August 1921, for example, Leonard Stein reported that 'rapprochement' was 'forbidden alike by Jewish self-respect and by Arab self-confidence'.[37] Yet, after the riots local Jews were free to maintain friendly contacts with local Arabs, until such time as a high-level 'national' policy on negotiating was decided.[38]

'Arab Work' and an Arab Policy

Whether the May riots had been the expression of a genuine 'national movement' or the work of an unscrupulously-incited primitive rabble, one thing was clear: the Jews could not afford to allow the Arab leaders (or 'agitators') an open field to continue their education of the masses to Zionist disadvantage. Under the impact of the May crisis, there were more Jews who felt the compelling need to take steps to organise those Arabs who were potential 'friends' into a political force in the country (see chapter 7, below).

As we have seen, the shaky state of Zionist finances had, perhaps more than anything else, hampered the launching of protracted and consistent 'political work' among the Arabs. If the prospects offered by Kalvaryski's committee in March and the disclaimers submitted by Dr Eder in April had not succeeded in squeezing the necessary funds out of the tight ZO budget, the May riots now provided the necessary urgency. Nahum Sokolow, the Executive member in Palestine at the time, called for the creation of a generous fund for political work. In London, the ZO Finance and Budget Commission responded by opening a 'special loan account' of £10,000 for the 'special needs of the Zionist Commission'.[39]

The ZO was not the only source of funds for 'Arab work' in Palestine. From its early experience, the Jewish Colonisation Association ('ICA') had learned how closely its main task – land acquisition – was intertwined with political considerations and relations with the Arabs. Even when the ZO officially assumed political predominance after the Balfour Declaration and the British occupation, the ICA continued for several years to protect its own interests by dealing independently with political aspects of its colonisation work. In so doing, the Association from time to time invested various sums of money *via* its agents and employees, among them H. M. Kalvaryski. Following the May riots, the ICA like the ZO, felt the pressing need for increased expenditure on 'Arab work'.

Throughout 1921 Kalvaryski was very much at the centre of the Yishuv's Arab affairs, serving as employee of the ICA, agent of the ZC, and member of the *Va'ad Leumi*. It is therefore not surprising that, in early March, he had suggested that two of his 'bosses' (the ICA and the ZO) pool their resources and provide him with an expense account which would place the work of winning Arab 'friends' on more solid ground. While this request had suffered the same fate as similar projects submitted at that time, after the May riots an arrangement for £15,000 along these lines was concluded between Nahum Sokolow, for the ZO, and James de Rothschild, for the ICA.[40]

With the promise of new funds in the summer of 1921, Kalvaryski went about his accustomed work with new vigour: continued support for the Jewish-Arab school near Rosh-Pina, contributions to charities, mixed clubs, press and propaganda. Added to this list was a new and more ambitious project: the creation of 'a large Muslim-Arab party favourable to our aspirations'.[41] The creation of the new party was by no means an easy chore, requiring 'enormous sacrifices' (i.e., finances) which Kalvaryski hoped would be forthcoming from London Zionists: 'We must stop at no sacrifice, however great, to reach this goal. Without the agreement all that we have built up over the last years will crumble.' Despite the unsteady flow of funds for his project, Kalvaryski was able in November 1921 to announce the birth and first activities of *al-Jamia al-Islamiyya al-Wataniyya* – the 'Muslim National Association' (MNA) through which, it was hoped, 'we shall weaken the baneful influence of the Muslim-Christian Association and we shall bring about the Jewish-Arab entente so needed and desired'.[42]

Other Zionists were equally concerned with the formulation of an effective programme of 'Arab work'. In July 1921 Dr Weizmann assigned Leonard Stein, Political Secretary to the Zionist Executive, to investigate the situation in Palestine, with special reference to the reorganisation of the Zionist intelligence service and the possibilities of the 'formation of a moderate Arab Party with which we could really co-operate politically and economically'.[43] Stein's comprehensive report, 'The Situation in Palestine, August 1921', contained an indirect but effective critique of Kalvaryski's 'Arab work'.[44] Stein regarded the creation of a 'moderate Arab Party' – i.e., precisely what Kalvaryski was doing at the time – as 'premature', although he did not rule out the possibility that one might 'eventually emerge'. What made such a party premature, in Stein's analysis, was the current inability of the Zionists to 'offer a quid pro quo' to the Arabs. Like Kalvaryski, Dizengoff, Tolkowsky and others in the Yishuv, Stein accepted the 'economic benefits' argument as the basis and starting-point for 'Arab work'. He underlined a widely-held explanation of those days when he stressed that 'the situation might have been less acute had Zionist activity brought the Arabs the material advantages they had been invited to expect from it.'

On the general question of 'Arab work', Stein spared no words in criticising the previous methods used by the ZC and its tendency to regard the Arabs 'as a temporary obstruction to be coaxed or bribed away'.

The signature of the professional petition-monger or the temporary benevolence of a venal editor have no appreciable effect on the situation; and in general little can be done by the mere distribution of casual bribes, except, perhaps, on a vastly larger scale than it is possible to contemplate.

Without having to mention names, such criticism clearly applied to the views and activities of men like Kalvaryski, Dr Eder and even Dr Weizmann himself.[45] In Stein's opinion, these 'spasmodic attempts to buy off opposition' would have to be replaced by a 'systematic and persistent effort to get at the root of the trouble' and 'to cultivate an entente with responsible representatives of moderate opinion'. Although several external factors (chiefly, the attitude of the Government) 'largely deprived the Zionists of their bargaining-power' in their relations with the Arabs, Stein noted that 'the failure of the Zionist Commission to develop a coherent Arab policy must be taken into account as an element in the situation'.

Stein was by no means either the first or the only person to point to the lack of a Zionist 'Arab policy'. In what appears to have been an 'open season' for political memoranda, the month of August also witnessed several local suggestions for a comprehensive programme embodying an effective Arab policy. Two such schemes which emanated from Yishuv quarters (and which mirrored many of Stein's observations) deserve mention here, especially as they reveal more directly the spontaneous concern felt in Palestine.

The proposals of Y. H. Castel and S. Tolkowsky began with the same premise: viz., that a clear 'Arab policy' had been sadly lacking, and that the gap had to be filled. Castel, whose ancestors had been in Palestine since 1492 and who served as head of the ZC Press Bureau, felt that[46]

Now, after the experience gained during the last three years, and having felt the "Bitter Existence" of our neighbours, there is no need to explain the importance of solving this [i.e., Arab] question.

Reflecting a growing body of Yishuv opinion, he urged that the Jews themselves had to face the issue squarely:

We must not pretend not to see its importance and to postpone its
solution with the sole hope that the ratification of the Mandate
will put everything right again, and that the Palestine Government ... will find the most desirable way out. Let us not rely
upon others ...

Castel presented a balance-sheet of the anti-Zionist and
pro-Zionist forces at work in the country and proposed an
elaborate scheme for 'Arab work', suggesting the correct
attitude to be adopted in every sphere of Zionist activity:
press, police, colonisation, public works, etc.

His conclusions were clear-cut. Zionists should base their
Arab policy on the assumption that 70 per cent of the Arab
population – 'the unorganised majority' – was a 'neutral factor', subject thus far to the predominant 'negative influence'
of the educated and 'effendi' classes. With the proper
attitude, the majority might 'equally fall under the healthy
sway of the Jewish colonies by the opportunities afforded
them to find employment with the Jewish farmers'. He noted
that, unfortunately, those Arabs who were potential 'friends'
– for whatever motives – were not organised and completely
without political support 'either from us or from the Palestine
Government'. In deference to what he felt was the innate
materialism of the Arab, he suggested that 'uninterrupted
practical and constructive work' was an essential precondition
to any lasting agreement: 'only then can the Arabs be sure of
the practical value of our colonisation.'

It was when Castel embarked upon his discussion of *political* fundamentals that he became a 'voice in the wilderness' in
terms of the prevailing mood of the Yishuv. It is nonetheless
interesting to contrast his independent views with those of the
recognised leadership of the organised Yishuv. While the
Va'ad Leumi clung to its generous interpretation of the 'true
contents' of the Balfour Declaration (p. 91, above), Castel
dared to conclude that the Jews had to recognise the '*bi-
national*' idea if any political agreement with the Arabs was to
be reached.

So long as we insist upon the principle "Palestine for the Jews as
England for Englishmen" [sic], our schemes for a peaceful
settlement will ultimately be of no avail; but, on the other hand, if

we come to the logical conclusion that "Palestine cannot be built up except on the basis of a Common State for our two Nationalities", like Belgium, Switzerland, etc., then we may succeed in realising the Balfour Declaration.[47]

To this end, he advocated that the Zionists should invite Mr Balfour himself to 're-write' the second part of his Declaration to read: ' . . . provided that they [HMG] shall develop the present National Home of the other inhabitants . . . and safeguard their legitimate rights to the country.'[48]

Samuel Tolkowsky, who also played an active role in 'Arab work' and in *hagana* organisation, was less daring than Castel, but no less concerned. He too felt compelled to compose a memorandum on the 'Arab Problem in Palestine',[49] which he asked Dr Weizmann to circulate privately (without mentioning the author's name) among delegates to the Twelfth Zionist Congress at Carlsbad (September, 1921). Like Castel, Tolkowsky felt that 'the present state of latent conflict between the Arabs and ourselves must be brought to an end', and that this could be done 'only by ourselves, through a well thought-out and systematically pursued Arab policy'. Also like Castel, he deprecated excessive reliance on the British, and identified the 'effendi' as the centre and origin of Arab hostility.

But, unlike Castel who ambitiously aimed at improving the situation on all fronts simultaneously, Tolkowsky argued that the single *point d'appui* of any Arab policy had to be 'the effendi'. He feared that Yishuv labour groups were behaving irresponsibly by frightening and alienating the 'effendi' with their attempts to 'awaken' the 'downtrodden' peasants (cf. p. 133, below). Had, he asked, the previous benefits which had accrued to the fellahin prevented them from taking part in effendi-inspired attacks on their places of employment? In Palestine, as in other Eastern lands, it was the 'effendi class' which 'makes the policy and uses the masses to carry that policy out'.

Convinced of the crucial importance of winning over the 'effendi', Tolkowsky stressed that constructive activity was an essential prerequisite to political success. He pointed out that too few land-purchases had been concluded since the war, leaving Arab landowners 'burdened with debts and disappointed in their hopes of great profits' on expected land-sales to the Jews. 'These persons have become once more our enemies. And, being land-owners and influential, they are dangerous enemies.'

Tolkowsky's memorandum urged a realistic acceptance of the 'fact, which we cannot change and which, therefore, we have to accept and reckon with, that the big majority of the Palestinian Arabs understand by "advantage" only material advantage.' Zionists must not shy away from giving 'baksheesh' to obtain political advantages. Otherwise, a 'laissez-faire' attitude (allowing economic forces to make the land 'flow with milk and honey' in the indeterminate future) would leave Arab 'agitators' an open field to do their work of poisoning Arab public opinion against the Jews. To Tolkowsky, as to others with real experience in trying to win Arab 'friends', it was inescapably a question of providing immediate and direct economic advantages.

Conclusion

The crisis of the May 1921 riots and their political aftermath produced, as we have seen, debates on the existence of an 'Arab national movement', new activity in creating a 'moderate' Arab party and soul-searching memoranda on a Zionist 'Arab policy'. All this reveals the new heights of Yishuv concern and awareness with regard to the 'Arab question'. While there were individuals who continued to warn against the perceived dangers and defects involved in activities on the Arab front, we cannot find the same consensus, which we encountered in 1919, daring to advocate *inaction*. Even individuals dedicated primarily to *hagana* began to admit that 'Arab work' could be regarded as a necessary adjunct to self-defence.[50]

Whether it received expression in vigorous 'Arab work' activity or in *hagana* preparations, the overall effect of the crisis of May and June 1921 was to foster greater Yishuv self-reliance. One corollary of this new self-reliance was the painful severing of the sentimental bond which had linked Palestine Jewry to Sir Herbert Samuel as the 'Jewish' HC.[51]

For, in his own efforts to resolve the problems of Arab hostility to Zionism, Samuel exerted much pressure on Zionist and Yishuv leaders to adopt a more conciliatory policy towards the Arabs. 'You yourselves are inviting a massacre', he warned Yishuv leaders in June, 'which will come so long as you disregard the Arabs.'[52] 'There is only one way', Samuel repeated, 'and that is an agreement with the inhabitants. Zionism has not yet done a thing to obtain the consent of the inhabitants, and without that consent immigration will not be possible.'[53]

One Yishuv reaction to this kind of advice was that 'in times of stern rule over the Arabs it is possible to negotiate, but not when the Jews feel themselves beaten'.[54] The Yishuv continued to regard the Arabs as, first and foremost, a threat to be held in check. In the meantime, Palestine Jewry was obstinate in rejecting Samuel's 're'-definition of the Balfour Declaration and clung firmly to their own broad and generous interpretation – which, we may note, had changed very little between 1919 and 1921.[55] The Yishuv was in no mood to go to the lengths advocated by Samuel in the hope of softening the Arab stand. Even though they had reached the stage where they regarded Arab hostility as 'temporarily menacing' and not 'properly or safely' to be disregarded,[56] Yishuv leaders did not choose to enter into a debate over which basic concessions in the full Zionist programme would have to be made in the quest for peace with the Arabs. At this stage, for the Yishuv to reckon with the Arab question meant only to foster 'moderate' Arabs and to strengthen the *Hagana*.

PART THREE

Consolidation under the Mandate

6

Yishuv Security after May 1921

In the three years following the May 1921 riots, the Yishuv was preoccupied with consolidating its position vis-à-vis an unwelcoming Arab population. 'Rapprochement' and 'mutual understanding' were mere phrases and nebulous goals at this time; in real terms, the necessary preconditions for such goals had yet to be created. As the Yishuv saw it, the basic, elementary requirement was the improvement of its own strength and security position: Arabs and Jews had to be able to interact on the common assumption that the latter were not to be eliminated by physical violence. This approach has become a basic feature of Zionist and Israeli policy, and can still be seen in operation today with the State of Israel's attempt to gain formal Arab recognition of its existence and to convince the Arabs of the futility of their hopes of eliminating the Jewish state.

Going one step beyond the basic security requirements, many Jews felt that an active attempt had to be made in the wake of May 1921 to counteract the evil influence of the 'extremist' opponents of the National Home. In this and the following chapter we shall take a closer look at security and 'Arab work' – two ways of dealing with the Arab question which were natural to the Yishuv and a product of direct local experience. In later chapters (8 and 9) we shall examine constitutional arrangements, and relations with the larger

Arab world – two other spheres which involved the consolidation of the Yishuv's position, but in which the initiative lay less with the local Jews than with the official Zionist leadership in London and Jerusalem.

Hagana after May 1921

If, immediately following the May crisis, Yishuv opinion was divided over the tactics of reacting to the British, over the true nature and extent of Arab opposition, or over the type of 'Arab policy' to be pursued, there was one thing which did evoke greater unanimity: that the strengthening of the *Hagana* on a far larger scale than previously had to become the Yishuv's most urgent preoccupation.[1] This point emerges most vividly not from the views of committed 'militarists', but from the reactions of those *Hagana* activitists who harboured 'pacifistic' leanings. The same Moshe Smilansky who had been among the advocates of the withering-away of *hagana* during Samuel's 'honeymoon period' wrote eloquently in July 1921 of the new era in which '*hagana* will take first place':

> We must and we can live in peace with our neighbours. But at the same time we must and we can be prepared to defend our existence from one moment to the next. If we ourselves are not "for" us, nobody else will be.[2]

A similar case is that of the *ha-Po'el ha-Tza'ir* labour leader, Yosef Sprinzak. Unlike Smilansky, who had served as a volunteer in the Jewish Battalions, Sprinzak had opposed the Battalions out of a deep antagonism to professional militarism and regretted that young blood was being diverted from the true colonisation work and pioneering spirit of labour-Zionism.[3] Nevertheless, his increasing support for the *Hagana* after December 1920 did not seem to conflict with his principles. If any further justification for his support of *hagana* were needed, it surely came in May 1921:

> The strong hand of Churchill [he told the *Va'ad Leumi*] did not put down or weaken the Arabs, and the strong hand of an Indian military escort [the Indian cavalry which saved Petah Tikva from destruction] will not subdue them. We shall never be at ease with English force [to protect us]. We shall not be able to go through our history with an English escort.[4]

Actual *Hagana* performance in May 1921 was, on the whole, a cause for concern and depression.[5] It had to be admitted that, without British military intervention, the situation in places like Hadera, Petah Tikva and Haifa would have been much worse. Many in the Yishuv felt that his dependence on British help would have to be reduced and replaced by a healthier self-sufficiency.

The urgency of improving the *Hagana* in 1921 did not flow simply from the memory of those who fell in the first week of May, but was continually underlined by the feeling of insecurity which persisted into the summer of 1921. In mid-June Eliahu Golomb felt that the Jews 'stood before the danger of war, not merely the danger of attack'.[6] Isolated cases of murder and violence against Jaffa Jews in June and July reinforced this feeling.[7]

Golomb, at the centre of the new *Hagana* reorganisation, anxiously witnessed the 'Arab movement' growing stronger and more united from week to week and received frequent reports indicating preparations for new outbreaks.[8] Obsessed with the fear of being caught off-guard again as in May, a core-group of activists fought an uphill battle to introduce improvements in defence and security. Effective intelligence, abandoned during the 'honeymoon period', had to be revived. The first 'officers' training course' was organised in August. Wherever possible, prospective immigrants would be given (while still in Europe) some elementary preparation, or even a weapon to smuggle into the country. Arms-smuggling was considered the most pressing need of all; by various subterfuges, more than 200 pistols were imported into Palestine during the six months following the May riots.[9] Improvements were gradually introduced, and the revived *Hagana* soon stood ready for its first real test in November 1921 (cf. pp. 117 f., below).

Legalised Defence

Alongside the illegal preparations for Jewish defence in Palestine, the ZO, Colonial Office and Palestine Administration all devoted their energies to restoring the sense of security still badly lacking in the country. Discussion of security schemes, interrupted by the May riots, was resumed. For Jabotinsky, now a member of the new Zionist Executive, the riots and especially the participation of the Arab police provided ample justification for the ZO and the *Va'ad Leumi* to rescind their previously-expressed, but reluctant, consent to participate in the 'Palestine Defence Force'.[10] In the name of the Executive, Jabotinsky cabled Sir Herbert Samuel on 6th May 1921, 'earnestly implor[ing]' him to reconsider the project of 'arming elements disloyal [to the] Mandate [and the] Balfour declaration' in the proposed mixed militia, which it was now 'morally impossible' for Jews to join.[11]

In the wake of the May riots, the Palestine Administration acknowledged the impossibility of going through with the proposed 'PDF', and instead turned its attention to the creation of a better-trained and better-paid gendarmerie.[12] New plans were also worked out for the defence of outlying Jewish colonies. A system of 'sealed armouries' – 'for use in self-defence against sudden and unprovoked attack' – and area defence committees (local leaders and British officials) was introduced in Palestine.[13]

The Gendarmerie scheme met with even less Yishuv enthusiasm than the former 'PDF' plan. Jewish recruits were forthcoming this time on the basis of the simple arithmetical calculation that 'every Jewish policeman [meant] an Arab policeman the less'.[14] For his part, Vladimir Jabotinsky continued to press for the rejuvenation of the Jewish Battalions as units within the British garrison in Palestine. Although heavy odds were against such a scheme, Jabotinsky refused to be inhibited or deterred. Within Zionist ranks he began the uphill battle of mobilising the necessary consensus and funds. Despite the record of mutual aggravation between the politically-minded and occasionally insubordinate Jewish soldiers and the British military authorities, Jabotinsky persistently pressed his case with the British. For him, the Jaffa riots had provided an eloquent and irrefutable argument in support of the thesis that Jews had to be protected by a *Jewish* military force. Writing to Churchill within days of the May riots, Jabotinsky invoked the 'mathematical' logic of the deterrent effect of Jewish troops:

... so long as there were 5,000 Jewish soldiers in Palestine, no riots against Jews took place, whereas after their reduction to 400 six Jews were killed in Jerusalem, and after their total disbandment over 30 were killed in Jaffa.[15]

Jabotinsky tirelessly went on to press his case in other directions as well: the Zionist Executive, the *Va'ad Leumi*, but most notably during the Zionist Actions Committee meeting in Prague (10–17.7.1921).[16] At the latter meeting, he successfully staked his continued membership on the Zionist Executive against the passage of a resolution in favour of the Battalions, supporting his case with another of his hard-hitting analyses of the nature of Jewish–Arab relations. In July 1921 Jabotinsky was able to draw on the May riots and the continuing incidents at Jaffa to remind his audience that the Arabs would 'always be opposed to Jewish immigration':

I don't know of a single example in history where a country was colonised with the courteous consent of the native population. It is not possible that there should be no friction.

For him, it was not a question of any 'misunderstanding' between Arabs and Jews:

They know very well that we do not want a Jewish state immediately, yet instinctively they are bent against Jewish immigration ... It is impossible to negotiate with people who say: We don't want Jewish immigration [and who] hope that, with the help of a few more acts of violence, they can put an end to it all.

After surveying, and pointing out the shortcomings of, the various methods which had been tried to remove or bypass this Arab opposition, Jabotinsky confessed that he could not see how it was possible to 'bridge this contradiction between us and the Arabs with words, gifts or bribery'. As he saw it, the contradiction was bound to express itself in a bitter and violent form, and this required the creation of an 'iron wall' – i.e., the Jewish Battalions – to stand between Zionist development and Arab attempts to halt that development. The Arab had to be forced to say to himself: 'Here stands an iron wall; the Jews are coming and will keep on coming; we are unable to prevent this; we cannot kill them.' Without this 'iron wall', Jabotinsky felt, it was immoral for Zionist leaders to send any more immigrants to Palestine – 'when we know what fate lies in store for them there'. But, once the 'iron wall' was built up, 'the door would open on the beginnings of a mutual understanding' with the Arabs.

Jabotinsky's arguments ran into opposition from a variety of quarters at the Prague meeting, chiefly pacifists, and those motivated by tactical considerations – e.g., not to 'provoke' the Arabs, or to give them an excuse to demand equal treatment in the form of a legion of their own. At the same time, Jabotinsky even alienated *Hagana* supporters. At the Prague meeting he argued that 2,000 Jewish soldiers would make 'a stronger impression on the Arab community than 10,000 armed civilians'. The continued existence of an illegal Jewish force would weaken the Zionists' bargaining-power with the British, and Jabotinsky denounced *hagana* so dogmatically that he cut himself off from many Yishuv elements with whom he still shared such basic assumptions as the paramount importance of security, and the absolute need to have Jews defended by Jews.[17] In the end, Jabotinsky's energetic campaign to have Jews defended by uniformed Jews under the Mandate came to naught, owing mainly to a lack of British support.[18]

The XIIth Zionist Congress

After June 1921 the political centre of gravity shifted away from Palestine to Europe. A delegation representing the IVth Palestine Arab Congress (29.5 – 3.6.1921) set off for England and Sir Herbert Samuel was most anxious for fruitful Arab–Zionist negotiations to result from this trip.[19] Zionist activity also shifted to Europe – not so much for the purpose of negotiations with the Arabs, as for a campaign to regain from the Colonial Office some of the losses incurred in Jerusalem on June 3rd.[20] In the ensuing 'tug-of-war' with the Zionists, Sir Herbert Samuel continued to impress the Jews with the need for two things: (a) immediate constructive activity, to prove to the Arabs that 'the success of Zionism will be to their benefit and not result in their destruction', and (b) an official Zionist declaration to reassure the Arabs in the same sense.[21]

To some extent, the fifth ('common home') resolution passed by the Twelfth Zionist Congress, which met at Carlsbad in September, could be seen as a response to Samuel's pressure. Indeed, the resolution was soon labelled 'historic', and, in view of the numerous occasions on which *parts* of it were subsequently quoted, let us consider its full text here:[22]

V. THE ARAB PEOPLE

With sorrow and indignation the Jewish people have lived through the recent events in Palestine. The hostile attitude of the Arab population, incited by unscrupulous elements to commit deeds of violence, can neither weaken our resolve for the establishment of the Jewish National Home nor our determination to live with the Arab people on terms of concord and mutual respect, and together with them to make the common home into a flourishing Commonwealth, the upbuilding of which may assure to each of its peoples an undisturbed national development. The two great Semitic peoples united of yore by the bonds of common creative civilisation will not fail in the hour of their national regeneration to comprehend the need of combining their vital interests in a common endeavour.

The Congress calls upon the Executive to redouble its efforts to secure an honourable entente with the Arab people on the basis of this Declaration and in strict accordance with the Balfour Declaration. The Congress emphatically declares that the progress of Jewish colonisation will not affect the rights and needs of the working Arab nation.

If this resolution succeeded, in its conciliatory sections, in evoking satisfaction from British quarters (see below) we cannot overlook the anger and determination which are intermixed with the call to peace.

Indeed, if we take the text of the resolution as a whole and view it in the context of the Congress atmosphere, it would appear that the concern for Yishuv *security* was the paramount consideration at Carlsbad, ahead of the desirable, but distant, 'honourable entente with the Arab people'.[23] Dr Weizmann set the tone of the Congress by affirming in his opening address that Zionists clung firmly to 'the rights guaranteed to us by the Balfour Declaration':[24]

[R]ecognition of this fact by the Arabs is an essential preliminary to the establishment of satisfactory relations between Jew and

Arab. Their temporary refusal to recognise that fact compels us to give thought to the means by which we can best safeguard our Yishub [sic] against aggression. Self-protection is an elementary duty ...

The Yishuv itself took its own security no less seriously than the Zionist leader. On the eve of the Congress a telegram from the *Va'ad Leumi* spoke of the Yishuv's 'desire for unity and brotherhood with the Arab people' – 'in spite of the depressing events of recent months'.[25] But, the message went on, it was the duty of the Palestine Administration to guarantee complete security of life and property and to afford 'the possibility for Jewish inhabitants to protect themselves against theft and murder'.

At the Congress, Berl Katznelson spoke even more forcefully for the Yishuv. Hardly in the spirit of a 'common home', Katznelson was annoyed with those who were arguing that the *Jews* had a moral duty to improve relations with the Arabs. As far as he was concerned, there was no doubt as to who was attacking whom: 'During the forty years of the New Yishuv, Jews have yet to attack an Arab village and there has yet to occur a case where a Jew has attacked an Arab.'[26] The labour movement, in whose name he spoke, had always preached 'deep words of brotherhood and peace' in the framework of national autonomy for both Jews and Arabs. And yet,

> Great is the distance between us and the Arabs ... We must guarantee the security of our own lives; only then will there be a basis for negotiations. We cannot concede our aspiration to become a majority in the country ...

It was, Katznelson concluded,

> obvious to everyone that our most crucial political activity must be: to renew our immigration; to strengthen our pioneering spirit; to reinforce *hagana*; and to fortify our positions in the country.

One final indication of the true tone of the 1921 Zionist Congress may be found in the less-quoted fourth resolution on the May riots, in which the Congress protested bitterly against the outrages and the stoppage of immigration, declaring 'before the entire world that the free immigration to Eretz Israel is an incontestable right of the Jewish people, of which in no circumstances it may be deprived'.[27]

> The Congress expresses its firm conviction that only a just policy of equal rights and equal duties for all sections of the population in Erez Israel [sic], only a strict and inexorable enforcement of justice and the protection of life and property, only an honest and consistent policy based upon the Balfour Declaration, can give peace to the country ...

Thus, while Samuel was searching for words of compromise in the fall and winter of 1921, Zionists both inside Palestine and abroad were preoccupied with one vital interest: security in the Yishuv and the strengthening of the Zionist position.

Jerusalem Disturbances, 2nd November 1921

Even after Carlsbad, security in Palestine continued to be 'the subject which [was] overshadowing all our own [i.e., Zionist] deliberations and all our negotiations with HMG.'[28] In Palestine itself, a sense of insecurity lingered long after the May riots. In fall 1921 almost every month brought false rumours of new outbreaks planned.[29] Samuel urged the Jewish colonies to complete preparations for their participation in the Government-sponsored defence scheme, and he assured anxious Yishuv leaders that security forces would do their duty to suppress any disorders.[30]

While the political situation in Palestine remained 'uneasy', the authorities gave every indication of taking the security problem seriously. Instructions issued to District Governors regarding the approach of 2nd November allowed them much discretion, and included recommendations for the 'prompt and effective employment of Force' to 'suppress the first signs of trouble'.[31] At the same time, the Administration followed up the Haycraft Commission findings regarding Arab attacks on Jewish colonies in May; searches for loot were conducted in implicated Arab villages and collective fines were levied.[32] Jews derived obvious satisfaction from this display of authority, and, generally-speaking, Eder felt

> convinced the Government [was] acting with much greater

firmness than heretofore. Sir Wyndham [Deedes] said: "We have had to adopt Turkish methods seeing that the more liberal methods have been misunderstood."[33]

When 2nd November was set by the Arabs as a day of mourning and protest, Eder reported with satisfaction that the Administration had sternly warned Arab leaders that they would bear full responsibility for any breach of the peace. 'Of course,' he went on 'no one can say that trouble may not arise, but I am satisfied the Government recognises the position and is taking measures to ensure the preventing and overcome [sic] any disturbances.'[34] But this new British firmness, although it gave greater confidence to the Jews, did not go so far as to produce any relaxation in the Yishuv's desire to 'take care of itself'. *Hagana* activities were kept up at a healthy pace in the fall of 1921. If there was a vague apprehension among the general public with the approach of 2nd November, *Hagana* circles were operating on the information supplied by an agent close to the Arab Delegation in London that disturbances were definitely being planned for that day.[35]

Defence committees, which had been set up in major Jewish centres since May, were placed on the alert for 2nd November. In Safed, for example, the committee organised a demonstrative Jewish street-march, to which it afterwards attributed a deterrent effect. Similarly, the *G'dud ha-'Avoda* 'Labour Battalion' despatched some of its members to Petah Tikva on 2nd November, with the happy result that the day passed quietly and several of the neighbouring Beduin camps 'flew white flags as a sign of peace'.[36]

But in Jerusalem the situation was more difficult.[37] On the morning of 2nd November Arab shops remained shut and crowds marched about shouting anti-Jewish slogans. All Jewish eyewitness accounts complained of a laxity on the part of the police towards the demonstrators. According to the same reports, the crowd seemed, if anything, *more* menacing after its leaders had conversed with the Governor, Ronald Storrs. Following an assembly (at which Storrs was present) inside the Haram ash-Sharif, crowds surged out to attack a nearby Jewish house, killing two of its occupants. A third Jew was killed in the streets while accompanying a party of women and children to the safety of a police station. The crowd then converged on the main street of the Jewish quarter of the walled city, which had been infiltrated (to the great relief of the Jews) on the previous day by a group of *Hagana* 'boys'. When it appeared that the small police contingent could no longer hold back the crowd, the Jewish defenders opened fire. The mob made several surges, but was driven back and was soon dispersed by a few grenades thrown by the Jews. Following this set-back, Arabs continued to drift about, assaulting the occasional Jewish passer-by, until order was gradually restored.

Subsequent British reports attributed the disorders to the 'hooligans and roughs of the City' and stressed that there had been 'no preparation nor concerted action'.[38] Even Dr Eder was prepared to certify that, although Storrs may have displayed some 'inefficiency', the Administration had taken 'all the necessary measures for the safety of the Jewish inhabitants'. In his view the attitude of the Government was, despite this unfortunate occurrence, 'in every respect much firmer' than it had been the previous May and it was 'therefore not desirable that we should keep on officially urging them to action, as the Government is undertaking it of its own accord'.[39]

But the Yishuv was hardly as generous towards the Administration. Despite satisfaction at the performance of the *Hagana* in the Jewish quarter (see below), the Yishuv's outward reaction consisted of an angry attack on the Administration. The very fact that crowds had been allowed to assemble and to 'get out of hand' – making *hagana* necessary – was proof enough of the bad faith of the authorities; to many, 2nd November 1921 was but a small-scale repetition of 4th April 1920. Some went further to argue publicly (as they had done privately in May) that this time was worse, because it had taken place under the *Jewish* HC. In fact, some of the criticism against Herbert Samuel which had been muted in May and June now came to the surface more freely. Ben-Gurion blamed Samuel directly for having left officials of the Military Administration at their posts, particularly Ronald Storrs. In this way, the Jewish HC had failed to remove the dangerous Arab belief that the Government was 'with them'.

Others continued to point to Samuel's 'gentle policy' in his relations with Arab 'extremists' as a contributing factor in the recent disturbances.[40]

Once again 'outside' Zionists had to do their best to calm the tide of Yishuv passions. But this could not prevent the *Va'ad Leumi* and other Yishuv bodies from insistently demanding the resignation of Ronald Storrs, upon whom full responsibility for the disturbances was cast.[41] Ben-Gurion defied all calls for self-restraint in a biting article in the labour weekly, *Kuntres*, of 11th November:[42]

> This time the moderates and "notables" among us will not be able to restrain themselves. Out of national sorrow and insult they call upon the successor of Pontius Pilate, the Governor of Jerusalem: Step down! ... The very fact of Storrs' presence in Palestine is a danger to the life of the Yishuv.

Yishuv Self-Reliance

All this may appear as an unduly hysterical and tedious over-reaction on the part of the Yishuv, especially when considering the extent of the disorders and the fact that they had been successfully contained by the *Hagana*. Yet, behind the familiar denunciations of the British which were given public expression in the wake of 2nd November, we can see a new maturity and self-confidence in the Yishuv. Behind closed doors Yishuv leaders wasted little time on analysing the British factor, and instead concentrated their attention on evaluating the rôle of their *hagana* and 'Arab work'. The disorders had come during an upswing of activity on both these fronts, and many considered 2nd November as the first 'trial by fire' of the Yishuv's new tendency to self-reliance in dealing with the 'Arab question'.

In the *post facto* analyses, adherents of *hagana* and 'Arab work' competed for the credit of the recent 'success'. Although the day had left five Jews dead and several dozen wounded, 2nd November was recognised by many as the 'coming of age' of the *Hagana*. No Jew was killed in the mob attack on the Jewish quarter, which was the only really defensible area. The Arabs were seen to withdraw with many casualties, including the death of the shaikh who had led the assault.

A new (but fragile) confidence was established between the aloof 'Old-Yishuv' Jews of Jerusalem and the 'New-Yishuv' Jews involved in *hagana*. Above all, the successful repulse of the Arab attack compensated for the poor showing of May, thus earning general Yishuv respect for the *Hagana* and also contributing to a greater feeling of Yishuv self-respect vis-à-vis British and Arabs in Palestine.[43]

At the 14th November meeting of the *Va'ad Leumi*, H. M. Kalvaryski wanted the Yishuv to appreciate that his new 'Muslim National Associations' (MNA) had also played a part in maintaining quiet on 2nd November in Haifa, Beisan and Nablus. He pointed to the fact that the disturbances had taken place in Jerusalem – where *no* MNA yet existed – as further proof of the usefulness of the Association, and announced that steps were being taken to include that city in MNA expansion plans.[44] Following his report, several speakers grudgingly accorded their passive neutrality or reserved approbation to Kalvaryski's MNA, whether as a 'provisional measure aimed at breaking the harmful atmosphere', or as a means of 'gaining sympathisers in our favour'.

The debates of November 1921 reveal a consolidation of the feeling which we noted after the crisis of May–June 1921: namely, that a proper balance of both forms of dealing with Arab opposition – *hagana* and 'Arab work' – was needed. The main thing – and on this point there was fundamental agreement – was that the Jews themselves had to continue to apply their own energies to the task of warding off or reducing Arab hostility.

Renewed Tension in 1922

At the close of 1921 tension in Palestine was beginning to ease somewhat. To the chagrin of Jewish labour and *Hagana* circles, some Jewish employers were feeling safe enough after 2nd November to resume more economical operations using cheaper Arab labour.[45] In January 1922 the Jaffa boatmen called off their boycott against the landing of Jewish immigrants (especially when it appeared that business might be transferred permanently to Haifa), and in March a peace agreement was concluded between the colony of Petah Tikva and the Arab villagers of Yahudieh, who had participated in the May 1921 attack.[46] The British attitude, too, continued to be firm and conducive to tranquillity. Punishments meted out to the Arabs implicated in the 2nd November disturbances were severe.[47] The addition of a unit of 762 'energetic' Irishmen (Black and Tans) to the new Gendarmerie in April 1922 was welcomed by the Jews inasmuch as it appeared to frighten the Arabs, and Zionist representatives were invited to (and, to a large extent, did) share in the growing British satisfaction at the overall improvements in the country's security arrangements.[48]

Despite these hopeful signs, and although we can see with hindsight that the 2nd November disorders were to be the last for more than seven years, *Hagana* elements in the Yishuv were slow to relax their guard. After 2nd November, *Hagana* devotees continued preparing against the prospect that the Arabs would soon be seeking 'another round'.[49] For people like Golomb, the building up of an arsenal and an organised secret military force remained the most important, and the most difficult, task facing Zionism: 'Without this,' he wrote in January 1922, 'in several years we won't be able to hold our own in the country.'[50]

Although no organised attacks took place as in 1920 and 1921, two major security scares gripped Palestine Jewry in the spring and summer of 1922. The first was the predictable rise in excitement which accompanied the approach of the Nebi Musa season. This year nobody in the British or Zionist camps was taking any chances. The authorities sought pledges from Arab leaders that order would be maintained, and they felt confident in assuring Jewish leaders that these pledges, accompanied by British security measures, pointed to a peaceful festival.[51] *Hagana* committees (and even the MNA) were on the alert, although Yitzhak Ben-Zvi and David Yellin, in accordance with an agreement made with the Administration, announced their confidence in the Government and warned the *Hagana* rank-and-file to remain well in the background.[52]

Some new external efforts were also directed at pacifying Arab feeling during the tense holiday season. On the private initiative of a Cairo Zionist, a call for peace was distributed in the name of the Egyptian Masonic Order to Muslim pilgrims in Jerusalem. Also in Cairo, a committee of Syrians who were at that moment secretly negotiating with the Zionists despatched an emissary to exert a pacifying influence in Palestine as a token of good faith to their negotiating partners.[53]

Whether as a result of one or more of the above 'preventive measures', the Nebi Musa of 1922 passed without violent incident. Yet, for the Yishuv, the tension did not ease overnight. Several weeks later a second and more serious threat seemed to be looming as discussion began in London for the final ratification of the Mandate for Palestine. Jews nervously watched the Arab press denounce the anticipated decision of the Council of the League of Nations, and, reading between the lines, saw hints that public disorders were likely to mark the event. The fears and predictions of certain *Hagana* activists since May 1921 now spread to a wider public, and by July 1922 there were strong apprehensions that a general rising or organised attacked were at hand.[54]

Adding to the tension surrounding the ratification of the Mandate, the Wailing Wall and the Muslim Holy Places were fast becoming a source of serious concern. Foreshadowing the ominous build-up of 1928–9, excitement about the Holy Places after April 1922 was threatening (in Deedes' words) 'to raise passions to a dangerous height'.[55] The report of the Palestinian delegation to an Islamic conference in Mecca exploited the theme of a Zionist threat to the Holy Places.[56] Apparently well aware of this campaign, the ZO's memorandum to the League of Nations on 'The Mandate for Palestine' included a stronger than usual paragraph categorically denying that the Jews had ever contemplated 'the smallest interference with the religious traditions or customs of the non-Jewish inhabitants of Palestine or with the Holy Places'.[57] In Palestine itself, local Jews needed no outside instruction to appreciate the explosiveness of the Holy Places issue. Discussing the matter at a *Va'ad Leumi* meeting, Ben-Zvi warned that, if not dispelled, these false accusations could endanger the position of Jews living in Muslim lands in the same horrible way that the 'Blood Libel' operated in Christian countries.[58]

As the excitement reached its peak, Jews and British

applied themselves to de-fusing the explosive atmosphere and to preparing against the possibility of Arab attacks. The 'great day' of the Mandate ratification, so long-awaited, was now almost a secondary matter. The Yishuv strictly followed British and 'outside' Zionist advice on the need for absolute 'tact'; the Jews were 'in no wise in a jubilant mood, but [would] await the result with equal calm whether the Mandate is ratified or indefinitely postponed.'[59] Instead of organising celebrations, Dr Eder co-operated with Deedes in matters of intelligence.[60] While the new Irish gendarmes were making their maiden public appearance, *Hagana* bands remained in the background in accordance with a tacit agreement with the Administration.[61] Kalvaryski's MNA, in addition to performing the external propaganda function of sending pro-Mandate telegrams and petitions abroad, again served, by its physical presence, as a counterweight to the Muslim-Christian Association in certain towns. In another product of 'Arab work', 'friendly' rural shaikhs in the Jerusalem region co-operated with the Jews by keeping their villagers away from the city during the tense period.[62]

Despite all these preparations, the security reports at hand on 10th July led the *Va'ad Leumi* to demand an even tighter British clamp-down on Arab leaders and 'agitators', and also an authoritative Government denial that the Jews were in any way interfering with the Holy Places.[63] But, as many in the Yishuv realised, for this last step to have any effect, the Jews themselves would have to issue a formal proclamation. Thus, on 12th July the *Va'ad Leumi* published an appeal to the 'Arab Nation in Palestine and the Greater Orient',[64] which stressed many of the elements which we have encountered in previous proclamations: e.g., that the Jews were returning to rebuild their ancient homeland, and that Jews and Arabs were semitic cousins, who would share equally in the progress and material prosperity which Zionism would continue to bring to Palestine and to the whole Middle East. In particular, the proclamation informed its readers that, against the Jews' desire to live and work in peace with their neighbours, there had arisen

a group of men whose objects are the introduction of disharmony, the promotion of internal strife, and the creation in our country of an atmosphere of hate, suspicion and perpetual conflict.

The *Va'ad Leumi* invited all Arabs to verify with any resident of Jerusalem that the photographs showing a Zionist flag on the Mosque of 'Omar were a complete 'fiction' and 'self-evident lie':

> Brethren, do not give credence to the tissue of falsehood circulated amongst you by agitators and mischief makers. Remember that only by means of a calm and peaceful life can this sacred land be regenerated. Do not heed those who provoke you to rise against your brethren who dwell with you in perfect confidence.

Ratification of the Mandate and After

The publication of the proclamation to the Arab nation coincided with the two-day country-wide general strike which was organised to demonstrate Arab displeasure at the impending ratification of the Mandate. The fears which had been building up among the Jews reached their climax during these two days, but were not realised, perhaps owing to the heavy security precautions, and also to the instructions from Arab leaders to refrain from any breach of the peace.[65] On 24th July 1922, the Mandate for Palestine was ratified, and the Yishuv received the news calmly and without celebration.[66]

But, before a collective sigh of relief could be heard from the Yishuv, a Jew was killed (on 27th July) along the Tel Aviv-Jaffa road, and this was followed by a succession of isolated acts of violence, including five more murders, in the course of the next month.[67] Although the killings were not considered in government circles to be 'political', their character was nonetheless undeniable; in no case was robbery the motive.[68] The Council of Jaffa Jews and other Yishuv bodies cried out to the Government for severe measures to put an end to what they were convinced was a 'Terrorist Society'. If the Government would not act, the Jewish public bodies could not be held responsible for controlling elements who wished to take the law into their own hands. They warned that a 'natural feeling of bitterness' was being increased by 'the impression that the Government [was] not doing everything it [could] and should do'; 'We have no one and nothing to rely on; no one to avenge *our blood*.' At least one Jewish revenge-killing of an Arab appears to have been committed before the wave of violence was stopped.[69]

Despite the effect of these latest threats and incidents of Arab violence on the mind and the nerves of the Yishuv, there could be no doubt that overall security in Palestine was, in fact, improving by the end of 1922, and would continue to improve thereafter.[70] This improvement could only lead to a decline in the general security-obsession and in the importance attached to *hagana*. Even so, the Yishuv was far from believing that the time had come to sit down with the Arabs to work out the terms of a 'mutual understanding'. The feeling that the Arabs constituted a potential threat to Jewish life and property – and to Jewish national aspirations – did not fade as quickly as did concern for *hagana*. As we shall see below, the experience of 1922–3 would justify Dr Thon's November 1921 warnings that the *Va'ad Leumi* should not forget that 'deep antagonism' still lay in the 'broad public' (and not only among the 'effendis' or the Christian Arabs); that negotiations, requiring sacrifices, would one day be necessary; and that 'in the meantime, all the methods' used to offset Arab opposition – viz., *hagana* and Arab work – were 'only palliatives' which in themselves would not 'bring about the settling of our relations'.[71] While physical attacks ceased, Arab public opinion would remain a long way from accepting the Jews on their own, Zionist terms.

7

Winning Arab Friends in Palestine

Supporting 'Moderate' Arab Parties

If, in the months and years after May 1921, many Jews were preoccupied with creating optimal conditions for self-defence against possible Arab attack, there was also a growing number who wished to go further: to engage in active political work among the Arabs with the object of winning 'friends' and reducing the likelihood of future attacks. Beyond the obvious need for effective explanation and propaganda to convince Arab public opinion that Zionist development would bring no injury but only benefit, political efforts of the ZC (and its successor, following the 1921 Zionist Congress, the PZE) were directed at organising 'moderate' Arabs into a 'party' which would make its influence felt in Palestinian politics to Zionist advantage. 'There are many ways', observed PZE press officer Yosef Haim Castel, 'of doing political work among the Arabs, and all of them point to one goal: to strengthen the forces and organisation of the moderates and to weaken the extremists.'[1] But this Arab work suffered from many inherent weaknesses, not the least of which was the dubious and elusive distinction which was made between 'moderates' and 'extremists'. Some of the more practical obstacles which were encountered included: a desperate shortage of funds; organisational confusion and internal

Yishuv divisions; and a decidedly unhelpful attitude on the part of the British.

Although a number of competitors emerged in 1922–3, H. M. Kalvaryski's MNA – the original 'moderate Arab party' – remained the major endeavour in the field. This project was undertaken with the backing of the ZC (and PZE) and the ICA, i.e., 'outside' bodies, and it remained in many respects foreign to the temperament of the Yishuv. Kalvaryski tried to keep his membership in the *Va'ad Leumi* and his participation in its various committees separate from his MNA work, but his overriding concern for Arab affairs led him to serve as an informal bridge between the Yishuv and this Zionist project.

Apart from his ambivalent position with regard to the Yishuv, Kalvaryski's status within the ZC was neither paramount nor well-defined. Although his MNA may have been the Commission's most valuable project, it was but one of the responsibilities of the Political Department under Dr Eder.[2] Through other local intermediaries, Eder was concerned with influencing the Arabic press, maintaining contacts with various Palestinian Arab notables, and dealing with Amir 'Abdallah's overtures for financial and political support.[3] In addition, Dr Weizmann, Pinhas Rutenberg (of the Palestine Electricity Company) and the ICA each had 'private' agents and commitments to 'Arab work'.[4]

When formulating a political budget for 1922, Dr Eder appraised Kalvaryski's contribution as 'valuable, but not as valuable as Kalvaryski claims, and … expensive'.[5] Financially, the MNA project was, despite the generous agreement between Sokolow and Rothschild, on no firmer ground than previous, less-ambitious undertakings. Being a man of great persistence, Kalvaryski kept the MNA from collapsing during 1921 and 1922 by borrowing heavily on his own private account, in the expectation that Dr Weizmann would arrange reimbursement. The latter was quite taken aback when Kalvaryski presented his 'bill' in early 1923, regarding it as 'improvident and unauthorised expenditure'; but the ZE soon appreciated that it had to settle with Kalvaryski out of moral obligation and in order to avoid a monstrous political scandal.[6]

Kalvaryski combined a sincere desire to 'win over' the

Arabs to Zionism with a down-to-earth assessment of 'Arab psychology'. While he considered himself an 'Arabophile' or 'Arab-lover', he simultaneously held the view that the Arab was 'by nature a materialist, and should he realise that no advantage will accrue to him by siding with us, he will naturally turn away from us'.[7] The correctness of this assessment was well illustrated by the halting and uneven flow of funds for the MNA. The establishment of each branch was a very practical affair, requiring an initial investment and regular monthly disbursements for the rental of premises and the payment of 'salaries' to local members and organisers. The Jerusalem branch, for example, was costing £285 per month in 1922.[8] The sympathy and loyalties of those Arabs who joined became precariously dependent on the flow of these subsidies, but for all his good intentions Kalvaryski proved to be a poor financial administrator. 'He gives out money very readily,' Eder noted at an early stage, 'to people who may be taking the money and laughing at us.'[9] On many occasions Kalvaryski overreached himself by promising, and then failing to deliver, payments which proved to be in excess of what his financial backers were willing or able to provide. Here, as in his previous efforts to 'win over' Arab sympathisers, Kalvaryski was arousing expectations which it would be difficult to fulfil. And, having accustomed the Arabs to expect generous, if sporadic, handouts, he had begun a kind of work from which it would be difficult to retreat gracefully. For, a subsidy once begun could not be easily withdrawn without running the risk of adding to the ranks of violent enemies.[10]

Apart from the inherent weaknesses of the MNA which stemmed from its reliance on Zionist money, the Association worked under the heavy, if not fatal, handicap of the public knowledge that it was a Zionist creation. This public knowledge, commented Sir Herbert Samuel, tended 'to excite suspicion against them and [gave] rise to rumours that people have been induced to join them by improper methods, and thus to nullify the good which these Societies might otherwise bring about'.[11] It became common for groups of Arabs to denounce Kalvaryski's 'bribing' of other Arabs who 'sell us out', and to ostracise 'Kalvaryski's Arabs' until they changed their minds and 'came to their senses'.[12]

Because of this public suspicion and the divisions caused in the Arab community, the British did nothing to favour the MNA, even though both Samuel and Deedes 'firmly believed' that Kalvaryski's motives were 'sincere'.[13] Jews too became equally aware that the effectiveness of the MNA suffered from the widespread knowledge that it was the artificial product of Kalvaryski's work. In fact, by summer 1922, one Cairo Zionist felt so embarrassed by the 'dangerous popularity' which Kalvaryski had acquired throughout the Arab world, that he suggested to the ZE that Kalvaryski should be seen publicly only with those Arab notables whom they *deliberately wished to compromise*! 'He should', recommended J. Hoefler, 'at all costs avoid keeping company with our friends.'[14]

Despite the drawbacks of financial instability and public notoriety, the MNA nevertheless achieved some short-term objectives. The Association sought to provide 'colourable evidence' for external consumption that there existed 'an important body of opinion in favour of Zionism' in Palestine.[15] In proclamations and in cables to British statesmen and to the League of Nations, the MNA challenged the right of the MCA to speak in the name of the people of Palestine; it welcomed the Jews as 'a brotherly people sharing our joys and our troubles and helping us in the restoration of our common country'; and it eagerly awaited the ratification of the Mandate as the dawning of 'a new era of peace and brotherhood'. In a more direct way, local MNA members used their physical presence during times of tension to deter or intimidate anti-Zionist agitators.[16]

The real test of the relative strength of the MNA and MCA came in the Legislative Council elections of 1923 (cf. pp. 153 f., below). During the MNA's gathering of pro-Mandate petitions from Arab villages in summer 1922, Dr Eder had already been thinking ahead to these elections, and he felt that the small cost of obtaining signatures (£6–7 per village) 'betokened at least that they [the Arab masses] were not at bottom very hostile'.[17] Eder was optimistic that a 'moderate party' could be formed to put forward candidates to counteract the anticipated boycott of the elections, and predicted that the MNAs would be 'of greater value in the future than they have been in the past'. Eder's successor, Col F. H. Kisch, entertained similar hopes for a substantial 'moderate' turnout at the polls, with the MNA serving as the main organisational nucleus. But when the hour of reckoning came the Jerusalem branch openly joined the boycott (reportedly 'owing to disappointments caused by Kalvaryski'), and the Association as a whole had little impact in the rest of the country.[18]

But even before this electoral test, Stein's August 1921 conclusion that a 'moderate Arab party' was 'premature' (p. 100, above) seemed to have been proven correct. The MNA had been unable to develop any esprit de corps or even rudimentary degree of countrywide centralisation. It was never more than the faintest shadow of a 'political party' in any sense of the word. It was a fair criticism levelled by Y. H. Castel in October 1922 that the 'moderate' Arabs in Palestine were still 'weak and disorganised, despite all the work and money which the founders of the MNA have invested to date'.[19] Castel's analysis of the balance of forces in the country (soon shared by other Zionists) was that there was no hope whatever of destroying the powerful anti-Zionist movement, or of dislodging the MCA and substituting 'moderates' in positions of influence. The conclusion for Zionists was that the most that should be expected from organisations like the MNA was the 'nuisance value' of harassing the 'extremists' – 'until such time as we are able to proceed quietly with our settlement work and become stronger in quantity and in quality in the country.'

At the end of 1922, the balance-sheet on Kalvaryski's MNA was even worse from the purely financial angle. In addition to the vast sums invested, Kalvaryski had left the PZE with almost £3000 of accumulated liabilities. While Col Kisch, in Jerusalem, was busy devising means to clear away these past debts so that he might begin his own Arab work with a clean slate, Kalvaryski himself (in Europe since September 1922) turned to Dr Weizmann with the first of many desperate pleas for reimbursement of another £3000 to pay off the *personal* debts he had incurred on behalf of the continued operation of the MNA.[20] Indeed, at this point Kalvaryski's personal story reached a pathetic low ebb. While his collapsing and discredited enterprise was being 'rectified' in

Palestine, he himself was in Europe virtually abandoned and burdened with debts. The ICA in Paris did not wish to renew his contract of employment for the coming year of 1923, and it was most likely on 'compassionate grounds' that the London Zionist Executive invited him to return to Palestine 'to give his services . . . with a view to the promotion of better relations between Jews and Arabs'.[21] But in view of Kalvaryski's past record, special instructions to his new 'boss', Col Kisch, stressed that Kalvaryski was 'in no circumstances to act otherwise than with your concurrence and under your supervision and . . . he is on no account to have any control over the expenditure of Zionist funds.'[22]

Before he could make a fresh start on the 'Arab question', which became one of his top priorities, Col Kisch had to deal with the Kalvaryski 'legacy'. This legacy included not only debts, but also contempt from Government circles, a crumbling edifice of clubs, and a long list of protesting ex-beneficiaries. With Kalvaryski working as his principal adviser on Arab affairs, Kisch displayed no radical departures from the previous orientation of Arab work. For all its recognised defects, Kisch maintained the existing MNA during 1923, while trying to derive more value for his money by slashing the size of payments and demanding more in return from his Arab 'friends'.

After the MNA was thoroughly discredited by its pitiful performance during the Legislative Council elections (February–March 1923), Kisch was convinced of the urgency of finding a new and more effective basis for the organisation of Arab 'moderates'.[23] The spontaneous appearance of the new 'National Party', composed of MCA dissidents, in fall 1923 seemed to provide new hope to Col Kisch. Yet, in the end, Zionists had to content themselves with only one virtue of the new party: 'the activities of the extremists [were] now devoted to defending themselves against the New Party rather than attacking us.'[24] Similarly, attempts to foster 'Farmers' Parties' during 1924–1925 brought only modest results. In the end, the PZE was unable to create a 'moderate' force capable of dominating Palestinian Arab politics and of destroying, once and for all, the power of the 'extremists'. For all their financial and moral support, Zionists had to satisfy themselves only with the decline of the once-omnipotent MCA after 1923.[25]

If the foregoing initiatives at fostering 'moderate' Arab parties could be classed as 'effendi'-orientated, brief mention should also be made here of the efforts of the Jewish labour movement to organise Arab 'fellahin' and workers.[26] While not engaged in the actual creation or support of Arab political parties, Jewish labour activists did see both socio-economic and national-political advantages in the project of helping to organise Arab workers in Palestine. Three types of schemes were discussed in Jewish labour circles: (a) 'joint organisation' of Jewish and Arab workers – i.e., mixed unions; (b) separate 'national sectors', under a central 'international' agency; and (c) 'parallel' organisations.[27] After much preparation, a single mixed union, the 'Union of Railway, Posts and Telegraph Workers', came into being in 1924.[28] In succeeding years, the moral support offered by the *Histadrut* to striking Arab workers was accepted on occasion, and several joint Jewish-Arab strikes were organised.[29] But such activity – even when intensified somewhat in later years – did not succeed in turning Arab workers or fellahin into an organised 'moderate' force sensitive to the benefits of Jewish immigration and Zionist development in Palestine.

Arab Work and the Va'ad Leumi

The increased interest in Arab work activity of the PZE and the Jewish labour movement was common to many Yishuv quarters. At first, those local leaders who had been emphasising the need for greater concern were pleased to note that many people who had previously been indifferent or hostile were at last becoming aware of the need for normal, friendly relations with the Arabs. But this trend continued into 1922 to the point where Y. Wilkansky – who four years earlier had preached to the 'Eretz-Israel Conference' on the need to recognise the reality and the difficulties of an Arab population in Palestine and a strong Arab movement outside it (above, p. 28) – felt that the Yishuv had gone 'from one extreme to the other':[30]

At the heart of the [new] Arab orientation there is also a new melody which is liable to be harmful. Honey-words ooze from our lips, and from this sweetness no strength will come ... It appears as though we would never have come to Palestine, had not the Arabs been here to serve us the objects of our improvements and philanthropy. This falsification will lead to perverse self-deception ...

As in the realm of words, so too in the realm of deeds many were beginning to worry that there was *too much* Yishuv 'Arab work' going on. At the first meeting of the newly-elected *Va'ad Leumi* (5th April 1922), Menahem Ussishkin was not alone in thinking that, of the errors committed in relations with the Arabs,

> ninety per cent result from what we are doing and ten per cent from what we are not doing; ... the damage comes from doing, not from lack of doing. We are all under the hypnosis that we must do something, and everybody is getting into the act.[31]

This state of affairs did not lead to recommendations for the stoppage of Arab work, but rather for the *Va'ad Leumi* to play a more effective role in controlling or directing the various activists who operated largely on their own authority.

The *Va'ad Leumi* Executive met the following day to consider what steps could be taken in this direction. Yosef Meyuhas recalled the many committees that had been created in the past without achieving anything, and he hoped that this time some real work could be accomplished.[32] He spoke strongly of the need for tight central supervision over the various agencies engaged in Arab work.

But there were members of the new Executive who were already committed to existing projects, namely Ben-Gurion and Ben-Zvi for labour work, and Kalvaryski for the MNA. In a sense, the Yishuv was fragmented internally along class lines, almost as if to correspond with the perceived 'fellah/ effendi' division in Arab society. Jewish activists who worked among Arab labourers and peasants were criticised for spreading ideas which threatened the entire Jewish community. The critics pointed out that labour's brand of Arab work – based on 'liberating' the 'fellah' from his 'effendi' oppressor – was already frightening the Arab 'ruling caste' and was undoing the small amount of good which had been accomplished by gaining some 'effendi' friends. If carried too far, it was argued, labour propaganda might well provoke the 'effendis' to protect their interests by taking a more active part in turning the Arab masses against the Jews.[33]

But labour spokesmen were equally dubious about the value of winning the friendship of the 'effendis', and insisted on the right to approach 'Arab work' in a way which corresponded with their own particular conception of the 'Arab question'. Thus, Ben-Gurion argued against proposals for a single Yishuv 'Arab policy' by invoking the principle, 'each [social] group on its own':[34]

We can accept the general view that the *Va'ad Leumi* wishes to create friendly relations with the Arabs. But let [the *Va'ad Leumi*] not take responsibility for what the Jewish socialists do to draw the Arab workers closer, or for what the other groups among the Jewish population do to win over other groups among the Arab population.

Thus, in spring 1922, although all Yishuv elements appreciated the need for pooling and exchanging information, no one was willing to abdicate his freedom of action to a central authority.

The continued independence of various brands of Arab work from any central Yishuv control was but one illustration of the *Va'ad Leumi's* inability to reign supreme over Palestine Jewry. Yet, even though it was unable to present its own coherent approach to the Arab question, the Yishuv soon chose this as one of the main areas where it challenged the political direction of the 'foreign' leadership of the Zionist Executive in London and in Jerusalem. It was not long before the accumulated murmurings of Palestinian Jews became open calls defying the PZE monopoly over political work and demanding a greater local voice so that 'things won't be done against our wishes'.[35] It became more common for Yishuv representatives to attribute difficulties with the Arabs to the ineptitude or incorrect attitude of the 'foreign' Zionists who made all the decisions.

This local self-assertion and rebelliousness reached new heights in late 1922 and early 1923. Yosef Meyuhas was among those who argued the case for 'local expertise' on Arab matters:

> Greater use should be made of the men who are experts in this matter – the local residents who have already had contacts with them [i.e., the Arabs] and who have managed to become familiar with and understand their mentality.[36]

Yishuv pressure for a greater voice in determining Zionist policy towards the Arabs led, in mid–1922, to the formation of a joint committee of delegates of the *Va'ad Leumi* and the PZE. But work on this committee brought absolutely no satisfaction to Yishuv participants, as it merely gave them a closer view of their own lack of influence and the PZE's complete discretion to ignore 'local advice'.[37] In July 1922, an exasperated Meir Dizengoff accused the *Va'ad Leumi* of cowardice and defied it to take the bold step of *demanding* that the PZE transfer almost total responsibility (and a budget) for Arab work to the Yishuv organ.[38] 'The Arabs approach only local Jews', he argued, whereas Eder and Ussishkin remained 'foreigners who don't know their language, customs, etc.' But, while most *Va'ad Leumi* members did agree that the Arabs preferred to deal with 'native' Jews ahead of 'foreign' Zionist representatives, they felt reluctant to take the bold step of demanding full responsibility for 'Arab work'.

Economic Involvement: Nissim Mallul and the Arab Secretariat

There were, however, two projects in which this local pressure for greater control over relations with the Arabs did find expression: the 'Arab Secretariat', and 'cultural work'. In summer 1922 the *Va'ad Leumi* opened its own modest Arab Secretariat under the direction of Dr Nissim Mallul, a native Palestinian Jew with experience as a journalist and as the Arabic 'press officer' attached to the ZO's Palestine Office before the War.[39] The general orientation of Mallul's work coincided with the views expressed in a lecture earlier in the year by a respected veteran on Arab affairs, Dr Yitzhak Epstein. Dr Epstein, who (in 1905) had been among the first to draw Zionist attention to the serious difficulties which the

existence of the Arabs and the methods of Zionist colonisation could cause to the hopes for Zionist success, was invited
on 5th April 1922 to lecture before the new *Va'ad Leumi* on
'Relations with the Neighbours'.[40]

Despite the abundance of activity in the sphere of Arab
work, Epstein was far from convinced that the Jews were
taking the 'Arab question' seriously enough, and he
denounced what he felt were examples of tactlessness and
stupidity (in the local Hebrew press), missed opportunities,
and assorted false or dangerous 'solutions' which were being
currently entertained. As far as Epstein was concerned, there
was only one way in which Arab opposition to the Jewish
National Home might be effectively overcome: viz., by

> involving the natives in all our activities. In actual practice we
> must take it upon ourselves – from the points of view of justice
> and necessity – to involve them in everything.

This, he felt, was a matter for direct 'local' initiative, and he
urged the *Va'ad Leumi* that it was *its* task (not that of the
PZE) to find ways of bringing about such joint participation,
beginning with seemingly trivial social intercourse during
religious festivities and meetings over tea.

These suggestions for improving relations with the 'neighbours' met with cold silence on the part of his listeners. Only
Yitzhak Ben-Zvi made specific mention of Epstein's suggestions in the ensuing debate, and expressed grave doubts
whether complete moral concern for the interests of the existing population, on the one hand, could be reconciled with the
full needs and priorities of Zionist immigration and settlement, on the other. If, in cases of conflict, the latter would
have to be subordinated to the former (as the tone of Epstein's lecture surely implied), then Ben-Zvi felt that it would
be 'impossible for us to agree to joint work'.

Yet, later in the year, there was an attempt to implement
these very ideas in the operations of the Arab Secretariat.
Although he worked with virtually no budget, Mallul enumerated the tasks of his Secretariat in long lists.[41] For our
purposes, we may divide his activities into three main
categories: (a) political assistance to the PZE; (b) opening up
Yishuv institutions for the benefit of Arab 'friends'; and (c)

revising Kalvaryski's system, during his absence, to render it more consonant with Mallul's own approach and general Yishuv feeling.

Mallul began with a flurry of activity. He drafted an appeal to King Husain regarding Jewish intentions and the Muslim Holy Places; disseminated Arabic leaflets encouraging Jewish-Arab understanding in Palestine; followed the proceedings of the Fifth Palestine Arab Congress held at Nablus (22.8.1922) through the reports of a 'friendly' participant; and travelled to Egypt to investigate the attitude of Egyptian journalists to the Jewish National Home.[42] Mallul toured northern Palestine several times to investigate Arab attitudes towards the coming Legislative Council elections, and actively encouraged individual Arabs who *were* interested in the elections to make their voices heard in defiance of the 'official' Arab boycott. From agents in Ramle, Haifa, Tiberias, Hebron, Gaza and other centres he received periodic reports which he summarised or translated for the benefit of the PZE.[43]

Perhaps the largest part of Mallul's day-to-day work did not directly concern Palestinian politics. As some had predicted, the very fact of creating an 'address' to which Arabs could write unleashed a flood of Arab communications: lavish protestations of friendship and offers of services; numerous complaints against unkept Jewish promises of favours or 'expenses' (sometimes accompanied by threats); vilification of Arab enemies or rivals; and an endless flow of requests and suits for Jewish assistance in obtaining employment (usually in the Administration[44]), loans, legal aid or intervention with the courts, medical care, or places for their children in Jewish schools. Some typical cases which illustrate the above may be cited here:

(a) A rural shaikh, who had a scheduled appointment with the HC, offered to say whatever the Jews wanted him to say, if only they could provide him with an automobile to drive him to and from Government House.[45]

(b) A Ramleh 'friend', smarting from a cut in funds, threatened Mallul as follows: 'Many letters are in my hands which I can use if necessary to publish a book, "The Secrets of Zionism", or to sell to others for a large sum. You know my friendship for the Jews which goes back over four years; and look how you are treating me! ...'[46]

(c) A Nablus notable, whose sister-in-law was receiving medical care at the Hadassah Hospital, asked Mallul to arrange for her to remain longer, since his brother was not yet ready to have her back home.[47]

It was in dealing with this tedious series of requests that Mallul was able to try his hand at implementing a programme of Arab 'involvement' in legitimate Jewish concerns so that they might better feel the benefits of Zionist progress at first hand. That Mallul did not meet with great success between August 1922 and April 1923 was certainly not due to any lack of persistence on his part. He energetically pressed 'friendly' Arab suitors on the various credit, commercial, welfare and educational institutions of the Yishuv, often prefacing his enquiries with the words: 'Since our position in the country requires that we strive to improve our relations with our Arab neighbours, [etc.] ...'[48] Mallul also wanted to systematise this branch of his work, hoping that Yishuv institutions would come to recognise letters of recommendation from his office as entitling the Arab bearer to equal consideration on a par with the firm's Jewish clients or users.

From a study of the correspondence between Mallul and the various Yishuv institutions on this subject, we are left with the impression that, while willingness to help was often expressed, lack of resources sharply minimised the results which Mallul was expecting. Among the positive replies we find: some *Alliance* schools willingly informed Mallul of the number of places available to Arab students; the *Kupat 'Am* savings association announced that it had no objection to Arabs becoming members; and, while the Silicate Company turned down the application of a Nazareth Arab for a local franchise (because it felt no need for a branch in that town), the same 'friendly' and enterprising Arab did win a contract for the supply of food to Jewish workers in Lower Galilee. But, on the other hand, almost all of the credit institutions canvassed by Mallul replied in the negative, and there were no openings to be found for teachers of Arabic recommended by him.[49]

At the same time as Mallul was getting nowhere with his

requests for loans for Arabs, the Hadassah director had the 'unpleasant task' of cutting down his budget for medical aid to Arabs, and various other Arab work projects seemed to be collapsing from lack of funds.[50] Six months earlier, Dr Ruppin had discouraged the PZE from trying to do very much for the Arabs 'in the material sense' because, frankly, they 'had not enough means at [their] disposal for [their] own needs'.[51] Unfortunately, the Yishuv and the Zionist movement were sinking into a particularly grave economic slump during the very months of Mallul's initiative of getting Arabs 'involved'. The PZE was literally on the verge of bankruptcy from month to month; road-workers were in a 'half-starved condition'; almost everyone in the Yishuv was 'burdened with debts'.[52] By late spring 1923 Mallul's activities also ground to a halt, as the PZE would not allocate the tiny amount needed to maintain his secretariat.

The 'Cultural' Approach: David Avissar and 'Halutzai ha-Mizrah'

While Mallul's economically-oriented work was proceeding with dubious success, there were some Jews in the Yishuv who thought that the 'Arab problem' had to be tackled at a more fundamental level: basic Arab attitudes to the Jews had to be changed by 'cultural work'. As in earlier periods, there was much talk of the need to found a respectable Arabic newspaper which would present the Jews, in general, in a more favourable light to readers throughout the Arab world.[53] Following several Va'ad Leumi discussions on this and similar topics, David Avissar, a native of Hebron, felt that the Jews could no longer afford to remain inactive on this front and presented a detailed proposal for the publication of leaflets in Arabic and Hebrew. The Va'ad Leumi shortly afterwards endorsed Avissar's suggestion and delegated the project to a group known as 'Halutzai ha-Mizrah' ('Pioneers of the Orient').[54]

Avissar's proposal of March 1923 was motivated by a sense of great urgency.[55] He was worried by the growing strength of the MCA, and particularly by Christian propaganda which exploited sharply anti-semitic themes to urge a united

Muslim-Christian front against the Jews. Citing a recent pamphlet published in Egypt ('Zionist Desires in Palestine') which invoked the Bible, the Quran, Aristotle and a host of sources (ending with the 'Protocols of the Elders of Zion') to denigrate the Jews, Avissar pleaded for action: 'Our people knows from experience the importance of the effect of such poisonous pamphlets; if we don't reply to our enemies, the naive will accept their words as the truth.'[56] He warned that if the Jews did not do something quickly towards educating a gullible and docile Arab public, then the seeds of hatred already sown by intriguing anti-semites would soon grow out of control, and 'the work of half a generation of national revival' would be wiped out in a short period. Jews, he believed, had to admit to some blame for having previously 'minimised the danger and thereby created an open field for the activities of our enemies'. Yet, if a counter-offensive could be mounted in time, Avissar was hopeful that the situation might be saved, since, he claimed, it was

> a known fact that, in occasional conversations with our neighbours on the Jewish question, they cannot deny our historic right to Palestine, they willingly admit that the advancement of learning was brought about jointly by Jews and Arabs in the Middle Ages, and only by forcing themselves do they remain silent on the reality of the great benefits which the Zionists are bringing into the country.

According to Avissar's plan, *Halutzai ha-Mizrah* would organise the publication of serious, learned, historical leaflets, written by real experts, so that *both* Jews and Arabs could prepare for future co-operation by learning about the little-known history of the two peoples, 'from their first meeting to the present day'. He wanted no mere 'propaganda', but rather honest studies which would automatically make the Arabs understand the justice and reasonableness of Jewish aspirations. By giving examples of previous Jewish-Arab co-operation, the leaflets were expected to encourage both parties to appreciate the possibilities and advantages of present and future co-operation.

Like the pre-War *'ha-Magen'* ('The Defender') group,[57] the *Halutzai ha-Mizrah* project was largely a 'native' or

Sephardi undertaking, whose initiators were conscious of
their special responsibility as a group which knew the 'neighbours' better than any other Jews. The necessary finances for
this cultural work were to be solicited from Jewish public
bodies in Palestine, wealthy individuals, and from Jewish
communities throughout the Arab and Muslim world. But the
project suffered the same fate as others, owing to the scarcity
of available means. The publishing venture got off to a slow
start: it was almost eighteen months before the first pamphlet
– 'Words of Truth and Peace' by Professor Joseph Klausner –
appeared.[58] Klausner attempted to show the groundlessness
of Arab fears by stressing the immense economic and other
advantages to be had from Zionist development, and by
pointing to the impossibility of Jewish political domination in
Palestine. Local Jewish community committees were given
the task of distributing copies to neighbouring Arab villages,
and they reported back to the *Va'ad Leumi* on the good effect
it had.[59] In spring 1925, the *Va'ad Leumi* began the slow
process of making enquiries for the launching of a second
pamphlet.

The British Attitude

No one who was close to the Arab situation in Palestine could
have been under any illusion that the cultural and economic
efforts of the period were making any great impact on Arab
attitudes to the Jewish National Home. Among other things,
the experience of these years seemed to prove the essential
correctness of Leonard Stein's economic analysis of the Arab
situation prior to August 1921:

> little Jewish capital [had] entered the country and ... there [had]
> been no conspicuous quickening of economic life. Zionist activity
> [had] not put enough money into the pockets of the Arabs to
> make any appreciable impression on their minds. Materialists as
> they are, they might have been reconciled to Jewish penetration
> by visible evidence of Jewish wealth ...[60]

As a general principle, successful Arab work seemed to
require the Yishuv to be enjoying 'years of plenty', so that it
would be in a position to deliver the 'economic benefits' which

the Arabs were being invited to expect. The experience of 1922–1923 also illustrated the negative side-effects of the independent Arab-work activities of Kalvaryski, Jewish labour and others: apart from the undesirable general absence of central direction, each brand carried with it its own particular dangers.

Yet, in the attempt to catalogue the explanations for the lack of success at Arab work during this period, the Yishuv and the PZE singled out one factor as more decisive than any of the above factors:– the attitude of the British.[61] It should be noted that there were, among Yishuv and Zionist observers, practically no exponents of the simplistic view that the British were deliberately attempting to sabotage every attempt at Jewish-Arab co-operation, out of 'divide and rule', imperialist motives; such 'explanations' were to become popular only later.[62] The negative and decisive British rôle was seen to be operating in a much subtler way.

As we have seen in previous chapters, it had been a constant complaint that the British consistently showed favour to 'extremist' elements, while indirectly ignoring – or actively persecuting – those Arabs who wished to be friendly towards the Jews.[63] Whenever they weighed their own standing in the country against that of the anti-Zionist forces, all the Jews could see was the Administration strengthening the latter at their expense. This was visible to them not only from major Government appointments (i.e., Hajj Amin al-Husaini as 'Grand Mufti'), but even from seemingly trivial episodes such as invitations to official social functions.[64]

As a general rule, many Jews believed that their prestige (especially as a minority) in the eyes of their 'Arab neighbours' depended heavily on a visibly favourable attitude on the part of the governing power. An illustration of the precarious dependence of Jewish 'prestige' in Arab eyes on the actions of the Government was the question, in early 1923, of the release and amnesty of Shakr Abu Kishk, who had been the principal leader of the May 1921 attack on Petah Tikva. The formalities of his release and the accompanying peace agreement between him and the Jewish colony were carefully scrutinised by the Jews, who were anxious to avoid the impression, current in certain Arab quarters, that the amnesty

was a result of MCA and Beduin pressure on the 'weak' HC.[65]
When it came to specific questions of 'Arab work', Jewish
credibility depended on the Arab belief that the Jews had not
only the broad sympathy of the Government, but also its 'ear'
on matters of appointments, concessions or other marks of
official favour. Not only Zionists, but also a number of British
observers, shared the view that Arab leaders had different
levels of integrity, and that many would have silenced their
anti-Zionist cries in exchange for a Government post.[66]

In this connection, exaggerated Arab notions of 'Jewish
power' over the Administration could appear distinctly useful
for the Jews, and there were times when the latter found it
advantageous not to contradict such beliefs. But on this point
the Jews were bound to come into sharp conflict with an
Administration, headed by a British Jew, which was from its
first days preoccupied with proving that it was *not*, as its Arab
critics claimed, 'bound hand and foot to the Jews'.[67] One
response to this problem came in the June 1922 White Paper,
which stressed that the PZE 'has not desired to possess, and
does not possess, any share in the general administration of
the country', and that future constitutional arrangements
allowing a special position to the ZO to 'assist in the general
development of the country' would 'not entitle it [the ZO] to
share in any degree in its Government'.[68]

The result of all this, as far as the Jews were concerned, was
that Arabs 'of moderate views' were 'rapidly coming to the
conclusion that if they desire, as all Arabs do, to have friends
at Court, the Jews cannot help them'.[69] Thus, the fact that the
MNA was known to be an artificial Jewish creation almost
automatically deprived its members of any hope of receiving
official favours from an administration which was sensitive to
charges of being 'all Jewish'. There was little doubt in Jewish
minds that the Administration's attitude to the MNA effectively doomed the project to failure. While Y. H. Castel
recognised other reasons for the decline of the Association,
he was emphatic that, in future,

> even if we chose the most perfect method of reorganising the
> MNAs and of strengthening them against the extremists by
> encompassing all the moderate Arabs – there is no hope of

success as long as the Government continues to approach the extremist leaders with apologies and concessions, in accordance with its policy of compromise, and to disregard the moderate leaders . . .[70]

The visibly contemptuous attitude of (British and Arab) Government officials to the MNA no doubt deterred many Arabs from joining, and even some Jews became embarrassed about associating their efforts with the Association.[71] And, far from seeing evidence of their own supposed 'Jewish power' over the Palestine Administration, local Jewish activists knew only frustration in their many attempts to obtain Government favours, appointments or promotions for their Arab 'friends', whether members of the MNA or not.[72]

While admitting that the MNA had indeed failed in its positive objectives, Kalvaryski argued that the very fact that the Arab masses were 'not yet entirely on the side of our opponents' had to be considered a substantial victory. Looking back, in June 1923, Kalvaryski noted that not only had those Arabs who had chosen to be 'friendly' done so at the cost of abuse and ostracism at the hands of their own Arab rivals, but also at the cost of incurring the contempt of the *Government*: 'To the MCA everything is permitted and the Government flatters it. By contrast our friends in the MNA are pushed aside, and the Government has decided to ignore them completely ... Under such conditions,' Kalvaryski concluded, 'it is a wonder that Arab opposition to us has not been stronger.'[73] This assessment underscores both the negative impact of the British on Zionist work among the Arabs, and also the negative standards by which the Zionists were forced to measure their 'success' in this sphere.

8

The Constitutional Struggle

The Constitutional Dimension

In the preceding chapters we have attempted to isolate the experience of the 'Arab question' which was peculiar to the Palestinian Jews, and in so doing we found the ideas of *hagana* and 'Arab work' to be most relevant. But the Zionist world as a whole, including the Yishuv, was called upon during the period under discussion to direct its attention to another aspect of Zionist–British–Arab relations – the 'constitutional-legal' dimension. In the first years of the British Mandate we can trace the development of a triangular relationship between: (a) Arab objections to the Zionist aspects of the new constitutional arrangements for Palestine; (b) successive British attempts to satisfy some of these 'constitutional grievances'; and (c) the endeavours of Zionists to safeguard their position during the course of the British-Arab tug-of-war on these questions.

To a large extent this struggle involved the non-Yishuv machinery of Zionist–British diplomatic relations and high-level representations both in Jerusalem and in London. Under these circumstances, the Yishuv and the *Va'ad Leumi* were relegated to relatively passive and secondary roles. Yet, if the local Palestinian Jews were not actively in control of the political manoeuvring which was affecting their constitutional fate, they were nevertheless keenly sensitive to the dangers and the difficulties, and were able, on occasion, to bring their views to bear on the situation.

The 'special features' of the Zionist claim to Palestine were a decided disadvantage in the new age of 'national self-determination'. On the eve of the Paris Peace Conference, the Jews were a scattered and divided people – a 'nation' *in potentia*, at best. The majority did not reside in the territory which was claimed as the homeland, and, to make matters worse, this claim was denied (however inarticulately at first) by those representing the population who could claim 'occupancy' and majority status there. The fact that the Balfour Declaration survived the diplomatic activity of 1919 intact – outliving both the despairing conclusions of British sympathisers that 'self-determination has caught on, and self-determination means an Arab-Palestine'[1] and also the visit of the King-Crane Commission – must be regarded with hindsight as the final great 'victory' of political Zionism. The subsequent San Remo decision and the ratification of the Mandate for Palestine made the position appear, in the international context at least, less awkward and even somewhat encouraging to the Zionists. For, by late 1922 Great Britain was formally pledged before the League of Nations to 'facilitate Jewish immigration under suitable conditions' and to 'encourage ... close settlement by Jews on the land' (Article 6), while the Mandate went even beyond the terms of the original Balfour Declaration to recognise 'the historical connection of the Jewish people with Palestine' and 'the grounds for reconstituting their national home in that country' (Preamble).

But these post-War pro-Zionist edicts of international politics also contained limitations in deference to what were termed the 'existing non-Jewish communities in Palestine'. Under the Mandate, nothing was to be done which might 'prejudice the civil and religious rights of existing non-Jewish communities' (Preamble), while the Mandatory Power was responsible for 'placing the country under such political, administrative and economic conditions' as would secure the development, not only of the Jewish National Home, but also of 'self-governing institutions' (Article 2).

If after 1921 Arab leaders in Palestine appeared to be abandoning violence as an effective political instrument in the fight against Zionism,[2] they continued to reject the Balfour Declaration policy and refused to recognise the Mandate or the Constitution which were based on that policy. In a positive way, they insisted on the fullest interpretation of the injunction against 'prejudicing' their rights, while their demands (made repeatedly since early 1919)[3] for some form of 'native national government' now appeared to dove-tail with Britain's Mandatory obligation to promote self-government in Palestine. This legitimate and constitutional campaign by the Arabs against the Balfour Declaration policy reached its peak during 1923, when successive British offers to establish a partly-elective Legislative Council, a nominated 'non-political' Advisory Council, and an 'Arab Agency' were made to induce them to co-operate in the administration of the country.

At an early stage Zionist observers realised that the constitutional demands of the Arabs were almost totally irreconcilable with their own demands and needs, and would have to be considered a 'threat' to be resisted. According to the analysis of Col Kisch of the PZE, there was indeed little room for manoeuvre on the constitutional question in mid-1923:

> ... so long as we need the Mandate at all, it is clearly impossible to contemplate any modification of those guarantees which it affords to our national aspirations. It is also clear that we do emphatically need the Mandate today, while we number only 11% of the population of which the remainder are ranged almost to the last man behind the banner of a hostile organisation. For these reasons it appears that we cannot to-day join the Arabs in demanding a change in the Constitution which would weaken the English control of the situation, a control which the English Government has introduced into the constitution in order to be able to carry out the pledges contained in the Mandate.[4]

For the British, the problem was to strike a balance between the Jewish National Home policy, on the one hand, and the Mandatory obligation to introduce democratic forms of self-government, on the other, in such a way that the full implementation of the latter would not – as was likely to be the case – make it impossible to fulfil the former, equally valid, obligation.[5] 'Gradualness' became the catchword for both Zionism and self-government under the British Mandate. During his visit to Palestine in March 1921, Mr Churchill made it quite clear that the present form of government would 'continue for many years' and that only 'step by step' would Britain 'develop representative institutions leading up to full self-government'.[6] As an indication of just how 'gradual' the process would be, Mr Churchill went on: 'All of us here today will have passed away from the earth and also our children and our children's children before it is fully achieved.'

However, like so many other cherished notions, the idea of the extremely gradual development of self-governing institutions did not stand up to the May 1921 riots. On 8th May Samuel wrote to Churchill suggesting 'the very early establishment of representative institutions'.[7] The Secretary of State was most reluctant to 'make such a concession under pressure', which would be, in his view, 'to rob it of half its value'; he was decidedly 'not of opinion that the morrow of the Jaffa riots was the best moment for such a concession'. But Samuel, looking for a way to restore Arab confidence in his Administration, asked for the authority to issue an official declaration to the effect that HMG were 'considering [the] constitutional question and that opinions will be taken into account of all sections' of the population. Mr Churchill gave his authorisation for a statement, but with the strong recommendation not to use 'any such words as "elected" or "representative" '. Samuel's 3rd June 1921 Statement of Policy thus contained the circuitously-worded, but very real, assurance that representative institutions for Palestine were under consideration. Over the next two and a half years Samuel displayed a great determination to introduce constitutional organs which would satisfy the Arabs as adequately responsive to their opinions.

Zionist and Yishuv Reactions to the Legislative Council Proposal

General Zionist fears of representative institutions for Palestine while the Jews formed only a small minority of the population are almost too obvious to require elaboration. Even before there were any actual plans for such institutions, experience under the Military Administration led Zionists to appreciate the dangers of allowing 'only the brutal numbers to speak' in Palestine. In 1918 and 1919 Dr Weizmann already felt the need to urge the British to recognise 'the fundamental difference in quality of Jew and Arab' and that the latter would not be 'fit for self-government for a very long time to come'.[8] Zionist publicists, too, sought skilful and tactful ways of presenting arguments against the introduction of democratic institutions in Palestine in the foreseeable future.[9]

The basic Zionist stand, as it developed in the early 1920s, continued to be that, while Zionists did not oppose the *gradual* development of self-governing institutions, it had to be recognised that Palestine would not be 'ripe' for self-rule for many years to come. They realised that it was impossible to say publicly that the proper time might come only when the Jews formed a majority (or near-majority) of the population. But it was by no means difficult for them to present the general European view that (quite apart from the question of Zionism) to grant full self-government to the Arabs of Palestine, with their primitive 'standard of education and political experience', 'would clearly be to run the risk of consigning Palestine to chaos'.[10]

For many, the riots of May 1921 seemed to strengthen the arguments that the Arab majority was quite 'unripe for civic responsibilities,'[11] and it was thus with particular distress that Zionists witnessed Samuel apparently discarding all the recent pronouncements on 'gradualness'. Samuel's attempt 'to deal with the Arab movement as a constitutional opposition' became as evident and as unwelcome to Zionists as his general tendency to take the Arabs 'too' seriously.[12] But Zionists were forced to appreciate that, however 'premature and in some degree artificial' the Arab demands for self-government may have been, they could not be 'indefinitely resisted' or deferred 'until the day, necessarily far distant, when there is a Jewish majority'.[13] Thus, during the interval between Samuel's Statement of 3rd June 1921 and the ratification of the Mandate in July 1922, Zionist leaders reluctantly accepted Samuel's determined lead on this question, but not without constantly stressing the need for adequate safeguards for the inviolability of the Balfour Declaration and the Mandate.

* * *

The fears of representative institutions which were acutely aroused in the Yishuv after May 1921 must be seen against the background of the peculiar constitutional arrangements which Palestinian Jews had been expecting to emerge from the Paris Peace Conference. As we have seen in Chapter 1, the 'Eretz-Israel Conference' of December 1918 had envisaged a post-war Palestine under predominantly Jewish and European governing bodies, with only token Arab representation. Yishuv leaders had immediately recognised the contradiction between 'pure' national self-determination and the type of régime which would be required for the development of the Jewish National Home. However much they wished to consider themselves 'democrats' by temperament or upbringing, they realised that, as a minority, the Jews could not *afford* to be 'democrats' with regard to their own claim to Palestine.

> We are afraid, [confessed Jabotinsky before the Conference] and we don't want to have a normal constitution here, since the Palestine situation is not normal. The majority of its "electors" have not yet returned to the country. If there is a normal constitution here, responsible to the "majority", then the majority of *us* would never enter, and even you – with all due respect – they would expel from the country.[14]

In 1918 Palestinian Jewry had put forward the demand for 'national-communal autonomy' for all groups as a legitimate alternative, more suited to the 'special' situation in Palestine than numerical or parliamentary democracy. But this concept of 'national-communal autonomy', as the Yishuv understood it, was never enshrined in the general constitutional apparatus of the country. It remained throughout the Mandatory period a cherished internal goal of the Yishuv. But the *Va'ad Leumi* never forcefully challenged Samuel's plans for a Western-style elective institution by suggesting an alternative system based on this 'national-communal autonomy'.[15]

Typical reaction of Palestine Jewry to Samuel's constitutional plans was simple fear and rejection. But representative institutions were indeed on the agenda of the HC, and after alluding to the dreaded subject in his 3rd June speech, Samuel summoned Yishuv leaders to give them an informal indication of the composition and functions of the intended Legislative Council. During the interview, the members of the *Va'ad Leumi* Executive took the opportunity of making clear their opposition to any form of elective institution, not so much 'because of our desire to deny the rights of others', but rather because they were of the firm opinion that 'in this case an elective institution makes difficult the realisation of the promises given to us by the League of Nations and the British Government.'[16]

In the prevailing atmosphere of Yishuv–Samuel relations during those weeks it is little wonder that local leaders were hardly impressed by Samuel's assurances that the special position of the Jews would not be endangered under any Council schemes. The feeling that an elective institution constituted a grave threat to Yishuv interests dominated the *Va'ad Leumi* meeting (28–30.6.1921) which heard the report of the interview with the HC. Only Y. Radler-Feldman (later to be, under the name 'Rabbi Binyamin', one of the binationalist leaders) was optimistic enough to suggest that there might perhaps be 'some party combinations among the Arabs favourable to us', and he urged the *Va'ad Leumi* to adopt 'a positive attitude' to the idea of an elected council.[17] Another speaker resurrected one of the ideas entertained at the 'Eretz-Israel Conference' of December 1918 when he suggested that the Yishuv might agree to participate in such a council only if the proportion of seats allotted to the Jews would reflect the ratio of the *world* Jewish population to the Palestine Arab population, while Dr Thon was prepared to accept a guaranteed quota of one-third Jewish seats. But, apart from these exceptions, the discussion focused entirely on what steps might prove most effective in averting the proposed Legislative Council. The general view was that the Yishuv would be quite foolish to lend its hand to a scheme from which no good could possibly come, and the resolution finally adopted by the *Va'ad Leumi* was unanimous in stating that

> so long as the Mandate, which fixes the political status of the country, the role of the Government and the rights of the Jewish people and the [other] inhabitants of Palestine, is not signed – the step of creating an elected council in the country is illegal and the *Va'ad Leumi* has no need whatsoever to concern itself with the idea.[18]

This Yishuv stand happened, in any case, to conform with the procedure which the British chose to follow, and the delay in the ratification of the Mandate, regretted for other reasons, provided the Jews with a welcome postponement of the plans for representative institutions. In the White Paper of June 1922, Mr Churchill announced the draft provisions for a Legislative Council in the hope of winning Arab and Zionist acquiescence in the new Constitution. But the Arab Delegation remained firm in rejecting *any* constitutional arrangements based on the Balfour Declaration and the draft Mandate.[19] Notwithstanding these Arab objections, ratification of the Mandate on 24th July 1922 was duly followed by the promulgation of Orders-in-Council for the Palestine Constitution and for elections to a Legislative Council. Within six months a Council – composed of twelve elected Palestinians (eight Muslims, two Christians, two Jews) and ten Government officials, under the presidency of the HC – was to come into being.[20]

Participation in the Legislative Council Elections

British hopes that the proposed Legislative Council would satisfy Arab constitutional demands were soon shaken. The Fifth Palestine Arab Congress, meeting in Nablus on 22nd August 1922, firmly rejected the new Constitution based on the Balfour Declaration policy, and resolved to boycott any elections to the proposed Council.[21]

In the months following the boycott decision of the Nablus Congress the attitude of Palestine Jewry was unclear. The *Va'ad Leumi* took no new official stand on the Council, but a number of its leaders appear to have been assuming that

Jewish participation would be inescapable. No one in the Yishuv relished the prospect of this Council in itself, but when it began to look like a battle between the Government and the boycotting 'extremists', Yishuv representatives had little choice. They noted with satisfaction that Samuel was – initially – not intimidated by the threat of the Arab boycott, and that he was prepared to suppress any anti-election activity 'as constituting an act against the Government'.[22] Some local Jews with experience in 'Arab work' unofficially assisted the PZE and the Administration by encouraging 'moderate' Arabs to defy the Nablus Congress boycott (cf. p. 138, above).

But Samuel's apparent resoluteness, and Yishuv satisfaction with it, were very short-lived. Almost within a month of the promulgation of the Elections Ordinance, and increasingly thereafter, Samuel was seen to display pathetic weakness and inactivity in the face of a boycott campaign which mounted in intensity and boldness. Beginning in late September 1922 Zionist complaints mounted steadily, and Col Kisch ended one of his reports in March 1923 with the opinion that 'the present lamentable situation' was 'the direct result of the application of the methods of English liberal administration to the government of an Eastern and backward people accustomed to the strong hand of Turkish misrule!'[23]

Initial optimism among the Jews that the elections would succeed, with the resultant boost to Government and (by extension) Zionist prestige, progressively faded. By the time detailed instructions for election procedure were issued on 7th February 1923, the difficulties of the situation and the Yishuv's own undefined position and internal problems were becoming unbearable for local Jewish leaders. Most would not deny the basic principle that the Yishuv would be far better off if the Council never came into existence; but the Jews were equally conscious of the fact that it was tactically impossible to reject the Council out-of-hand, following only their 'healthy and simple instincts'.

In the absence of a clear stand by the *Va'ad Leumi*, the Jewish population appeared divided on the advisability of taking part in the elections for the unwanted Council. With only one week remaining before the voting was to begin, the *Va'ad Leumi* met (14–15.2.1923) to resolve the lingering uncertainty with regard to Yishuv participation.[24] The theme of the first day's debate was: how to make the best of a bad thing. Interspersed throughout the discussion were hypothetical questions illustrating the continuing anxieties of the Yishuv with regard to this constitutional innovation: how would the Jews react if the Arab members on the Council immediately demanded its dissolution and elections for a fully democratic body? How would the Jews react to Arab attempts to use the Council to interfere with internal Yishuv matters? Were there two Yishuv personalities of sufficient dignity and weight to 'hold their own' against twenty Arabs and officials?

On the immediate question of participation in the elections, however, only Meir Dizengoff stated categorically that he would not place himself in the absurd position of casting his vote for a 'fictitious' mock-parliament which was, at the same time, visibly dangerous to Jewish interests. Other speakers adduced a variety of tactical considerations to justify a decision in favour of participation in the unwanted institution. A successful election with substantial Arab participation, some argued, would be a welcome defeat of the 'extremists', and would amount to Arab recognition of the Constitution and the Mandate. Col Kisch also reminded local Jewish leaders that even if the elections were to be called off owing to insufficient *Arab* participation, a co-operative and loyal Yishuv stood to gain from the subsequent gratitude of the Administration.

It was clearly less out of any love for Samuel or for representative institutions, than out of fear of Musa Kazim Pasha, that Yishuv representatives appeared prepared to participate in the elections. At this particular meeting and elsewhere, the refusal to make common cause with Musa Kazim was the most frequently and strongly argued rationale of the local Jews. A different argument, advanced by only a few, was that the Jews should not waste the chance – however slim – that some 'moderate' Arabs (the only ones who would dare to run for election) might serve on the new Council. At the end of the debate a motion was passed in favour of participation

by ten votes to one, with abstentions from the labour representatives.

But the matter did not end here. One unknown factor
which had hovered over the day's discussion was the separate
stand which the *Histadrut* would take on the issue. At the first
day's meeting, labour representatives had spoken only in
their private capacities. Participation in a patently undemo-
cratic and 'effendi'-oriented institution involved some
embarrassing compromises of their social-democratic
instincts, but labour elements too were sensitive to the tactical
complications of a Jewish boycott. In the current depreciated
state of the *Va'ad Leumi*'s command over various 'separatist'
and dissident groups within the Yishuv,[25] many Jewish leaders
desperately hoped that the anticipated *Histadrut* decision
would not be so 'radical' as to lead to an open breach with the
Va'ad Leumi, which might prove a death-blow to the credibility and authority of the Yishuv's supposedly supreme
organ.

Since the proposed Legislative Council was seen to
endanger, in particular, Jewish autonomous development and
immigration, *Ahdut ha-'Avoda*, the dominant partner in the
Histadrut, had decided to announce to Samuel that its participation in the elections would be conditional on two points: (a)
immediate Government recognition of the Yishuv's autonomy by giving final sanction to the much-delayed draft Communities Ordinance;[26] and (b) an assurance that ultimate
control over immigration would be in Jewish hands. While it
was a foregone conclusion that the second condition would be
rejected, the labour party considered it important enough not
to be passed over in silence, especially in view of the 'Immigration Committee' which was to be attached to the proposed
Council. *Ahdut ha-'Avoda* was prepared to concede the
immigration precondition, once the point was registered, but
it would regard the demand on autonomy as an ultimatum. Y.
Sprinzak, on behalf of *ha-Po'el ha-Tza'ir*, the second largest
group in the *Histadrut*, informed the *Va'ad Leumi* of his
concurrence in the *Ahdut ha-'Avoda* stand.

In order to avoid splitting the Yishuv into two (or more)
camps on the elections issue, the *Va'ad Leumi* decided after
much debate to reverse its ten–one decision of the previous

day, and it formally adopted the workers' minimum demands regarding national-communal autonomy as its own considered position. The resolution which was finally passed at 2 a.m. read (somewhat incoherently):

> The *Va'ad Leumi* regards as a prior condition to its participation in the elections the sanction of the Communities [Ordinance] and its autonomous rights before the convening of a Legislative Council; otherwise it is certain that there will not be the desired participation in the elections, the abstention of important sections is to be feared, and the necessary moral prestige for Jewish participation in the elections will be lacking.

A delegation was chosen to bring the matter before the HC.

It would be wrong to interpret this last-minute balking at the impending elections merely as proof of the feeble *Va'ad Leumi's* inability to stand up to the determined labour movement. The attachment to 'national-communal autonomy' was genuine, and the Yishuv leaders became instilled with a new confidence by following the labour lead in juxtaposing this demand against participation in unwanted representative institutions. But apart from these considerations, and the instinctive fear of seeing 'democracy' perverted in the hands of Arab 'extremists', there was a more basic issue at the root of the Yishuv's attitude to the Legislative Council proposal: confidence in Sir Herbert Samuel's ability to remain faithful to the interests of the Jewish National Home in the course of his attempts to develop 'self-governing institutions' for Palestine.

We have only to look back to the *Va'ad Leumi* debates of 2nd–3rd January 1923 to feel the intensity of the bitterness and frustration in the Yishuv with regard to the Administration on a number of issues. Quite apart from its disillusionment at the glaring evidence of Government timidity in the face of the Arab election boycott campaign, the Yishuv's dissatisfaction with Samuel's record on the questions of immigration and land-acquisition facilities had mounted steadily since the ratification of the Mandate.[27] The idea of an inevitable confrontation with Samuel was already brewing then, as Ben-Zvi reflected the growing feeling that

> Samuel's whole policy is based on the belief and the assumption

that the MCA is the power and that we are not; and if we don't show our strength, we won't be able to influence him.

The same undercurrent of discontent with Samuel was evident during the February debates devoted to the question of participation in the elections. David Ben-Gurion noted drily that his party was 'responsible neither for his appointment, nor for his resignation', and that there was therefore no need to weigh the merits of the *Ahdut ha-'Avoda* ultimatum against the possibility of Samuel resigning.[28]

During his interview with the *Va'ad Leumi* delegation on 16th February Sir Herbert Samuel was noticeably taken aback by the bitterness and dissatisfaction of the Yishuv representatives.[29] No doubt preoccupied in recent months with the Arab campaign of boycott and non-cooperation, Samuel had been taking for granted that the Palestinian Jews would appreciate that they shared a common interest with him for the success of the elections. Fed up at precisely this point – being 'taken for granted' – the *Va'ad Leumi* delegation now took the opportunity to make clear its disappointment on the Government's recent record and, in particular, it insisted on receiving some assurance that the Communities Ordinance would be approved in exchange for organised Jewish participation in the elections. The Yishuv spokesmen stressed that any forthcoming *Va'ad Leumi* support would, in any event, be given against the better judgment of the Yishuv and only owing to force of circumstance.

In replying to the Yishuv delegates, Samuel attempted to convince them of the political wisdom of their participation in the elections mainly by referring to the strong anti-Zionist and anti-Mandate lobby in England, which would use a combined Jewish-Arab boycott as ready ammunition in its campaign for complete abandonment of the Palestine 'burden'. He hinted further that, in the event of a joint boycott, he and Bentwich would see little point in continuing 'to sacrifice the best of their forces here'. On the other hand, Samuel did show much sympathy for the Yishuv position. Although he was unable to give a definite commitment that the Communities Ordinance would be sanctioned before the Council was convened, Samuel did succeed in convincing the *Va'ad Leumi* delegation that he was sincerely and energetically supporting the Ordinance in its difficult passage through the Colonial Office.[30]

The crisis over participation in the elections passed, as the *Va'ad Leumi* reconvened two days later to learn the results of the interview. The feeling was unanimous that the Yishuv had been as successful as could have been expected in having its position understood at Government House. In the short time available Yishuv leaders devoted their energies to the internal and organisational problems of preparing the population to participate in the elections.

The primary elections held between 20th and 28th February returned more than the required number of Jewish and Druze secondary electors, but only 82 of the 722 places allotted to Muslim and Christian Arabs. The HC extended the deadline, but the number of Arab secondary electors rose only to 126. On 4th May 1923 an Order-in-Council in London declared the elections 'null and void', and on 29th May Samuel announced this officially to the people of Palestine – who had not 'fully availed themselves of the opportunity afforded to participate in the Government of the country through elected representatives'.[31]

To the extent that the elections had been a battle between boycotting 'extremists' and 'moderates' who wished to co-operate with the Administration, the resounding victory of the former was obvious well before Samuel's formal announcement. Although the 'extremist' victory was to be regretted as such, many Palestinian Jews were clearly relieved that the unwanted Council would not be created, and satisfied that they could not be reproached for having failed to do their 'duty' by supporting Samuel. During the *Va'ad Leumi's* post-election analyses, only a few voices expressed disappointment that the Jews had not done more to ensure a larger Arab turnout.[32] But Ben-Zvi and Yellin reiterated the official *Va'ad Leumi* view that the main business of the Yishuv had been to bring Jews out to the polls, and, having done so, there was no need to mourn the demise of the Legislative Council scheme. Any work for Arab participation, it was noted, had been the private affair of individuals.

The New Advisory Council Offer

The offer of a Legislative Council in 1921–1923 represented Sir Herbert Samuel's major effort in the direction of 'self-governing institutions' for Palestine. But, even after the failure of this project, Samuel persisted in his search for another appropriate constitutional modification which would allow the Arab population to feel that the Administration was sincerely interested in taking its views into account. His initial optimism was, however, substantially diminished, and in mid-1923 he realised that it would be very difficult

> to find any solution which the Arabs will accept short of the transfer of the government to their own hands, with the purpose and the result – whatever paper guarantees might be given – that the Jewish enterprise will be destroyed.[33]

In his proclamation of 29th May, Samuel announced the imminent formation of a nominated Advisory Council.[34] Aware of the failure of the proposed Legislative Council in early March, the HC had taken the trouble to consult members of the Arab Executive (AE), and had been informed that the Executive could see nothing objectionable in an appointed advisory body to co-operate with the Government on administrative matters only, leaving the sensitive political question completely aside. Feeling that he had now overcome the defeat of the Legislative Council proposal, Samuel was hoping that the country might soon return to its 'normal' business, with the thorny constitutional question temporarily resolved and the battered prestige of the Government somewhat restored. Zionists, too, welcomed the Advisory Council announcement and predicted a 'favourable change' in the political situation.[35]

But the AE soon had second thoughts about allowing the Administration too easy a victory. Strong pressure was exerted on the Arab nominees to withdraw their acceptances, or to demand conditions, such as a Government stipulation that it recognised that their participation did not amount to Arab acceptance of the validity of the Constitution.[36] Negotiations between the Arab nominees and the Government – accompanied throughout by vigorous public and private

reminders of the proper patriotic attitude – continued unresolved through the summer of 1923.

While this was going on, Yishuv representatives, for their
part, expressed disappointment that the new distribution of
seats gave them only two (compared with three on the 1920–
21 Advisory Council).[37] But they did not strenuously argue
this point. Yellin and Kalvaryski, the two Jews elected by the
Yishuv to sit on the Council, were on the whole quite satisfied
with the new arrangements. They considered only one of the
ten Arab nominees an 'extreme opponent', and expressed the
hope that the Council might provide a useful stimulus to
informal Jewish-Arab contacts.

But the real 'constitutional struggle' over the Advisory
Council centred on the Government-Arab negotiations, and
this left Yishuv leaders on the sidelines with little active role
to play. The PZE took a more active interest in a Government
victory over the 'extremists'' campaign to obstruct the operation of the new Advisory Council.[38] But these efforts bore
little fruit. By mid-July, the fact that the Advisory Council
had not yet succeeded in meeting (with or without the full
complement of nominees) was already being interpreted as a
second victory for the MCA and the AE.[39]

The 'Arab Agency' Proposal

After these two successive failures at having the Arabs 'play
the constitutional game' and channel their opposition through
participation in Government organs, Zionists were beginning
to feel that the limit had been reached. They had reluctantly,
but loyally, endorsed the policy of the June 1922 White
Paper;[40] likewise, they had gone along with the Legislative
Council scheme at Samuel's insistence, but against their own
better judgment. The fact that Samuel had not yet succeeded
in winning Arab confidence was, in their view, no Zionist fault
and should not entail any further futile concessions, which
could only be at Zionist expense. True, the Balfour Declaration policy itself had not been overturned in the last two
years, but the very process of making offers to conciliate the
Arab non-cooperation movement was doing only harm: it
threatened to diminish the major Zionist 'diplomatic' vic-

tories of recent years; it did nothing to enhance Government prestige in Arab eyes; and it had already decreased Jewish confidence in the Government.

Such was the Zionist feeling in July 1923, as a special Cabinet Committee on Palestine began meeting in London. This feeling was transmitted officially and unofficially to British policy-makers by Zionists in the form of pleas that 'any new concessions to the Arabs'

> would not only be of no value as a means of conciliating the Arab extremists, but would . . . give an impression of [British] weakening which would have a most disheartening effect on Zionist opinion.[41]

In the Yishuv as well, many were hoping that, after the 'lessons' of the Legislative and Advisory Councils, the British would now resume direct, 'efficient, if not representative' rule.[42] Yishuv confidence in the British – and in Sir Herbert Samuel – had not improved since early 1923, and in July the Jerusalem weekly, *ha-Tor*, looked uneasily to London, where both Samuel and a delegation of the Sixth Arab Congress were currently visiting:

> Both London and Jerusalem have adopted a policy of keeping peace at the highest price – compromising on everything and listening to the threats of the Arabs. Who will protect Jewish interests against the intrigues of Musa Kazim and Co.? The High Commissioner . . .? Why, it is due to his policy and leniency that these people now speak in the name of the Arab people. It was he who allowed the Arab leaders to boycott the elections. He has allowed the Arab extremist movement to grow by trying to suddenly introduce British liberalism into the country of Jamal Pasha's scaffolds. Will he be able to protect Jewish interests now?[43]

Nor was this sense of insecurity confined only to 'unsophisticated' local elements in Palestine. Col Kisch gave his candid views in a secret letter to Dr Weizmann several months later:

> I have always been terrified of any attempt *by the Government* to come to an understanding with the Arabs. The CO and HC have both shown themselves so ready to make concessions on our policy while getting nothing in return, that I have ever dreaded

what they might be tempted to do against some possible advantage . . .[44]

Notwithstanding all the Zionist hopes and suggestions that no new concessions would be offered to the Arabs, the Cabinet Committee was indeed contemplating a third 'palliative' to induce the Arabs to adopt a more positive attitude to the Constitution and administration of Palestine. This was the idea of inserting a 'counter-poise' to the Jewish Agency provision in the Mandate, an idea which had first suggested itself to Samuel under the impact of May 1921, but which had been rejected by the then Secretary of State, Winston Churchill.[45] On 4th October 1923 the Secretary of State, the Duke of Devonshire, wrote to Samuel to inform him of the final outcome of the recent deliberations on the Palestine policy.[46]

Acknowledging that the most frequently cited of all Arab constitutional grievances was the privileged position of the Zionists under Article 4 of the Mandate (which recognised 'an appropriate Jewish Agency', in practice, the PZE, as a 'public body for the purpose of advising and cooperating with the Administration' on matters affecting the Jewish National Home and the Palestinian Jewish population), the British Government was now prepared to accord 'similar privileges to an Arab Agency', which would enjoy 'a position exactly analogous to that accorded to the Jewish Agency'. On the questions of immigration (Article 6) and public works (Article 11), the Arab Agency would also enjoy the parallel right to be consulted with regard to the 'rights and position of the other (i.e., non-Jewish) sections of the population'.

One week later the HC convened a 'fully representative' assembly of Arab notables and read a statement containing the gist of the Secretary of State's letter. Samuel invited those present to accept, on behalf of the Arab population, this 'opportunity . . . to share in the conduct of the country's affairs', and added that, contrary to recent misrepresentations in the press, HMG were definitely not considering any constitutional modifications beyond the present proposal. This 'take-it-or-leave-it' offer was rejected by the assembly as not satisfying 'the aspirations of the Arab people'. Musa Kazim al-Husaini, on behalf of the assembly, 'added that the Arabs, having never recognised the status of the Jewish Agency, have no desire for the establishment of an Arab Agency on the same basis'.

In London, the Duke of Devonshire received the Arab decision 'with great regret' and informed Samuel on 9th November that HMG were 'reluctantly driven to the conclusion that further efforts on similar lines would be useless' and had 'accordingly decided not to repeat the attempt'. He authorised Samuel to resume the administration of Palestine with an Advisory Council or according to his statutory discretion. In December it was announced that the HC would be governing henceforth with an 'Executive Council' composed of senior Government officials.[47] Practical consideration of any new proposals for the 'development of self-governing institutions' would be resumed only when the Arabs themselves took the initiative and expressed their 'readiness to participate'.[48]

Owing to the circumstances in which the offer was made and rejected, Zionist and Yishuv reactions were almost entirely theoretical and after the event. If the 'Arab Agency' proposal had not amounted to a real and practical danger, its contents were felt to have been far more disturbing than either of the previous Council schemes. The fact that the 'Arab Agency' was very quickly a 'dead' issue did not detract from the serious need which Zionists felt to register their unambiguous denunciation of the project. The Yishuv and the Zionist Executive took separate but similar post facto stands on the 'Arab Agency' proposal.[49] There were two main reasons for the severe displeasure of both bodies. First was the very fact that the British could have contemplated 'tampering' with the Mandate (and, worse still, so soon after its coming into effect on 29th September 1923); this could only dangerously undermine the sanctity and authority of that 'unalterable and solid international document' and the Zionist position enshrined in it. Secondly, the offer made to create an Arab body 'exactly analogous' to the Jewish Agency had apparently overlooked the 'distinctive characteristics' of the Jewish Agency as a body representative of the interests of *world* Jewry with regard to Palestine; this 'oversight' might lead to the disastrous conclusion that Britain recognised that the *Arab world* had a parallel right to be consulted on internal Palestinian matters. A third anxiety, expressed particularly in Yishuv circles, was that immigration – 'the most elementary of the Jewish rights' – should have been specifically mentioned among the subjects on which the Arabs had a right to be consulted.

But, counterbalancing all the negative reactions, the 'Arab Agency' episode did leave in its wake valuable compensating features. Samuel's reaffirmation of the inviolability of the Balfour Declaration and his overall tone of firmness on 11th October were welcome and refreshing to the Jewish public. The Declaration and the Mandate had now survived three successive offers of 'constitutional palliatives', and the British appeared for the time being to have realised that there was no point in further concessions.[50]

Despite the noticeable Zionist relief following a difficult constitutional struggle, the Arab demand for representative 'national' government was to remain a permanent feature of Arab–Jewish relations in Palestine. In the years after 1923 Yishuv leaders would look only with dread on the recurring possibility that the British might again decide to try to satisfy the Arab desire for 'native national government'.[51]

9

The Palestine Question and the Greater Arab World

The Broader Arab Perspective

In many respects the turn of 1923–1924 marked the end of a six-year 'settling-down' period for Zionism in post-War Palestine. Even if an understanding with the Arabs was not yet imminent, the security aspects of the Arab question were now well in hand; the opposition led by the MCA was visibly weakening; and the international diplomatic gains of the peace settlement were at last safely enshrined in the Mandate for Palestine, unaltered by the recent Arab non-cooperation campaign. But the struggle for the consolidation of the Zionist position had simultaneously involved meeting challenges on yet another front: the Arab world beyond the boundaries of Palestine. Let us now go back over the period to place the local, Palestinian, Arab-Zionist confrontation in this broader perspective.

At a very early stage, many Zionists had found it necessary to regard Palestine – and the problem of winning local Arab acquiescence in the Zionist programme – in the larger context of the Arab world as a whole. There were three sides to this outside Arab world. (a) One side was fearful and threatening; 'pan-Arabism' or 'pan-Islam' often showed a fanatic animosity to Westerners in general, or to Zionist Jews in particular. But the other two sides appeared in a quite positive light.

(b) On the one hand, non-Palestinian Arabs usually presented more hopeful prospects for reaching a negotiated settlement than could be expected in the purely local, Palestinian context, while (c) on the other hand, placing the Palestine question within its larger Arab context afforded some justification for the claim to a 'Jewish Palestine'.

The present chapter will illustrate Yishuv concern for all three faces, although we shall find the threatening side to be by far the dominant concern. The Yishuv – largely excluded from the Zionist diplomatic activity of the period and preoccupied with the local conditions of the day – was on the whole slow to appreciate the possibilities of a solution to the Palestine problem through the greater Arab world. Yet there was little hesitation among Palestinian Jews to point to the outside Arab world in the context of their justified demands for a Jewish homeland in Palestine. More than a mere propaganda or rhetorical device, it has been in many cases sincerely believed that, in all good faith, the Arabs – as a nation endowed with many lands – ought to be 'reasonable' (as the European Powers were) and 'magnanimous' enough to permit the Jews to return to their only historic homeland which was situated in 'tiny' Palestine.

To strengthen this general justification, Zionists also invoked supplementary negative arguments to show that Palestine was not central or indispensable to the awakening 'Arab national movement', as it *was* to the Jewish 'national movement'.[1] In the period immediately following the War, Zionists found further support in presenting their case against Palestine falling within the legitimate scope of pan-Arab national aspirations by the accepted European stereotype of the 'true Arab type' of the desert. Zionists learned much on this score from 'experts' like T. E. Lawrence, G. F. Clayton and William Ormsby-Gore, the sympathetic liaison officer attached to the Zionist Commission in 1918 (and later Colonial Secretary, 1936–38). The latter frequently expounded on his contempt for the degenerate 'Levantinized' elements of Palestine and Western Syria, and urged the Zionists to distinguish between the 'real men' of Faisal's movement and the 'so-called Arabs of Palestine'.[2] Zionists accepted and repeated the view that the Palestinian population was not 'pure'

Arab, but rather riddled with backward, 'dishonest, unedu-
cated, greedy, ... unpatriotic', etc. elements, and hence a
matter quite distinct from the 'real' Arabs of the 'real Arab
national movement'. By extension, it was sometimes argued
that Palestine had no claim to become 'Arab' under the
doctrine of national self-determination.[3]

Even though such views were sincerely believed or widely
held, appeals to Arab 'magnanimity' or unflattering distinc-
tions between 'real' and 'so-called' Arabs did little to convince any Arabs of the justice of the Jewish claim to Palestine.
What was needed was an effective *policy* based on such
beliefs. Even before the War, Richard Lichtheim had realised
the advantages of taking the following line in his negotiations
with non-Palestinian Arab representatives in Constantinople:

> The Arab question is much more extensive than the Palestine
> question. If the Arabs allow us to buy land in Palestine and to
> colonise ..., they will be able to win through our agency the
> goodwill of the European press and eventually of Jewish financial
> circles for the development of Arabism.[4]

After the War, the idea of proposing an 'exchange of services'
to non-Palestinian Arabs was to prove by far the most promising avenue to resolving an apparently impossible local dead-
lock. Many rounds of Zionist–Arab negotiations followed a
common pattern: Zionists would agree to support Arab
national aspirations *outside* Palestine, in exchange for (a) a
specific Arab recognition of the Zionist position in Palestine;
or (b) passive non-intervention in Mandatory Palestine; or (c)
such intervention as would exert a 'moderating' influence
over the local opponents of the Jewish National Home. Thus,
for example, Ben-Gurion – who could see 'no solution' to the
contradiction between Jewish and Arab claims in 1919 – later
became more hopeful by employing a 'pan-Arab' perspective:

> They [the Arabs of Palestine] regard this land as theirs, and we
> regard it as ours ... Our wishes are opposed to those of the Arabs
> of Erez [sic] Israel, but they are only a small part of the Arab
> people as a whole.[5]

In his talks with Arab leaders during the 1930s, Ben-Gurion would frequently propose an 'exchange of services' in which a 'Jewish Palestine' would bring immense benefits to the Arab nation as a whole.[6]

The Threatening Side of Pan-Arabism

It was in their association with Faisal that Zionist leaders had their first real opportunity to attempt to resolve their difficulties in Palestine in the context of the Arab world as a whole. In spite of all the frustrations and the ultimate failure, their relations with the Amir still represented the closest the Zionists had – or would – ever come to a global agreement with the Arab world over the Palestine question.[7] And, to this day, the Weizmann–Faisal agreement has a place in Zionist propaganda as evidence both that the Zionists did desire to come to terms with the Arabs, and that an authorised representative of the Arab world had been willing, at one point, to welcome the Jews to Palestine.[8]

But there is little evidence that Palestine Jewry was as patient or as indulgent with Faisal, or that it shared Dr Weizmann's hopes for an agreement through his auspices. Following the advance of French troops and Faisal's flight from Syria, Jews in Palestine experienced relief at seeing 'the most dangerous element – [Arab] Damascus – ... leaving the stage'.[9] After Faisal's expulsion, the greater Arab world continued to be seen by the Yishuv more in its role as a potential threat than as the source of any real hope for an agreement. While the new French régime at Damascus temporarily stilled Palestinian agitation for a greater Arab Syria, it was not long before the Islamic world as a whole was caught up in a general anti-European ferment. The 'pan-Islamic revival' did not single out Zionism as a specific target,[10] but both Zionists and British were equally interested in insulating Palestine from the effects of this general unrest. The Zionists, as 'foreigners' in the Middle East, knew very well their precarious position in the face of 'a premature pan-Arab renaissance' which might 'mean the end of all European control from Morocco to the Persian Gulf'.[11]

In addition to hoping that the British would, in the course of protecting their own interests against this anti-European movement, also defend the Zionist position, Zionist leaders were conscious of the need to do their own 'public relations' work in the wider Arab world. Going beyond simple plans for influencing the Arabic press, the idea of 'external Arab work' with a 'cultural' or 'intellectual' slant was suggested by Max Nordau in the months following the 1920 Jerusalem riots.[12] During the course of 1921–1922 other Jews came to see how the Arabs of Palestine partook in, and were stimulated and nourished by, intellectual and political currents which originated *outside* the country.[13] The corollary for action was that an 'Arab policy' should not be confined to Palestine, but would be more effective 'in the real centres of Arab politics, that is, in Baghdad, Cairo and Damascus'.[14] During Col Kisch's term of office as the political head of the PZE, Zionists took a greater interest in promoting the friendship of Egyptian Muslim personalities as a means towards consolidating their position in Palestine.[15]

Although the Jews of Palestine were no doubt aware of the pan-Arab dimension of their 'Arab question', their attitudes to this external factor were far more suspicious and hostile than those of the official Zionist leadership. The 'pan-Islamic revival' of the early 1920s was strongly felt in the Yishuv and indeed forced local Jews to widen their perspective on the Arab question to include the outside Arab and Muslim worlds. But this 'awakening' was hardly a positive phenomenon.

In his lecture of April 1922, Dr Yitzhak Epstein urged the *Va'ad Leumi* to look on the Arabs of Palestine as forming a part of a greater Arab nation, and on the 'Arab movement' as a very real political phenomenon.[16] 'Whether we like it or not,' he declared, the Yishuv had to 'seek a *point d'appui* in the Orient'. 'If only,' he went on, 'we had begun from Damascus, and not from London! We must reconcile ourselves to all the peoples of Islam; if we don't, we are lost.' If the great European Powers were being forced to take this movement into account, how could the Jews – a minority in Palestine – afford to neglect it? Although he felt it was premature to actually 'draw up a covenant with the Orient', the Jews were nonetheless obliged to prepare for the day when this necessary covenant would be possible. The Palestinian Arab reaction to the Turkish victory at Ismir later in 1922 further opened Yishuv eyes to dangerous inspiration which local Arabs drew from abroad.[17] In his diary at the time, Hamar Ben-Avi reveals an obsession with the dark forces of Islam:

> The Islamic wave and stormy seas [?] will eventually break loose, and if we don't set a dyke in their way by an agreement with the Arabs, they will flood us with their wrath . . . Tel Aviv in all her splendour, our coast and all its beauty will be wiped out . . .[18]

Likewise, Y. H. Castel sought to remind Zionists at this time that

> we live in an Arab world and are surrounded on all sides by a sea of Arabs, and, whether we like it or not, we must open a small door to this big world and look into it with open eyes.[19]

The stress given by both Castel and Epstein to 'whether we like it or not' indicates that their audiences were in some need of coaxing to face an unpleasant situation squarely.

'Abdallah and Arab Confederation Schemes

The *Va'ad Leumi* itself had little competence or inclination to take any bold steps into the Arab world outside Palestine. This 'foreign policy' was left to Dr Weizmann and the PZE. The extent of the Yishuv's ventures into this sphere consisted of Dr Mallul's trips to Egypt; the *Va'ad Leumi's* proclamation to 'The Arab Nation in Palestine and the Greater Orient'; and a telegram sent to King Husain denying Jewish designs on the Muslim Holy Places (cf. pages 124 f. and 138, above).

The true extent of the decidedly negative attitude of the Yishuv to an 'active' policy in the larger Arab world can be seen from its reactions on learning that official Zionist leaders *had* been secretly engaging in such a policy. The two central issues of 1922–1923 in this regard were relations with 'Abdallah of Transjordan and the discussions for a confederation of Arab states. Early Zionist interest in the Amir 'Abdallah had been merely a hope that he might bring more settled conditions to Transjordan, which was for some time a word synonymous with 'anarchy' in the Zionist vocabulary.[20] This interest in the Amir became more 'political' in October 1921,

when Dr Eder heard rumours that the French might allow
'Abdallah to rule at Damascus. The Amir's agents suggested
to the Zionists that, if they helped him win French approval,
then 'Abdallah at Damascus would be 'well disposed' to the
Palestine Government and to the Zionists.[21] Eder and London Zionists reacted cautiously, although not negatively, to
this 'speculative' and 'fantastic' possibility; but they were on
the whole relieved when nothing came of the rumours.[22]

A year later, 'Abdallah travelled to London amid similar
rumours that the British and French might co-operate to
make him 'Prince of Trans-Jordania and Syria'. But, by this
time Zionists had experienced the White Paper of June 1922
and the exclusion of Transjordan from the Jewish National
Home clauses of the Mandate, and Dr Weizmann now feared
that if such an Anglo-French scheme came into being, 'the
whole Arab situation would assume formidable dimen-
sions'.[23] 'Abdallah negotiated his future relations with Britain
in October 1922, and at the same time held a series of secret
talks with Weizmann and the Zionist Executive. With the
Zionists the Amir discussed (a) financial support for Transjordan, and (b) recognition of the Jewish National Home in
exchange for his becoming the ruler of a re-united Palestine
and Transjordan. While it seems unlikely that anything
definite was concluded at these talks, the fact that they had
taken place did not remain secret, and conflicting rumours
reached Palestine, causing much excitement in both Jewish
and Arab circles.[24]

When Dr Weizmann visited Palestine in late November,
Yishuv leaders were most anxious to have the matter
authoritatively clarified. At a meeting of the *Va'ad Leumi*,
David Ben-Gurion requested that Dr Weizmann take local
leaders into his confidence about 'Abdallah and 'Arab policy'
in general, noting that 'secret diplomacy' could be 'disastrous'. The Yishuv, he claimed, had a right to be informed, not
so much because local people claimed to be more 'compe-
tent', 'but because we – those who live here in Palestine – . . .
will have to live with the policy which will be laid down.'[25] Dr
Weizmann informed the *Va'ad Leumi* that he had had five
'very interesting and serious' conversations with the Amir,
but that he could not elaborate further at this 'public' meet-

ing. He would willingly disclose more information at a private
session with members of the *Va'ad Leumi* Executive: 'then
you will see that I was right not to make a [public] announcement at this time.'

Having thus stimulated Yishuv curiosity (and apprehensions) to new heights, Weizmann made – and then apparently
failed to keep – an appointment with the Executive to disclose
his important revelations. Yishuv leaders were unanimous in
condemning this as a deliberate evasion, and Weizmann's
personal reputation was called into serious question.[26]
Rumours of 'Abdallah's expansionist ambitions persisted,
and the Yishuv was becoming convinced that it was Weizmann's 'Arab policy' which was to blame for encouraging the
Amir to think lightly of the Zionist position. Amid the uncertainty, the Yishuv's temper was further aggravated when
Ittamar Ben-Avi, who was then acting as Dr Weizmann's
secretary, published an article which implied that the 'Arab
policy' of the Zionist Executive was, in fact, sympathetic to
the idea of a strong Arab state under 'Abdallah, in exchange
for the Amir's recognition of the Jewish National Home.[27]
Yishuv anger was aimed directly at Dr Weizmann for what
was considered to be both a dangerous 'foreign policy'
escapade, and an official 'sell-out' of the Jewish claim to
Transjordan as part of the National Home.[28]

The ' 'Abdallah question' happened to overlap at this time
with more general public discussion surrounding the possible
creation of a 'confederation of Arab states'. Just as August
1921 had been an 'open season' for internal suggestions for a
coherent 'Arab policy' for the ZO (pp. 100 f., above), so too
was winter 1922–1923 a time for British, Arab and Zionist
proposals for an Arab confederation. Following his spring
1922 Cairo talks, Dr Eder became a more convinced advocate of the eventual creation of a 'Confederated States of the
Middle East'; Dr Weizmann's follow-up talks in Egypt in
December also centred round this topic; while in London
Jabotinsky was simultaneously drawing up his own plan for a
political agreement with the Arabs, also assuming a con-
federative pattern. In the same month, Deedes and Samuel
submitted their ideas for a loose confederation which might
satisfy Arab 'national feeling', while at the same time pre-

serve and strengthen the Jewish position inside Palestine.[29]

Whenever the subject came up for private discussion, Dr Weizmann had 'always insist[ed] that it is our duty to encourage this idea and in exchange secure Arab consent to the National Home policy in Palestine'.[30] Weizmann did not consider these views particularly radical or dangerous, but he was soon forced to realise that he would never be able to be cautious enough in his Arab 'foreign policy' to please the *Va'ad Leumi*. It is possible that he had little patience for Yishuv warnings, and, in the absence of persistent personal reassurances and explanations on his part, local leaders were left to assume the worst. Basing itself largely on the 'information' revealed in Ben-Avi's article and on coloured reports of Dr Weizmann's secret meeting with only some Yishuv representatives, the *Va'ad Leumi* meeting of 2nd–3rd January 1923 dwelt on what was supposed to be the 'new' and reckless Arab policy of the Zionist Executive, and the devious ways in which Dr Weizmann was attempting to implement it against Yishuv wishes and 'behind our backs'.[31] Several speakers saw a 'deal' with 'Abdallah as a question serious enough to require the express sanction of a Zionist Congress. 'No one', declared Ben-Gurion,

> has the authority to conclude any agreement with 'Abdallah. Dr. Weizmann has already failed once with Faisal, and he must be careful not to do the same this time. We must therefore not pass over this matter in silence . . .

Amid cries of 'treason', some declared that the Yishuv would never agree to go along with this disastrous policy. One speaker was quite explicit in giving reasons for not 'negotiating with the Arabs and helping to unify them, so that they will agree to the [Palestine] Mandate':

> Anybody who has any political sense will understand how dangerous this is for us. Any unification of the Arabs imperils our future. If it is true that there have been negotiations and that the highest authorities [i.e., the Zionist Executive] are assisting [the Arabs], this is assistance in our death . . . This policy which they have now begun shall under no circumstances win our consent . . . It reminds me of the situation of the Armenians . . . we must not allow this idea to be implemented [etc.].

When the persistent rumours soon took the specific form of Palestine and Transjordan being reunited into a single state under 'Abdallah, Yishuv excitement was 'intense', and (with the exception of Ben-Avi) opposition to 'Abdallah enthroned in Jerusalem was fierce and unanimous.[32] Col Kisch attempted to calm the local hysteria by reminding the Jews that (a) much of this was speculative gossip; (b) the British could be counted upon to preserve the terms of the Palestine Mandate should any political rearrangements ever take place; and (c) for their part, Zionist leaders had always insisted in their talks with Arab representatives that in any pact Palestine would have to become 'quantitatively and qualitatively Jewish'.[33] With these 'safeguards' in mind, Kisch recommended that Jews should force themselves to listen to the current talk of an Arab confederation with 'diplomatic sympathy'. Not only would this attitude cost the Jews little, but it would have the advantages of gaining some Arab good-will 'and thus obtain increased security during the next few years while our numbers were dangerously low', and of earning from the British 'the credit of having shown ... good-will towards the Arabs'.[34]

Although Yishuv leaders remained suspicious of, and hostile to, Weizmann's and Kisch's 'soft' stand on 'Abdallah, Dr Weizmann was insistent that his attitude had done nothing to endanger the Zionist position.[35] Whatever had been contemplated in October 1922, Dr Weizmann was quite aware after his visit to Palestine that no real hopes could be attached to an 'exchange of services' with 'Abdallah. It was, he had concluded, 'very doubtful whether the Emir carries any weight in Palestine or even in Trans-Jordania itself, and whether his promises and guarantees do represent a political asset of any real value'; furthermore, the Zionist leader was now well aware that 'Jewish public opinion in Palestine and in the World generally ... would no doubt resent such a project'.[36]

For two months, Palestine heard little more of the ' 'Abdallah question'. But on the very day that Kisch was reporting to London that the subject was virtually a dead issue, fresh rumours were sparked off by a *Daily Mail* article which claimed that the Colonial Office was now entertaining the idea of re-uniting Palestine and Transjordan under the

Amir.[37] While Kisch pressed London and Jerusalem for denials, Kalvaryski (on behalf of the PZE) set about reassuring the greatly upset *Va'ad Leumi* leadership that there was no foundation to these reports. Again Yishuv voices cried 'Never!' to the prospect of living under 'Abdallah's rule. The rumours were soon officially denied, but for many weeks the Jews of Palestine remained uneasy.[38]

If 'sensible' Zionists could now feel secure that there was no real danger of the 'Abdallah rumours materialising, even Col Kisch was alarmed when he suddenly became aware that all the previous 'harmless' talk of an Arab confederation had 'now advanced far beyond the stage of mere Arab gossip and speculation'.[39] During a conversation with Gertrude Bell and the HC, Kisch learned that the British were actively considering some form of confederation (possibly under King Husain), and that Miss Bell had been discussing the idea with local Palestinian notables. This new situation, he felt, called for a firm Zionist demand to be kept informed of this matter which so closely affected the interests of the Jewish National Home. And, anticipating the likely Yishuv reaction to this new 'threat', Kisch tried to prepare local leaders for future developments by counselling them generally that they should not 'shut their eyes' to the fact that the Arabs in Palestine had broader 'national aspirations', and that the British were interested in satisfying these aspirations as far as possible – but 'without injury to our aspirations here'.[40]

No amount of advance preparation by anybody could have adequately conditioned the Yishuv for the 'bombshell' publication, on May 18th 1923, of a telegram from King Husain to Musa Kazim al-Husaini, informing the Arabs of Palestine that Allah had granted him and Great Britain the 'great gift' of being able to fulfil their agreement of 1915:

> according to Anglo-Arab treaty [under negotiation at the time] ... His Britannic Majesty actually guarantees the foundation of a general compromising [? comprehensive] unity to include Iraq and Palestine Trans-Jordania and other Arab countries except Aden.[41]

The effect of this telegram on the population of Palestine was similar to that of the Syrian Congress resolution of March

1920; intense excitement among the Arabs at the prospect 'that they will be the Government' (and will abolish the National Home), and corresponding insecurity among the Jews at the thought of being left to the mercies of the whole Arab world.[42] In his interviews with Kisch and with *Va'ad Leumi* leaders, Samuel stressed that Husain's telegram had been 'wholly unauthorised' and was deliberately misleading; that an official denial would be forthcoming from London; that any federation would be bound by the loosest of ties (trade, customs, etc.); and that, if the confederation should ever come into being, Zionists would have nothing to fear, since the Jewish National Home policy would remain in force in Palestine, and there would be the possible advantage of 'peace and quiet' in the country should Arab sentiment be satisfied by the new arrangement.[43]

The official British clarification was not made for two weeks, and this allowed Yishuv apprehension to grow. The fact that Sir Herbert Samuel had mentioned in his interview with Yishuv representatives that Dr Weizmann had supported the idea of an Arab confederation perhaps had the opposite of the intended effect of calming local uneasiness.[44] Basing himself on Samuel's unofficial reassurances, Kisch was sending fairly optimistic reports to London, but secretly even he was beginning to share the Yishuv's apprehensions. In a secret despatch he expressed his doubts whether the British had been 'playing the game with us' on the 'Abdallah and Husain questions:

> The actions of the British Government in these matters have given the impression in this country that the Government is acting in the Arab question without taking into consideration Jewish rights in Palestine, the feelings of the Jewish community or the political position of the Jewish Home.
> I confess that this impression is not altogether unjustified.[45]

As for the *Va'ad Leumi*, its lack of confidence in Weizmann and Kisch was absolute during these weeks, and the meeting of May 30th 'cross-examined and heckled [Kisch] on the [Husain] matter until the early hours of the morning'.[46] The Zionist Executive was the direct target of the Yishuv's attack. Kisch's expressions of sympathy with local annoyance at the telegram, and his repeated assurances that Jewish interests were being fully protected, did not prevent one speaker after another from venting his anger on the official Zionist leadership, accusing it of: (a) having irresponsibly encouraged these 'terrible' developments in the Arab world through its defective Arab policy; (b) having known about the British–Arab negotiations all along, and having kept them secret from the Yishuv; and/or (c) *not* having known about this issue, and hence having been dangerously negligent in its defence of Zionist interests. Most of those who bothered to address some of their remarks to the actual confederation question saw only the danger of an intended 'loose' economic association serving as a convenient platform from which the Arabs would work their way to full political union, the ultimate result of which they saw as the destruction of the Jewish National Home. Several speakers doubted whether all this 'high politics' with Arabian kings and princes could have any positive effect on the actual attitude of the Arabs of Palestine to the Jews.

The British Government reacted to King Husain's telegram in early June with a statement containing an authoritative extract from the draft treaty.[47] It now became clear that King Husain would be bound by the treaty to recognise the 'special position' of Great Britain in Iraq, Transjordan and Palestine, and 'to do his best to cooperate with His Britannic Majesty in the fulfilment of his obligations' in those countries. Under the impact of this authorised version, the pattern of public reaction in Palestine was reversed: the storm inside the Yishuv died down, while the Arabs of Palestine began – predictably – to display increasing resentment towards Husain.[48] Although Zionists were relieved by the official statement, representations were made to the Colonial Office stressing the need for the most explicit and careful wording to safeguard the Jewish position in Palestine: attention should be directed not only to the strict legal phraseology, but also to the 'impression' which the treaty as a whole might make 'on the public mind' and to the 'political consequences which it may eventually involve'.[49]

Visit to 'Amman

As the Anglo-Hejazi treaty appeared to be receding as a practical possibility, King Husain paid a visit to his son 'Abdallah at 'Amman in January 1924. By now Palestinian *Arab* opposition to inclusion in a confederation which included recognition of the Balfour Declaration policy had become as firm as Yishuv opposition to being ruled by an Arab king.[50] Col Kisch immediately saw in Husain's visit an opportunity for a diplomatic move of great public-relations value: the ceremonial reception by the King of a Jewish deputation from Palestine. Kalvaryski informally arranged with his friend Riad as-Sulh, then in 'Amman, for invitations to be sent to Kisch, and the latter began preparing to take with him some representatives of the Yishuv.[51]

But, in the coming days, both Kisch and Herbert Samuel were forced to use their most persuasive arguments to convince the reluctant *Va'ad Leumi* leaders, who took the view that there was 'no need for the Yishuv to send any deputation' to 'Amman.[52] This reluctance, perfectly consonant with the Yishuv's hostile and suspicious reaction to all the pan-Arab politicking of the past two years, was based on the specific fear that a visit of this kind would likely be construed by the public as recognition of Husain's claims to rule an Arab confederation which included Palestine. But this time Col Kisch was not worried, and felt that far more good than harm would come from such a visit. He had plans for attracting valuable publicity in the Arab world for the resolutions on the 'Arab question' passed by recent Zionist Congresses, and he regarded the mere receipt of an invitation from King Husain as 'virtually amount[ing] to a recognition of political Zionism and the progress already made' in Palestine.[53]

The formal invitation which Kisch soon received from Husain was accompanied by private British assurances that the King was 'ready to say nice things' to the Jews.[54] Kisch, David Yellin and Rabbi Jacob Meir proceeded to 'Amman on January 27th 1924, and their formal audience with the King lacked nothing in the way of pomp and ceremony.[55] Amid exchanges of greetings and expressions of mutual good-will and friendship, Kisch handed Husain a testimonial in which he had skilfully pieced together extracts and sentiments from the 'common home' and the 'awakening of the orient' resolutions of the 1921 and 1923 Zionist Congresses.[56] Yellin spoke of the common semitic ancestry of Jew and Arab, and of the joint co-operation during the Middle Ages for the advancement of knowledge, pledging that:

> now, as we return to inhabit our land, only one feeling fills our hearts: that we shall be able to do our work of regeneration energetically and in peace with our Arab brothers.

Husain, in reply, did not disappoint Zionist expectations of hearing 'nice things'. The King sought to relieve the Jews of their apprehensions arising from the recent public controversy over the confederation and the Anglo-Hejazi treaty:

> All the rumours circulating in Europe regarding the aims of the Arabs are false. The Arabs aspire only to defend their national rights and they are prepared to accept Jewish assistance towards this aim. He himself [Husain] made no distinction between Jew and non-Jew. The King then opened his robe, adding: "My heart and my country are open to receive the Jews. I am prepared to give land to the Jews as a gift, on condition that they enter by the door and not by breaking down the walls." The future would see decisive proof of his integrity and would prove to the Jews that they had no reason to fear the Arabs.

Following a royal banquet, the Amir 'Abdallah and H. St. John Philby (British Representative in Transjordan) invited the Jewish deputation for a private and more practical discussion which focused on the meaning of Zionism and Jewish aims in Palestine. The Amir was rather guarded during the talks, and challenged the Jews that their deeds were 'apparently not as good as their words'. In reply to the 'historic connection' arguments advanced by Kisch and Yellin, 'Abdallah argued that the Palestinian Arabs seriously feared for their rights:

> I feel and I understand the feelings of the Jewish people which longs for its homeland and its country, and I would have been very glad had it not been expelled from its country 2000 years ago. But we must consider the political rights of the Arab people in Palestine, and if only the Jews would declare their consent to

recognise these rights, they would be able to come into the country and develop it freely.

While the Yishuv itself was not visibly affected for better or for worse by the royal visit, Col Kisch could not have been more delighted with the diplomatic success which he had scored.[57] The encounter at 'Amman provided useful propaganda material for Dr Weizmann, who was then touring America, and, as Kisch had hoped, the Zionist declarations of peace and good-will found their way into the Arabic press.[58] Kisch himself made and consolidated new contacts with several members of Husain's and 'Abdallah's entourages, and became highly optimistic about future relations between the Zionists and the outside Arab world. As for 'Abdallah's undisguised and undying ambitions to reunite Palestine and Transjordan under his rule, Kisch was now more confident than ever that neither Palestinian Arabs, nor Jews, nor British, nor other Arab leaders (including Husain) supported the Amir.[59]

Although Husain's visit to 'Amman had not led to any Zionist hopes for a new 'exchange of services' on a grand scale, the visit did mark the end of a period in which the outside Arab world had been showing its threatening face.[60] After the visit Zionist interest in, and Yishuv apprehensions of, the greater Arab world were to fade for a period of several years. The decline of Husain, following his self-proclaimed and little-recognised assumption of the Khalifate and after the Wahabi attacks on his kingdom, marked the end of a chapter for both the British and the Zionists. The collapse of the Hashemite-centred plans for a measure of Arab unity seemed to underline the 'lesson' that the Arab world was still not sufficiently unified, and hence not yet ready to become a reliable negotiating partner in an ideal 'exchange of services' over Palestine.[61] In the interim, Zionist leaders would passively keep their eyes open for a rising Arab leader or party which might conceivably be capable of 'delivering the goods' in an agreement.[62] But this was still in the realm of 'high politics', leaving the cautious Yishuv on the sidelines, sceptical of the chances and wary of the dangers. It would only be in the 1930s, when local Palestinian leaders like Arlosoroff,

Ben-Gurion and Shertok would occupy important positions of power in the Palestinian Zionist establishment, that a less suspicious appreciation of the advantages of an 'exchange of services' would be visible among Yishuv spokesmen.[63]

Conclusion

Conclusion

The 'Equilibrium'

In the preceding pages we have described the uncertainty, the crises and the difficulties which accompanied the consolidation of the Zionist position in Palestine during the years immediately following the Balfour Declaration. The original, far-reaching expectations which many Zionists, and Yishuv leaders in particular, had attached to British promises underwent a painful revision in a process usually described as the 'whittling down of the Balfour Declaration'.[1] The experience of the post-War years had also forced at least some Zionists to recognise Arab opposition as a factor which needed to be taken more seriously than they had originally anticipated. By the end of 1923 the uncomfortable period of post-War uncertainty seemed to be coming to an end. All signs began to point to a tendency for both Arabs and Jews in Palestine to be 'tiring of politics'. 'Equilibrium' was a term often used to describe the improvement. With the coming into effect of the Mandate, the collapse of the Arab non-cooperation movement, and the decline of the MCA, the British, no less than the Zionists, felt justified in concluding that the population was at last settling down to the business of everyday living.[2]

If there had been no single, coherent 'Arab policy' which had guided Zionist and Yishuv leaders through the period which preceded the new 'equilibrium', the various 'Arab policies' all seemed to have shared a common, double-edged object: to prove to the Arabs that (a) no power could prevent the return of the Jews to rebuild what they considered their homeland in Palestine – i.e., that Zionism would proceed whether the Arabs liked it or not; and, at the same time, that (b) the advent of Zionism was, or could be, (economically) 'good' for the Arabs. In terms of such an approach the 'carrot' and the 'stick' were inextricably intertwined, and the 'equilibrium' which was apparent during 1924 and after was due to partial success at showing the Arabs the 'stick', and perhaps even a glimpse or promise of the 'carrot'.[3]

At the end of 1924 H. M. Kalvaryski saw fit to write that, following a period of 'exaggerated excitement and the over-rating of obstacles', Jewish-Arab relations had entered a new phase:

> We know now that there is an Arab question, that it is very serious, and that we must find a solution to it. On the other hand, there is no more nervousness among us, the wrath has passed, and so is the tendency to believe that it was possible to change the world-order overnight. The atmosphere which has been created by the decrease of irritability on both sides has made it easier to search for the proper solution, and correspondingly the hope has grown that such a solution will be found.[4]

As we shall see below, Kalvaryski's appraisal of the continuing seriousness of the Arab question went far beyond what most of his Yishuv colleagues would have written.

But in welcoming a new and healthier atmosphere Kalvaryski was wildly outdone by the general and official Zionist press, in which enthusiastic spokesmen described a great improvement in Jewish-Arab relations, with some even going so far as to proclaim that the 'Arab problem' was now 'in process of solution'.[5] Without attempting to separate the exact percentages of wishful thinking, morale-boosting and genuine belief in such statements, we may assume that there was a fair dose of all three. But the fact remains with us today that the 'Arab problem' was *not* 'solved', either in those years or during other occasional periods of optimism, and in the following pages we shall attempt to discover the true nature of the 'equilibrium' in Yishuv-Arab relations which was sensed during 1924–1925.

In fairness to the 'optimists' of those years, it may be said that their rosy forecasts of the 'disappearance of the Arab problem' were not made in utter and cynical defiance of facts which told an obviously different story. In certain respects there did seem to be sufficient justification for optimism, as even British officials were beginning to admit.[6] In a general way, improved economic conditions were bringing in their wake a certain reduction of popular discontent. As for the Yishuv, the successive challenges, threats, and crises which it had lived through – physical attacks, MCA incitement and opposition, Legislative Council and Arab confederation schemes – had all passed and were no longer present in their acute form. True, there appeared to be no strong Arab leader or party on the horizon openly welcoming the Zionists to Palestine; but to have apparently arrested the development of a menacing Arab opposition was a 'negative gain' not to be despised. Such an achievement was important and necessary, in the Zionist analysis, as a precondition to the further and more positive stages of Jewish-Arab co-operation which were still to come. A full political rapprochement (on the terms on which the Zionists were insisting) was considered, even by optimists, to be some distance away, and there was still much ground to be covered before a satisfactory level of co-operation was achieved in the social, economic and cultural spheres.

With these 'negative gains' of 1918–1923 behind them, and with an improvement in the financial position of their movement, Zionists began to think more of proving the truth of the 'economic blessings' argument, and to begin to deliver the promised economic goods which they had thus far failed to do. As we have already seen, Zionists were quite aware of their failures in this sphere, and also of Herbert Samuel's disappointment in them.[7]

In theory, there was supposed to be a direct connection between the power of economic forces and the disappearance of Arab opposition. As Zionist practical work and economic development gathered momentum in 1924, some thought was given to the concrete benefits which the Arabs might be made to feel. Kisch stressed the importance of the oft-suggested idea of founding an agricultural-loans bank for the benefit of Arab farmers – a step which would earn Arab gratitude ('we would be hailed as saviours of the people') while at the same time weaken the hold of the malevolent 'rich Arab effendis' over the masses.[8] This idea was to be implemented only several years later, but in the meantime a smaller step was taken in this direction when a philanthropic grant enabled the PZE to provide agricultural tools to selected Arab farmers, members of the 'Peasants' Parties'.[9]

Zionist propaganda lost no time in indicating that the Arabs were already beginning to feel and to appreciate the new 'economic blessings', and that this was a factor making them more receptive to Zionism.[10] While there were some British officials who confirmed this to a certain extent,[11] there was also a noticeable Arab reaction in the opposite sense. In 1924 a vigorous press and obstructionist campaign began in response to the increased pace of Zionist 'penetration' by economic means.[12] A full analysis of the overall effects of economic development on the Arab attitude to Zionism would take us beyond the scope and also the period of the present study, but looking ahead to the 1930s it is not difficult to see that the Zionist hopes that increasingly prosperous Arabs would more easily 'swallow the Zionist pill' were to be disappointed. Even when the Zionists would be able to prove statistically something which they had been claiming for years – viz., that Arab villagers who were in contact with Jewish settlements enjoyed a higher standard of living than those living in purely Arab areas[13] – this did not help to produce the desired psychological effect of making Arabs welcome the prospect of Palestine becoming progressively more Jewish. As David Ben-Gurion felt forced to conclude in 1936, 'economic blessings' had no effect on the Arab leaders:

> even if they admit – and not all of them do – that our immigration brings a *material* blessing to the land [, t]hey say – and from the Arab viewpoint I think rightly so – "None of your honey and none of your sting".[14]

'Arab Work'

Since it is too early in 1924–1925 to consider 'economic blessings' as a major factor contributing to a fundamental revision of the Arab attitude to the advent of Zionism, we must, for our assessment of the 'equilibrium' of those years, confine ourselves to an examination of those negative gains which had been achieved. Again we focus on the two principal areas in which the Yishuv attempted to deal with its Arab question, 'Arab work' and defence, and in both spheres we find that there were important limitations to the successes that were scored.

The truly negative character of the 'equilibrium' of 1924–1925 is perhaps most apparent when we look at 'Arab work'. For a variety of reasons, the original, positive, aims of such activity – to strengthen, organise and increase the number of Arab friends – were gradually abandoned as unworkable, and 'Arab work' became primarily the business of weakening or obstructing enemies. As the novel and artificial Muslim-Christian alliance[15] was identified from the start as the prime force operating against the Zionists, most efforts at 'Arab work' had been aiming, implicitly or explicitly, and with varying levels of tact, at weakening this alliance.[16] Jews often suspected that friendly overtures from Muslims were not necessarily 'out of love for Mordecai', i.e., the Jews, but more often 'out of hatred for Haman', i.e., the Christians.[17] It was simply good politics to encourage any potential dissidents from the MCA, whether these dissidents were motivated by political, religious, family or personal reasons.

The 'equilibrium' of 1924–1925 was to a large extent the product of the disintegration of the organised opposition to Zionism which had reached its height between 1918 and 1923. It would be wrong to attribute this disintegration too much to the credit of Zionist 'divide and rule' efforts, or to take at face value the claim of H. M. Kalvaryski that

> this favourable change in the attitude of the Palestine Arab population is the result of continuous and persevering work ... and the effect of multiple causes, of which the main one is undeniably the formation of new Arab political parties, which has greatly contributed to the weakening of the MCA.[18]

If the decline of organised Arab opposition was in part due to Arab-work successes, it was probably in greater part due to the inherent inability of that opposition to remain organised.[19] General economic improvements and the non-realisation of the prophesies of doom and destruction of the Arab population at the hands of the Zionists also took some wind out of the sails of the anti-Zionist campaign.

Ben-Zvi, Yellin and other local leaders frequently pointed to prevailing Arab disorganisation and disunity, not so much as an excuse for complacency, but as a stroke of good luck which offered the Jews valuable time and an opportunity – which should not be wasted – to try to win over certain friendly 'islands' in the Arab sea which surrounded the Yishuv.[20] Yet, on more than one occasion in the history of Yishuv-Arab relations Jews would be simply grateful that they had been saved from disaster by 'the incurable political incapacity of the Arab opposition'.[21] 'The strongest guarantee for the security of our interests', Kisch noted in March 1923, 'is the inability of the Arabs generally to agree among themselves.'[22]

Another weak point in Zionist Arab work was the tenuous assumption of the existence of an animal called the 'Arab moderate'. To the extent that this creature could be defined, there was often a visible connection between professed 'moderation' and 'baksheesh', or a desire to 'milk the Zionist cow'. Labels such as 'moderate' or 'extremist' no doubt had their value in public-relations exercises, and Zionists maintained this dubious distinction for many years. But those people closely connected with Arab work were privately aware of the limitations of this terminology. Kisch admitted, on the eve of the Legislative Council elections, that he could not confidently predict that a 'moderate' Arab, once given a position of power, would remain a 'moderate', and Meir Dizengoff was less reserved in his low opinion of the value of such 'moderation': 'We all know', he told the *Va'ad Leumi*, 'that the moderates ... are the baksheesh-takers who will oppose us if we don't pay them.'[23]

Such a remark evoked the sarcastic comment, 'Since when are we so sensitive that we won't deal with those who take baksheesh?' and other indications that the Jews had little choice; such imperfect 'moderation' was better than nothing.[24] Under the circumstances, the buying-off of opposition appeared a natural, and – for some – the only effective, way of dealing with that opposition.[25] But, if the fact that Arab opposition could be easily bought off led some Zionists to conclude that Arab hostility was not a serious obstacle, the fact that 'baksheesh' was almost the *only* way of winning 'friends' was a more telling indication of the slim chances that the Arab community would ever come to an acceptance of Zionism which could be embodied in an 'honourable' and enduring political agreement.

Security

Notwithstanding occasional incidents or localised security 'scares' after 1922,[26] there is no doubt that a feeling grew among the Jewish population that, whatever the defects in its attitude on other matters (see below), the Palestine Administration was now reasonably conscientious and efficient in maintaining public order in the country.[27] Increased confidence in the British ability to protect Jewish life and property was reflected in a drop in Yishuv concern for the preparation of independent self-defence. During the 'quiet years' after 1923, the general public was relieved, as it had been for a shorter time during Samuel's 'honeymoon period', to feel that it could now turn to the 'real' work of building up the National Home in the belief that this work might proceed without disturbance. The warnings of the small group which espoused *hagana* as a way of life affected a progressively smaller number of listeners. Eliahu Golomb found little response for his arguments that it was *precisely* during these years of 'general stagnation' that the Jews could make their most effective preparations for the next – and, as he firmly believed, inevitable – 'hour of upheaval'.[28] For the general public, as for many leaders, it was a more eloquent fact that the imminence of physical attack continued to recede, and it would require the serious shock of the 1929 riots to recreate the high level of concern for the *Hagana* which had been shown during 1921–1922.

Despite a drop in the 'security-obsession' as evidenced in

the decline of clandestine defence preparations, both British officials and the Jews themselves were aware that the welcome improvements in security were not, in themselves, equivalent to improvements in Jewish-Arab relations. Samuel made a point of this in two reports which he submitted in December 1922. The first was a lengthy and optimistic survey which stressed the observable decrease in tension in Palestine. The second was a supplementary despatch a few days later, with the obvious intention of preventing the Colonial Office from deducing 'too' optimistic conclusions from the first report:

> ... although I consider the position to be more satisfactory than it has been, I am far from thinking that we have reached stability ... If there is less indication of any serious disturbance in the near future, the inflammable material is still there and the danger always exists. Were the present state of things to continue permanently no one would be satisfied.[29]

Sir Wyndham Deedes likewise balanced his cautious optimism regarding security improvements and the decreasing level of tension in 1922 with explicit reservations that the basic question of Jewish-Arab relations was not showing similar improvement.[30] This theme was to be repeated many times in British reports of 1923 and 1924. The HC, CS, and District Governors directed their comments separately to the general tranquillity, on the one hand, and to the friendliness or frequency of Jewish-Arab contacts, on the other; optimism was usually restricted to the former.[31]

Among Yishuv leaders, too, there was no mistaking better security for a qualitative improvement in Jewish-Arab relations. Ben-Gurion, Katznelson, Golomb and Jabotinsky had indeed stressed that 'diplomatic relations' alone would not prevent 'pogroms', and that without real security there could be no talk of 'agreements' with the Arabs. But it was equally true that improved security was not sufficient, in itself, to bring about a resolution of the differences which continued to separate the Yishuv from its 'Arab neighbours'. A fundamental and inescapable fact of the situation was that it would require more than a few years to erase from the mind of the Yishuv the memory of the Jerusalem and Jaffa 'pogroms'.

Previous prejudices – that the Arabs were *'basically'* hostile and prone to primitive violent outbursts – were confirmed by the experience of 1920–1921. If the Jews could subsequently feel that there was greater security in the country, few believed that this was because the Arabs had suddenly accepted either the inevitability or the benefits of Zionism. The improvement in security was more likely seen as the result of a general prosperity and the fact that the British were keeping the situation 'in hand'. In the back of their minds, few Jews doubted that, should the Arabs be 'allowed' (by British negligence or intrigue) to be distracted from their peaceful everyday pursuits and to be incited by 'agitators', then there was a very real possibility that the Yishuv would once more be the victim of attacks.

The deep and persistent Jewish mistrust of the Arabs spilled over into areas where political choices were involved. Yishuv socialists, for example, often justified their collaboration with British 'imperialism' by pointing to this elementary security factor. Ben-Gurion reports that he informed a Polish Zionist critic in the 1920s that

> what we had suffered at Arab hands up to then [i.e., the Jaffa riots] was child's play compared with what we might expect in the future . . . [S]o long as we are few and weak . . . we must try to maintain the Mandate regime.[32]

The same absence of basic trust also precluded any bold response to proposals and overtures which would have involved drawing 'closer' to the Arabs in a way which reduced the benevolent protection afforded by the British connection. In the light of what we have seen of the Yishuv's reactions to 'Arab confederation' and Legislative Council schemes, it does not seem exaggerated or unreasonable that Col Kisch should have rejected a confederation proposal, without the British mandate, on the grounds that 'for some time to come the Jews would not feel safe alone in the country with the Arabs';[33] or that Leonard Stein should have expressed lack of enthusiasm for the prospect of the Jewish National Home under 'Abdallah's rule partly on the grounds that

> both the history of the Arabs, and the present condition of such Arab states as existed, suggested that political stability was

hardly to be expected of the Arabs as a whole and that little confidence could be felt in their ability to guarantee security either of life or property.[34]

Thus, while the Zionist press was raising morale by proclaiming, in 1924 and 1925, that the 'Arab problem' was 'in process of solution', the real feelings of the Jews in Palestine were more accurately reflected in the words which Kisch reported he had used in conversation with Hasan Sabri in Egypt:

whatever the future may render possible, the lack of confidence created by the anti-Jewish actions of the Arabs has produced a situation which makes it impossible for us to agree at present either that Palestine should be included in any sort of Arab Confederation, or that Palestine should have a so-called "National Government". We desire that the Arabs should recognise our rights, and also the right of the Mandatory Power to guarantee them.[35]

The British Factor

A closer look at Yishuv sources for 1924–1925 reveals views which were often widely divergent from the contemporary public proclamations heralding a new era of peace and stability. One area in which the discrepancy is perhaps greatest is in the Yishuv's attitude to the British. As we have tried to show above, the Yishuv's relations with its Arab neighbours were considered to depend heavily on the proper attitude of the British. In times of turmoil it was the British 'firm hand' which the Yishuv called for, and in broader political terms the 'key to an Arab-Jewish rapprochement' was seen to be 'in British hands'. 'The essential condition for any sort of compromise', declared the Political Report of the ZE to the 1921 Zionist Congress, was

the establishment of an unmistakable and active pro-Zionist attitude throughout the whole British administration, and a system of prevention and retribution which would discourage any dreams of successful and unpunished violence.[36]

In times of relative quiet Zionists hoped for an 'understanding' attitude from the British in order to facilitate their 'Arab work' and make it more productive, while during the years of 'equilibrium' they sought a favourable and activist British policy to quicken the pace of the economic growth of the National Home.

The extent of Zionist dependence on the British for a 'proper solution' to all aspects of the 'Arab question' seems to have been surpassed only by the extent of the disappointment. At the grass-roots in Palestine this disappointment was especially pronounced, and was scarcely affected by the optimism which characterised the Zionist press. Yishuv disillusionment was accompanied further by a stubborn and primitive suspicion of British intentions, and on several occasions Col Kisch was annoyed that local leaders refused to appreciate the fact that British good faith could, to a fair extent, be relied upon, and that the Administration deserved *some* credit for governing the country in accordance with a policy which was unpopular with the majority of its inhabitants.[37]

Nonetheless, local people saw no reason to cease their public or private accusations against the unchanging hostile and conspiratorial behaviour of British officials, or to refrain from occasionally comparing British 'liberalism' unfavourably with the methods of the Turks, who, whatever their faults, nevertheless 'knew how to demand respect from one race and religion to another'.[38] Preparing for the visit of the Colonial Secretary, Mr Amery, in 1925, Yitzhak Ben-Zvi warned the *Va'ad Leumi* not to allow the impression to be created 'that we explicitly agree to the British administration without any changes: we cannot agree to this because, in fact, we have no confidence in the British administration'.[39] And when the Palestinian Jews returned from their interview with Mr Amery, they were confirmed in the conclusion which they had bitterly reached in the dark days of June 1921 – 'that the Government [was] not thinking of actively helping in the creation of the Jewish National Home' and that 'we ourselves will have to build up our own National Home'.[40]

The HC's final *Report* on his administration of Palestine both reflected and stimulated the rosy optimism which was then prevalent in many – but not all – circles. The survey of Samuel's five years as HC included a long and sympathetic description of the achievements of the Zionist enterprise in Palestine. In his concluding passage on the development of the Jewish National Home, Samuel contrasted the Arab accusations that his Administration had favoured the Jews unduly in promoting this development with the frequent Jewish complaints that the Government had not done enough. So far as there was any truth in these criticisms, Samuel admitted that 'the latter ... has the most substance', and he proceeded to summarise the evidence to prove that the Jews were, in fact, being forced to become 'self-dependent' in the absence of practical assistance from the Administration.[41] His final words on the subject were no doubt intended as a flattering tribute to 'the Jewish movement':

> if it has been able to rely on the Government of Palestine to maintain order and to impose no unnecessary obstacles, for all the rest it has had to rely on its own internal resources, on its own enthusiasm, its own sacrifices, its own men ... But this one factor, at least, is propitious: that the building of the National Home has not been the work of any Government; it is not the artificial construction of laws and official fostering. It is the outcome of the energy and enterprise of the Jewish people themselves.

Samuel left Palestine much as he had come: in simple dignity and modest ceremony, and amid words of touching sentiment from his 'brother Jews'.[42] But among those elements who had come to appreciate the overall negative results of having had a liberal British Jew as HC there was a decidedly unsentimental reaction to the *Report* which he had left behind.[43] Berl Katznelson saw absolutely no reason why the Yishuv had to accept as either complimentary or 'propitious' the fact that all Zionist achievements had been '*in spite of* the methods of the Government which was appointed to execute the Mandate'. In a long article which dissected and challenged Samuel's optimistic *Report* on many matters, Katznelson stated plainly that the HC's words of 'affection' were not good enough, and he urged his readers to note that *words* were all that the Administration had been prepared to pay to the Yishuv:

> Every reader must not allow himself to be bought off by the tender words of sympathy, but should dwell on the political methods of the Mandatory Administration and its spokesman in order to recognise the realities ... in which we must operate.

The *Report*, in Katznelson's view, would have 'most dangerous consequences' if, by its flattery, it were to succeed in

> teaching us to go along with the violation of our rights and the
> lowering of our stature, and to accept the injustice against us *with
> love* . . .
> One gets the decidedly incorrect picture [from the *Report*] that
> the Yishuv has accepted the infringement of its rights and the
> injustice against it willingly and submissively. Why is the political
> character of the Yishuv distorted to such an extent? And what
> right has the HC to brush aside all the claims of the Yishuv, even
> in his hour of departure, at a time when he himself admits that
> our complaints have some substance to them?

One final passage from Katznelson's critique of Samuel's
Report may be quoted here as reflecting a real fear of the
effect which this official 'apologia' for Zionism might have on
the Arab mind. Despite its 'good intentions' and its more than
obvious aim of 'pacifying' the Arabs, Katznelson felt that
Samuel's *Report* had presented a dangerous image of 'the
Jew' to the Arab reader:

> Which Arab [he asked] who fears the ultimate aim of Zionism
> will be calmed when it becomes clear to him that, instead of
> methods of aggressive political conquest, we have adopted a
> system of political infiltration; that we have replaced an upright
> approach by a clandestine one? Is not the true story, as told in the
> *Report*, that despite the absence of any assistance from the Gov-
> ernment; despite restrictions on immigration; despite the decla-
> rations weakening the contents of the Balfour Declaration;
> despite the balancing of [the Declaration] in favour of others – [in
> spite of all this,] *our numbers have doubled in five years*? Does
> this not confirm that the "Zionist danger" is greater than all the
> exercises of maximalist declamation and extremist political posi-
> tions? In this sense, Samuel has hardened the mystical fears of
> the Arab patriot.

Other Dissenters

Katznelson was only one of a number of naive children in the
Yishuv who spoiled the general jubilation of 1924–1925 by
being unable to see the emperor's new clothes.[44]

Despite the examples which were adduced at the time to
show that Jews and Arabs were coming into more frequent

and friendlier contact,[45] there is also credible evidence that this was not really so. One factor which definitely caused a reduction in the number of Jewish-Arab interactions (of a certain type) was the gradual but deliberate termination of 'Arab work' between 1923 and 1927 by Col. Kisch, and the stopping of similar *Va'ad Leumi* efforts in 1923–1924 owing to lack of funds.[46] The overall quantitative drop in Jewish-Arab contacts was critically noted by Kalvaryski in May 1925:

> We all admit the importance of drawing closer to the Arabs, but in fact we are growing more distant like a drawn bow. We have no contact: two separate worlds, each living its own life and fighting the other.[47]

Perhaps the most devastating contemporary critique of the false optimism of 1924–1925 came from someone outside the Yishuv, but who nevertheless understood its spirit better than most 'foreigners': Vladimir Jabotinsky. One of Jabotinsky's basic premises, shared by many Palestinian Jews, was that the local Administration was 'an unfriendly government'. Samuel's *Report* was, for him, an 'eloquent *feuilleton* ... published under the disguise of a White Paper', and in July 1925 he refused to believe that the 'Arab question' was by any means 'resolved':[48]

> I understand as well as anybody [he wrote to Kisch] that we've got to find a *modus vivendi* with the Arabs; they will always live in the country, and all around the country, and we cannot afford a perpetuation of strife. But I do not believe that their reconciliation to the prospect of a Jewish Palestine can be bought either by the bribe of economic uplift, or by watered and obviously falsified interpretations of Zionist aims à la Samuel ... [J]ust because I want peace, the only task is to make them lose every vestige of hope: "neither by force, nor by constitutional methods, nor through God's miracle can you prevent Palestine from gradually getting a Jewish majority" – this is what they must be made to realise, or else there will never be peace ...

In Jabotinsky's analysis, the Arabs were still a long way from having relinquished their hopes of sabotaging the Zionist policy. They had turned from 'pogroms' to 'constitutional abstraction', but their aim was still the same and the Zionists had to direct their best defences against any renewed proposals for a legislative council. Jabotinsky's critique went on to note that under the influence of the self-proclaimed 'equilibrium', Zionists were guilty not only of relaxing their guard, but also of 'wantonly ... destroying the only valid argument by which we can fairly combat this [legislature] scheme: the Arabs' unflinching opposition to the Jewish National Home idea'. He concluded:

> We shout from the tops that it is all over, the Arabs are ready to welcome us, etc. It's a lie; but still worse – it's a direct invitation to the government to assume that there is no longer any contradiction between a local parliament with an Arab majority and the spirit of the Mandate. I consider this policy suicidal; and it can only be combated by making the Arabs say openly what they think of us ...
>
> One day we shall pay dearly for Kalvarisky's bribes and Weizmann's peace-lies. This campaign of hiding the danger encourages the government to reduce the garrison; still worse, it encourages our own men to leave the police service – why rot in barracks and bear bullying when the danger is over? I've never seen, never heard of, such a display of irresponsible light-headedness ...

'Solutions'

In our examination of the relatively short period 1917–1925, we were able to see the stages of the Yishuv's increasing awareness of an 'Arab question':– the 'Eretz-Israel' Conference (December 1918); the King-Crane Commission and the *Va'ad Zmani* debates of June 1919; the tense build-up which culminated in the Jerusalem riots (March-April 1920); the optimism of the Churchill visit (March 1921), followed by the rude shock of the Jaffa riots and Samuel's reactions (May-June 1921); the Jerusalem disturbances of November 1921; the increasing activity around 'Arab work' and *hagana*; the threats of Samuel's constitutional palliatives; and 'Abdallah's ambitions and Arab confederation schemes. That the Arabs *existed* was hardly in dispute; that the Arabs were fundamentally *opposed* to Zionist goals became increasingly obvious, notwithstanding Zionist propaganda to the contrary.

But 'awareness' of an Arab question was not synonymous with having 'solutions' that would remove Arab opposition.

The gradual learning experience which the Yishuv underwent in the period under discussion – and which it would continue to undergo in later periods – by no means led to any unanimous conclusion about what had to be *done* in response to this problem of Arab opposition. The growth of awareness did not automatically point to the adoption of specific policies; least of all did it provide any consensus that there were certain concessions or sacrifices which had to be made in the effort to de-fuse the 'Arab question'.

As we have seen above, only a few individuals in the Yishuv actually believed that Arab opposition had to be answered by a 'peace plan' which would have included some reduction in the aims of the Zionist movement. Instead, the majority goal seemed to be to keep the situation in check, a 'holding operation', and various policies were advocated in realms of internal and external 'Arab work' and of *hagana*. These options seemed to reflect the fundamental belief that strengthening the numbers and the economic resiliency of the Yishuv, while simultaneously advancing the basic goals of Zionism, was the best way of dealing with the 'Arab question'.

To illustrate this latter tendency, we shall conclude by discussing a relatively minor episode – one which occurred at the end of our chosen period, and which touched, it would seem, only indirectly on the 'Arab question'. In 1925 the *Va'ad Leumi* was called upon to give its opinion on how it wished to see the Government execute the bequest of a wealthy Shanghai Jew, Sir Ellis Kadoorie, for the founding of an agricultural school, or schools, in Palestine. Yishuv reasoning and the final decision on this question are an excellent indication of the preference to resolve the problems of Arab hostility not by means of political formulae or agreements with the Arabs, but rather by concentrating on internal growth and development.

When the Kadoorie bequest became available, the Administration favoured, and Kalvaryski supported, the creation of a mixed Jewish-Arab school. Most Yishuv leaders, however, were eager to use this opportunity to take another step in the direction of strengthening their communal autonomy and separate development. Kalvaryski, a convinced advocate of the benefits of mixed education for the relations of the future generation of Arabs and Jews, was squarely confronted with the decided 'exclusivist' tendencies of most of his colleagues, and his impassioned appeal to the *Va'ad Leumi* meeting of 13th May 1925 was yet another illustration that Kalvaryski was still the 'lone wolf' and the 'outsider' whom we first encountered in 1919.[49]

The choice involved in the Kadoorie bequest decision was largely one of 'togetherness' with, or 'separateness' from, the Arab neighbours. Kalvaryski attempted to dissuade his colleagues from opting for the latter course first by pointing to the fact, already known to many Jews, that the separate Arab (i.e., Government) educational system was fast becoming a dangerous breeding-ground for a future anti-Zionist generation more convinced and more effective than the present one. But Kalvaryski also went beyond this narrow aspect to warn that a *Va'ad Leumi* decision for separate schools would expose Jewish 'hypocrisy' for all the world to see:

> The contradictions between the public declarations of our desire to come to an agreement with the Arabs and our actions in the country are so obvious that it is impossible not to arouse an attitude of lack of faith [in us] ... Of course, we never miss an opportunity, whether at Zionist Congresses, *Va'ad Leumi* meetings, or in the press, to declare that we aspire to common work with the Arabs. Sometimes we are able to fool even the most astute of the "goyim" and to lead them to believe that we really do want to work together and that it is only the mischievous effendis who are rejecting our approaches ...
>
> Gentlemen! Even in mere declarations there is sometimes something useful, but declarations with no reality behind them bring in their wake only disappointment ...

If Kalvaryski had really hoped, by this bitter reproach, to 'shame' Yishuv leaders into renouncing their preferred separateness for a happy togetherness with the Arabs, then the obstinate rebuttals which his harangue received must have come as a severe blow. Just as his 1919 programme for an Arab-Jewish entente had been denounced as 'absurd' and 'dangerous' in its day, so too was his 1925 plea for mixed education greeted as 'premature' and 'surprising'. While speakers favoured 'general cultural rapprochement' or the teaching of Arabic in Jewish schools as a way of drawing closer to the Arabs, they saw a real danger in a mixed school, which would 'expose our children to Arab influences'.[50] Other reactions reflected more than simple 'exclusivism', and indicated a belief that the new era of 'equilibrium' had not really brought about any real change in the mutually antagonistic positions of Jews and Arabs in Palestine. Yosef Meyuhas, not one to treat the 'Arab question' lightly and a veteran advocate of the study of Arabic language and Arab studies in Jewish schools, was surprised that Kalvaryski had presented arguments which were completely at variance with the lessons of previous experience. He pointed out that 'effendis' sons' who had been educated in *Alliance* schools became 'alienated' from any pro-Jewish sentiment once they found government posts:

> Such is the relation between the weak and the strong . . . Among us and among the Arabs nationalism is bubbling over, and if we bring together poisoned Arabs and Jews in one place, the contact will only strengthen the hatred and will bring about dangerous consequences . . . It appears that Mr Kalvaryski has forgotten that we still need, for a certain period, much caution in matters of education.

From this clash of views on a relatively minor issue we are reminded of two basically different approaches inside the Yishuv. The 'optimistic' minority maintained that a 'solution' to the contradictions between Zionist and Arab interests existed and had to be sought, and that there were a number of special steps that should be taken to prepare the ground for a future 'agreement' with the Arabs. One practical expression of this view in 1925 was the formation, by Dr Ruppin, Kalvaryski and others, of a discussion group which was subsequently known as *Brit-Shalom* ('Covenant of Peace') and which adopted the programme of a 'bi-national' Palestine as the most promising solution by which Zionist and Arab aspirations might be harmonised.[51] The 'pessimistic' majority, on the other hand, was not so sure that there existed a solution, in the rationalist sense, to the 'Arab question'; hence, it was considered wasteful and perhaps demoralising to chase after formulae which might serve as the basis of a signed agreement, or to take any steps which might weaken the tiny

Yishuv vis-à-vis the Arab majority. In a practical way, their less specifiable – but no less real – 'answer' to the 'Arab question' was to use every available month and year of 'quiet' in order to realise the final aims of Zionism which meant presenting the Arabs as quickly as possible with the fait accompli of a Jewish majority and a prosperous and irremovable Yishuv.

During the years 1918–1923 the 'Arab question' had presented itself in a form which could not be ignored, and the Yishuv was forced to deal with the Arab opposition in ways which fell short of any ultimate solution or agreement. But once the 'Arab question' in its threatening form appeared to recede from immediate view, the Yishuv reverted to its basic tendency to 'solve the Arab question' by first solving the 'Zionist question'.[52] The guiding principles for such an approach were a stress on correcting the Yishuv's numerical and physical weakness, on the one hand, and a certain isolationism and caution in external relations with 'the neighbours', on the other. These guiding principles were also operating in subsequent periods, and we must conclude that even today the best that either side can hope for is not a 'resolution' of the conflict, but rather an uncomfortable accommodation superimposed (likely from outside the Middle East) over latent and 'permanent' conflict. Such an accommodation would not be the result of any peace-plans or global 'solutions' as such, but would be built on a stand-off or balance of strengths – political, economic, technological, social, moral and, of course, military.

Appendix I

The following pages are a reproduction of the 'Heads of Scheme for the Provisional Government of Palestine', as prepared by Akiva Ettinger, Yitzhak Wilkansky and Vladimir Jabotinsky for discussion at the 'Eretz-Israel' Conference held at Jaffa, 18–22 December 1918.

The handwritten revisions were inserted following deliberations at the Conference and by a Revision Committee elected by the Conference (David Ben-Gurion, A. Ettinger, V. Jabotinsky).
Source: CZA, J1/8766/I.

The final reprinted 'Heads of Scheme' used by the Yishuv Delegation to London and Paris in 1919 (identical to the original as revised, below) may be found in CZA, A153/149.
[Cf. pages 23 f., above]

HEADS OF SCHEME

for the provisional Government

OF PALESTINE.

ראשי פרקים

לתכנית שלטון זמני

בארץ ישראל.

דפוס א. איתן וש. שושני, יפו.
Printed by A. Itine and S. Shshany, Jaffa.

רב"ז .

PREFACE.

The following scheme is founded on two fundamental assumptions:

a) that the claim of the Jewish People that Palestine should become ~~its National Home~~ *Jewish Commonwealth* will receive international sanction at the Peace Conference;

~~this is to say,~~ *and* that the Powers will recognise that in all matters of the Government and administration of Palestine a decisive voice belongs to the Jewish People throughout the world:—

b) that the Powers will appoint Great Britain as their representative, or Trustee, to whom they will entrust the Government of Palestine ~~and~~ *with* the task of assisting the Jewish people in the building up of ~~its National Home~~ *the Jewish Commonwealth.*

הקדמה.

התכנית הזאת מיוסדת על שני תנאים עקריים:

א) כי דרישת עם ישראל, שא"י *תהיה לעם ישראל* תקבל אשור אנטרנציונלי בועידת השלום.

כי הממשלות *יכירו*, שבכל עניני שלטון א"י יש זכות-דעה מכרעת לכל עם ישראל בכל ארצות התבל.

ב) כי הממשלות תבחרנה באנגליה בתור בא-כחן, או .טראסטי". אשר בידיו יפסר שלטון א"י *ותעודה* לעזר לעם ישראל בבנין בניתו *ביתו*.

I.

FUNDAMENTALS.

Palestine will include all the territory within the frontiers specified in the special memorandum annexed hereto, ~~with the exception of the «Holy Places».~~

The official name of the country ~~in Hebrew~~ will be «Erez-Israel», which means the Land of Israel.

The Zionist flag will be the official flag of the country, ~~together with the colours of the Trustee Power.~~

The national status of any person born or naturalized in Palestine will be described as «citizen of Palestine», with mention of ~~membership of~~ *his relationship to* the Trustee State. *The capitulations will be abolished. Sabbath and the Jewish Holidays will be the official days of rest.*

without prejudice to the religious rights of non-Jews.

יסודות.

.ארץ ישראל" תכיל את כל השטח הנמצא בין הגבולים המפורטים בתזכיר המיוחד הצרוף לזה.

שמה הרשמי יהיה .ארץ ישראל".

הדגל הציוני יתקבל בתור דגלה הרשמי של הארץ.

המעמד הלאומי (הנתינות) של כל מי שנולד או נתאזרח בארץ יהיה זה של .אזרח א"י, בהוספת נוסח המעיד על מדינת ה.טראסטי".

--- 2 ---

II.

THE GOVERNMENT of PALESTINE.

1. THE RESIDENT.

At the head of the Government of Palestine will be a ~~Resident~~ *Governor General* appointed by the Trustee Power.

The ~~Resident~~ *Governor General* will guard & defend the rights and the equality of the legal status of all the inhabitants of the country irrespective of race or creed.

2. THE EXECUTIVE COUNCIL

The ~~Resident~~ *governor general* will exercise the functions of government through on Executive Council composed of the heads of all governmental departments.

A special Minister for Arab Affairs will also form one of the Executive Council.

The Executive Council, under the control of the ~~Resident~~ *Governor General*, will exercise legislative and administrative powers in all matters appertaining to the government of Palestine, except as follows:

a) military & foreign affairs, as left ~~entirely~~ to the competence of the Trustee Power;

b) the 'Holy Places,' ~~as entrusted to a special International Commission;~~

c) matters of religion, education, and communal organisation, ~~as left entirely to the competence of the respective national communities.~~

There will be a special ~~Wakf~~ *of non general Welfare* Department under the Minister for Arab Affairs.

The ~~Resident~~ *Governor General* will have the right to veto any decision of the Executive Council. In case of such veto the Council may appeal to the Trustee Government.

In matters concerning Customs duties the Trustee Government will consult the Palestinian Executive Council.

ממשלת א"י.

1. הנציב.
(הגוורנר-גנרל)
בראש ממשלת א"י יעמד נציב מטעם ע"י ה.טראסטי.

הנציב ישגיח וינן על זכויותיהם ושויון-משפטם של כל תושבי הארץ, מבלי הבדל הגזע והדת.

2. ועד השלטון.

הנציב ימלא את תפקידי הממשלה ע"י .ועד השלטון המחבר מראשי כל הוזרות.

וזיר מיוחד לעניני הערבים יחשב גם כן לחבר ועד השלטון.

ועד השלטון, תחת השגחתו של הנציב, יחוקק ויפקד בכל עניני הממשלה בא"י, חוץ מאלה:

א) עניני צבא ועניני חו"ל — אשר יםסרו בידי ה.טראסטי;

ב) עניני .המקומות הקדושים" (הבלעדי-הבלאדית) בידו ועד אינטרנציונל מיוחד;

ג) עניני הדת, ההשכלה והסתדרות הקהלות —

המשרד לעניני הקרש (הקף) יבא תחת רשותו של הוזיר לעניני הערבים.

לנציב יש זכות הוסמו על כל ההחלמות ועד השלטון, ואז יוכל ועד השלטון לערער לפני ממשלת ה.טראסטי.

— 3 —

III.

THE ZIONIST ORGANISATION.

until the creation, for the building up of a Jewish commonwealth, of an all Jewish congress

The Universal Zionist Organisation will be recognised by the Powers as representing the Jewish People in its relationship to Palestine.

A representative of the Z. O., selected by mutual agreement, will enter the Government of the Trustee Power with the rank of «Permanent Under-Secretary for Palestine.

the members of the Palestinian Executive council will be elected by the Congress

~~He will submit to the Trustee Government a list of all candidates to be appointed as members of the Executive Council for Palestine, with the exception of the Minister for Arab Affairs.~~

The Trustee Government will have the power to veto any candidate so proposed.

In special cases, On the initiative of the Under-Secretary, the Trustee Government will have the power to legislate for Palestine concerning any matter, except religion, education and communal organisation.

IV.

The COLONISATION ASSOCIATION.

The Universal Zionist Organisation will form, with the sanction of the Powers, a National Colonisation Association.

The statutes of the Association shall be framed so as to secure the permanence of Zionist leadership in the Executive.

The Association will be granted the following rights:

1. The rights to organise the immigration of Jews from any country into Palestine and to prepare the latter country for their reception and establishment.

ההסתדרות הציונית.

הממשלות בתור באת-כח של עם ישראל ביחסו אל ארץ ישראל.

בא-כחה של ההסתדרות הציונית יתקבל, בהסכם שני הצדדים, לתוך ממשלת ה.טראסטי בתור סגן-חזר לעניני א״י.

חבר ועד הטלטון העולה העברי יתמנו

למטשלת ה.טראסטי יש זכות הויטו בנוגע לשטות המוצעים.

במקרים מיוחדים ולתגלי אינציאטיבה של סגן-החזר לעניני א״י, תוכל ממשלת ה.טראסטי לחוק חקים בשביל א״י בנוגע לכל מקצעות חייה, חוץ מעניני הדת, ההשכלה והסתדרות הקהלות.

החברה לישוב א״י.

ההסתדרות הציונית העולמית תיסד, באשור הממשלות, חברה לאוטית לישוב א״י.

תקנות החברה יבטיחו את ההברעה הציונית בהנהלתה.

החברה תקבל את הזכית דלמטה:

1. הזכות למדר אימיגרציה של יהודים מארצות הגולה לא״י, ולהכין את הארץ לקבלתם והתישבותם.

— 4 —

2. The ownership of all Turkish crown- and government lands as well as of all lands uninhabited or unclaimed, or uncultivated, or waste, or desert.

3. All the rights reserved by the Ottoman Government to itself in granting railway concessions, or any other concession in Palestine in the past.

4. The sole right to exploit all underground, or other natural resources and forces.

5. The sole right to construct railways, harbours and irrigation works.

6. The Administration of the Ottoman Government's Agrarian Bank, and the sole right to found new institutions of agrarian credit.

7. The right of pre-emption in all transactions dealing with land, underground resources, natural forces, means of communication or transport, or with any institution appertaining to the exploitation of the afore said branches.

8. The sole right to grant concessions for all & any of the purposes mentioned above.

9. Generally, the right to purchase, own, hire, lease, or sell any kind of property and to undertake any sort of public works, or to found any kind of establishment deemed necessary for the development and sanitation of the country, for the progress of its agriculture, commerce & industry and for the success of Jewish colonisation.

The Government will promote such measures, especially land legislation, as may be necessary for the above purposes.

.2 הזכות על כל קרקעות השולטן וממשלה התורקית, ועל כל קרקע בלתי מיושב, בלתי מעבד או שומם.

.3 כל הזכיות שהממשלה התורקית השאירה לעצמה בעבר, בעת שנתנה קונצסיות לבנין מסלות ברזל או למטרות אחרות בא"י.

.4 הזכות היחידה לנצל כל האוצרות הטמנים באדמה ויתר אוצרות הטבע וכחותיה.

.5 הזכות היחידה לבנין מסלות ברזל, חפים, ומכוני השקאה.

.6 הזכות לנהל את הבנק הקרקעי של הממשלה העותומנית, והזכות היחידה ליסד מוסדות חדשים לקרדיט חקלאי.

.7 זכות הקדימה בכל מקרי מקח-וממכר של קרקעות, אוצרות אדמה, כחות הטבע, אמצעי חבור או אמצעי הובלה, ושל כל המוסדות המשמשים לנצול המקצעות האלה.

.8 הזכות היחידה לתת קנצסיות בנוגע לכל המטרות הנזכרות למעלה.

.9 בכלל, הרשות לקנות, לחחזיק, לשכור, להשכיר ולמכר כל מיני רכוש, לעסק בכל מיני עבודות צבוריות, וליסד כל מיני מוסדות, הנחוצים לפתוח הארץ או הבראתה, לקדמת החקלאות, המסחר והתעשיה בארץ, ולהצלחת התישבות היהודים.

הממשלה תעשה את כל הצעדים, בפרט בנוגע לתקן חקי הקרקע, הנחוצים להשגת המטרות הללו.

V.

LOCAL SELF GOVERNMENT.
(MUNICIPAL).

Every town, colony or village will receive the right of self-government in matters of municipal management, sanitation and police, the right of taxation, and the right to enter into federation with each other.

Any section of a town, delimited by clear boundaries and counting a certain minimum of inhabitants, the majority of whom belong to one & the same nationality, may demand separate municipal rights as an independent township.

Town & Township Councils will be elected on the system of proportional Representation.

שלמון-עצמי מקומי (מוניציפלי).

כל |עיר, מושבה וכפר יקבלו זכות שלטון-עצמי בעניני המשק המוניציפלי, הבריאות והמשמרה, זכות תרומת מסים והרשות להתאגד.

כל חלק-עיר מאוחד ומגבל, אשר רב תושביו הם בני אומה אחת ושמספרם מגיע למינימום ידוע, יוכל לדרש זכויות מוניציפליות נבדלות בתור שכונה ברשות-עצמה".

העיריות תבחרנה עפ"י השיטה הפרופרציונלית.

VI.

NATIONAL-COMMUNAL AUTONOMY.

Any national or religious group, in any town, township, colony or village, will be considered as a national community and will enjoy full & complete autonomy in all its internal affairs, to wit:

a) in matters of religion, including marriage, divorce and forms of succession;

b) in matters of elementary, secondary or university education, general as well as special;

c) in matters of jurisdiction between members of the respective nationality;

d) in matters of social relief & welfare.

A national community will embrace compulsorily all the members of the respective nationality in the locality concerned.

National Communities will possess the right of taxation, the right of petition

שלמון-עצמי לאומי.

כל קבוץ לאומי או דתי בכל מושב וישוב יחשב לקהלה לאומית", ויקבל זכות שלטון-עצמי גמור ושלם בכל עניניו הפנימים, כלומר:

א) עניני הדת, עם דיני נשואין, גטין ואופני הירושה.

ב) עניני ההשכלה לכל מקצעותיה ומדרגותיה.

נ) עניני משפטים בין בני האומה.

ד) עניני הסיוע החברותי לכל ענפיו.

בקהלה יכנסו באופן הכרחי כל בני-אומתה הגרים במושב.

לקהלות יש זכות תרומת מסים, הרשות לפנות לממשלה בפטיציות בכל ענין הנוגע לארץ או לאומה, הרשות להתאגד.

to the Government on any matter affecting the country and the nation, & the right to form federations with one another.

~~Any national community may, if it so desires, transfer its rights and entrust its functions to the local Municipal Council.~~

VII.

LANGUAGE REGULATIONS.

In all Offices of the Palestinian Government, including Law Courts, Hebrew and Arabic will be treated on a footing of complete equality.

All documents emanatig from and all symbols used the Government will be expressed in ~~both languages.~~ *Hebrew and Arabic*

Should the Trustee Power so desire its language will enjoy the same rights.

In intercourse with Jews or Jewish public bodies, all Government Offices will use Hebrew only, both orally and in writing.

All the above rules will equally apply to all municipal offices in any town or independent township the population of which includes both Jews and Arabs.

Hebrew will be the only official language :

a) in all municipal offices of purely Jewish localities ;

b) in all Jewish communal institutions ;

c) in all offices of the Colonisation Association which, however, will also employ interpreters for Arabic and English.

דיני הלשונות.

בכל המוסדות של ממשלת א"י, ובכלל זה גם בבתי-המשפט, עברית וערבית תחשבנה לשפות רשמיות על בסיס שויון גמור.

כל דוקומנט או סמל ממשלתי יהיה ~~מנוסח~~ 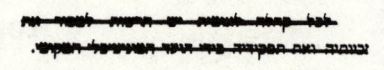 *עברית וערבית.*

אם תדרש ממשלת ה.טראסטי, תנתנה הזכיות הנ"ל גם לשפתה היא.

במשא ומתן עם יהודים או מוסדותיהם, כל אורגני הממשלה ישתמשו רק בעברית, גם בכתב גם בדבור.

כל החקים הנ"ל ישלטו גם במוסדות המוניציפליים של כל עיר, או שכונה ברשות-עצמה, אשר יש בהן גם יהודים גם ערבים.

עברית תהיה הלשון הרשמית היחידה :

א) בכל המוסדות המוני-ציפליים של מושב יהודי בלתי-מעורב ;

ב) בכל מוסדי הקהלה העברית ;

ג) בכל מוסדות ה.חברה הלאומית לישוב א"י ; ואולם ישתמשו מוסדותיה גם בתרגמנים לערבית ואנגלית.

Appendix II

Biographical Glossary

Note: b. = born
   f. = founded
   a. = emigrated to Palestine (*'aliya*)

AARONSOHN, Aaron (1876–1919) – b. Rumania; grew up in Zikhron Ya'akov. Agronomist. Set up an agricultural experimental station in Athlit with American help. Advocated employment of Arab labourers on Jewish farms, which led to friction between him and Jewish labour circles. Founder and organiser of *Nili*, the pro-British spy network in Turkish Palestine during World War I. After 1916, worked directly with British intelligence. Undertook various missions for the ZO in the US, UK and at the Paris Peace Conference. Disappeared in plane crash over the English Channel.

AARONSOHN, Alexander (1888–1948) – b. Zikhron Ya'akov, brother of Aaron. Engaged in agricultural research, 1910–15. A co-founder of the *Nili* spy network, and later served directly in British intelligence (1917–18, 1936 *et seq*.). Active in recruitment of the Palestinian Jewish Battalion of the Jewish Legion (1918). Founder and first President of the *B'nai Binyamin* farmers' association (1921–24). A founder of the Jerusalem Hebrew daily, *Doar ha-Yom*.

ALMALIAH, Avraham R. B. (1884–1967) – b. Jerusalem, to family of Moroccan origin. Founder-member of *ha-Magen*, 1913. Represented Sephardi community before the King-Crane Commission (1919), at the London Zionist Conference (1920) and before the Peel (Royal) Commission (1936). Journalist and contributor to Hebrew and Arabic publications. Member of the first and second *Assefat ha-Nivharim*, 1920–31, and of the *Va'ad Leumi*. Member of Jerusalem Municipal Council (1935 *et seq*.)

ARLOSOROFF, Dr Haim (1899–1933) – b. Ukraine, raised in Germany. a. 1924. Active in *ha-Po'el ha-Tza'ir* and later *Mapai*. Member of Yishuv Delegation to the League of Nations Mandates Commission, 1926. Solid supporter of Dr Weizmann at the XVIIth Zst. Cong. (1931). Headed Political Department of the JAE following that Congress until his assassination by unknown assailants on a Tel Aviv beach.

AVISSAR, David (1887–1963) – b. Hebron, later moved to Jerusalem. Educator. Founder and Chairman of *Halutzai ha-Mizrah*. Sephardi representative on the *Assefat ha-Nivharim*, *Va'ad Leumi*, Jerusalem Jewish Community Council and Pro-Jerusalem Society, as well as to several Zst. Congs.

BEN-AVI, Ittamar (1885–1943) – b. Jerusalem, son of noted lexicographer Eliezer Ben-Yahuda (and the first Jewish child to be brought up to speak modern Hebrew). Journalist, who introduced the spirit and colour of modern European journalism into the Palestinian Jewish press. Founder of *Doar ha-Yom*, which he edited from 1919–29; edited *Palestine Weekly* (1924 *et seq.*). A founder of the *B'nai Binyamin* farmers' association (1921). Moved to the USA in 1939.

BEN-GURION, David (1886–1973) – b. Poland. a. 1906. Active in the socialist-Zionist *Po'alei-Zion* party, and played a leading rôle in the creation of its successors, *Ahdut ha-'Avoda* (1919) and *Mapai* (1930). Edited the *Po'alei-Zion* newspaper, *ha-Ahdut*. Expelled by the Turks in 1915; went to America where he organised the *he-Halutz* movement and recruitment for the Jewish Legion. Returned to Palestine in 1918 with the Hebrew Battalions. Served as first Secretary-General of the *Histadrut* (1921–34). Headed the Political Department of the JAE (with Moshe Shertok-Sharett), 1933–35, and then became Chairman of the JAE, a post which he held until 1948. First Prime Minister and Minister of Defence of Israel, 1948–53; returned to office 1955–63. Retired from active politics in 1970.

BEN-ZVI, Yitzhak (1884–1963) – b. Ukraine. Follower of Borochov and a founder of the *Po'alei-Zion* movement (1906). a. 1907. Devoted much study and writing to the history of Eretz-Israel and the ethnography of its dispersed peoples. Founding editor of *ha-Ahdut*. Active in *ha-Shomer* (f. 1909) and the *Hagana*. Like Ben-Gurion, was expelled from Palestine during World War I and returned from America with the Hebrew Battalions. Appointed to the Palestine Government's Advisory Council (1920–21). Member of the *Assefat ha-Nivharim* and the *Va'ad Leumi*, serving on its Praesidium (1920–25), as Deputy-Chairman (1925–29), Chairman (1930–44) and President

(1944–48). Member of the Jerusalem Municipal Council, 1927–29, 1934 *et seq*. Second President of Israel, 1952–63.

BERLIGNE, Eliahu Meir (1866–1959) – b. White Russia. a. 1907. Among first residents of Tel Aviv. Founding member of the *Va'ad Zmani* and subsequently the *Va'ad Leumi* (taking responsibility for finances in the Education Department). A director of the *Bank ha-Po'alim*, 1921–28.

BLUMENFELD, Efraim (David Bloch-Blumenfeld) (1884–1947) – b. White Russia. Active in *Po'alei-Zion*. a. 1912. Helped establish labour offices and workers' settlements. Represented the labour movement on the *Va'ad Zmani* and *Va'ad Leumi*. Founding member of *Ahdut ha-'Avoda* (1919) and the *Histadrut* (1920). Deputy Mayor (1923) and Mayor (1925–27) of Tel Aviv.

CASTEL, Yosef Haim (1899–1968) – b. Jerusalem. Served with the Turkish Army in World War I. Journalist and poet. A founder of *Halutzai ha-Mizrah*. Directed the ZC Press Bureau and acted as Secretary to Dr Eder and Col Kisch. After 1928 did Zionist publicity work in London and Paris.

DIZENGOFF, Meir (1861–1936) – b. Serbia. a. 1892. Headed committee of Jaffa Jews who founded Tel Aviv (1906), and later served as its Mayor (1921–25, 1928–36). Founded *ha-Ezrah* citizens' movement. Served on *Va'ad Zmani* and *Va'ad Leumi*. Also worked for the PZE Department of Trade and Industry (1927–29).

EDER, Dr Montague David (1866–1936) – b. England. Psychoanalyst and Fabian socialist. Helped organise recruitment for Jewish Legion. Worked on ZC, becoming Dr Weizmann's personal representative and effectively its political head. Held high-level negotiations with Syrian Arab nationalists in Cairo, 1922. Member of the London ZE (1925–28) and President of the EZF (1930–32). Actively opposed the Jabotinsky group at the XVIIth Zst. Cong. (1931).

EPSTEIN, Dr Yitzhak (1862–1943) – b. White Russia. a. 1886. Studied and taught agriculture and languages. After 1918, became Chief Inspector for Zionist schools in Palestine.

ETTINGER, 'Akiva (1872–1945) – b. Russia. Agronomist, worked on Jewish settlement projects for the ICA in Bessarabia, Argentina and Brazil. a. 1918. Played a leading rôle in the ZE's and the JNF's colonisation departments.

FRIEDENWALD, Harry (1864–1950) – b. USA. Ophthalmologist. President, Federation of American Zionists, 1904–18. Visited Palestine, 1911, 1914 and 1919, in the latter year serving as Chairman of the ZC.

FRUMKIN, Gad (1887–1960) – b. Jerusalem. One of the first

Jewish lawyers in Palestine under the Turks. Appointed to the Palestine Supreme Court, 1920–48. Participated with Pinhas Rutenberg and others in a private initiative to negotiate an agreement with the Arabs during the 1936 general strike.

GOLOMB, Eliahu (1893–1945) – b. Belorussia. a. 1909. Active in recruitment for the Palestinian Jewish Battalion (1918). Founding member of *Ahdut ha-'Avoda* (1919), the *Histadrut* (1920) and *Mapai* (1930). Founder, guiding spirit and uncrowned leader of the *Hagana*. Served on *Va'ad Zmani* and *Va'ad Leumi*.

HOOFIEN, Eliezer Siegfried (1881–1957) – b. Holland. a. 1912. Banker and public figure. Member of the *Va'ad Zmani*. General-Manager of the APC (later *Bank Leumi le-Israel*), 1924–47. Founder of the Jaffa-Tel Aviv Chamber of Commerce, 1923. Consul-General of the Netherlands, 1923–47. Economic Co-ordinator, Prime Minister's Office, 1948–49.

JAFFE, Bezalel (1868–1925) – b. Lithuania. a. 1909. Among the founders of Tel Aviv, serving as President of the Jaffa-Tel Aviv Jewish Community Council. A founding member of the *Va'ad Zmani*; also a member of the *Assefat ha-Nivharim* and the *Va'ad Leumi*. Board Member of the PLDC.

KALVARYSKI, Haim Margaliut (1867–1947) – b. Poland. a. 1895, after completing studies in agronomy. Administrator of ICA colonies in Galilee, 1900–22, and helped acquire extensive areas for Jewish settlement. Active in promoting a Hebrew-Arabic school near Rosh-Pina and political negotiations with Arab nationalists, beginning in 1914. Member of the Palestine Government's Advisory Council, 1920–23, and the *Va'ad Leumi*, 1920 *et seq*. Employed by the PZE to advise on Arab affairs, 1923–27, and recalled to head the 'Joint Bureau' on Arab affairs, 1929–31. Active in promoting groups favouring Jewish-Arab understanding: *Brit-Shalom* (f. 1925), *Kidma Mizraha* (f. 1936), the League for Jewish-Arab Rapprochement and Co-operation (f. 1939) and *Ihud* (f. 1942).

KATZNELSON, Berl (1887–1944) – b. Belorussia. a. 1908. Wrote and spoke extensively on the Jewish labour movement: its rôle in the fulfilment of Zionism, and the need for unity of the Jewish working class. Joined the Jewish Legion, 1918–20. Founding editor of *Kuntres*, the organ of *Ahdut ha-'Avoda*, and of *Davar*, a daily published under the auspices of the *Histadrut*. A Director of the JNF. Abstained from work on the *Va'ad Leumi* or the ZE, but was widely respected by all community leaders.

KISCH, Col Frederick Herman (1888–1943) – b. India, where his father was in the British Colonial Service. Served the Military Intelligence Section of the British Delegation to the Peace Con-

ference, 1919–21; resigned to accept Dr Weizmann's invitation
to head the political department of the PZE in 1922. Subsequently elected Chairman of the PZE, which he served until
1931, when he went into business in Haifa. Continued to advise
the Yishuv on security matters. Killed in action in North Africa
while inspecting a minefield.

KLAUSNER, Professor Joseph (1874–1958) – b. Lithuania, raised
in the Ukraine. a. 1918. Hebrew author and literary historian.
Active Zionist, attending many Zst. Congs. Co-edited *ha-Shiloah*
(1903–26) and *Betar* (1932–33). After 1930, identified with
Jabotinsky, the Revisionist Party and *Herut*.

LICHTHEIM, Richard (1885–1963) – b. Germany. Zionist
ideologist and publicist. Edited *Die Welt* (1911–13). Worked in
the Zionist Office in Constantinople (1913–17), where he took
part in talks with Arab representatives. Member of ZE, 1921–23.
Joined the Revisionist Party, 1925. a. 1934.

LUDVIPOL, Avraham (1865–1921) – b. Russia. Hebrew journalist, active in *Hibbat-Zion* movement. a. 1907. Active in public life
of Tel Aviv. Founding member of editorial staff of *ha-Aretz*.

MALLUL, Dr Nissim Ya'akov (1892–1959) – b. Safed, family of
Tunisian origin. Began press work for the Zionist Office in 1911.
A founder of *ha-Magen* secret society, and promoted Jewish-
Arab understanding. Had contacts with the Arab Decentralisa-
tion Party and the Committee of Union and Progress. Served in
the Jewish Battalion. Published widely in Hebrew and Arabic on
Jewish-Arab affairs. Edited *as-Salam* and assisted the PZE and
the *Va'ad Leumi* on Arab affairs.

MEIR, Rabbi Ya'akov (1856–1939) – b. Jerusalem. Chief Rabbi of
Salonika, 1908–19. Sephardi Chief Rabbi of Palestine, 1921–39.

MEYUHAS, Yosef Baran (1868–1942) – b. Jerusalem. One of
early exponents of the development of modern Hebrew. Teacher
and writer. A leader of the Sephardi community, and President of
the Jerusalem Jewish Community Council, 1920–31.

RADLER-FELDMAN, Yehoshua ('Rabbi Binyamin') (1880–
1957) – b. Galicia. a. 1907. Hebrew journalist, known for his
outspoken opinions. Active in the *Mizrahi* Party. Edited *ha-Hed*
(1926–53). A founding-member of *Brit-Shalom* (1925).

REMEZ, M. David (1886–1951) – b. Belorussia. Member of
Po'alei-Zion. a. 1913. Active in the formation of *Ahdut ha-
'Avoda* (1919), the *Histadrut* (1920) and *Mapai* (1930).
Secretary-General of the *Histadrut*, 1935–45. Chairman of the
Va'ad Leumi, 1944–48. Israeli Minister of Transport (1948–50)
and of Education (1950–51).

RUPPIN, Dr Arthur (1876–1943) – b. Prussia. Writer, economist and sociologist. a. 1908, when he established the Palestine Office and the PLDC. The 'father of Zionist settlement', he headed the Colonisation Department of the ZC and later served, almost continuously, on the ZE and the JAE until 1935. A founder of *Bank ha-Po'alim*. A founding-member of *Brit-Shalom*, which he later abandoned. Founder and head of the Institute for Economic Research (1935).

RUTENBERG, Pinhas (1879–1942) – b. Ukraine. Prominent in revolutionary movement. Served under Kerensky. Active in the creation of the Jewish Battalions during World War I. a. 1919. Played a leading rôle in the *Hagana* in Jerusalem (1920) and Tel Aviv (1921). Founder of the Palestine Electric Corporation, and a pioneer of modern industry in Palestine. Attempted to mediate between feuding labour and revisionist factions during the 1930s. Participated, with Moshe Smilansky and others, in a private initiative to negotiate an end to the Arab strike and rebellion in 1936.

SAPHIR, Ascher (1893–1942) – b. Jerusalem. During studies in Constantinople, established contacts with Arab nationalists. Participated in Zionist-Arab negotiations, 1922. Moved to Paris in the 1920s to work in finances, returning to Palestine in 1935–38.

SCHILLER, Shlomo (1879–1925) – b. Poland. a. 1910. Educator and Zionist writer. Settled in Jerusalem.

SMILANSKY, Moshe (1874–1953) – b. Russia. a. 1890. Agricultural pioneer and Hebrew writer, settled in Rehovot. Opposed exclusive Jewish labour on Jewish colonies. Published Hebrew stories on Arab life. Active in the formation of the Federation of Judaean Colonies and the Farmers' Union, whose paper, *Bustenai*, he edited from 1929–39. Participated with Gad Frumkin and others in a private initiative to negotiate an end to the Arab general strike of 1936.

SPRINZAK, Yosef (1885–1959) – b. Russia. A founder of *Ze'irei-Zion* (1905). a. 1908. A founder of *ha-Po'el ha-Tza'ir* in Palestine. Founder and leading member of the *Histadrut* (1920) and *Mapai* (1930). Active in the *Assefat ha-Nivharim* and the *Va'ad Leumi*. Member of the Tel Aviv Municipal Council. First labour representative to sit on the ZE. Headed PZE Labour and 'Aliya Departments, 1921–27. Secretary-General of the *Histadrut*, 1945–48. Speaker of the *Knesset*, 1948–59.

STEIN, Leonard Jacques (1887–1973) – b. England. Staff Officer in the British Military Administration in Palestine, 1918–20. Appointed Political Secretary of the London ZE, 1920–29, after which he served the JAE as legal adviser. President of the Anglo-Jewish Association, 1939–49. Author of *The Balfour Declaration* (1961).

TABENKIN, Yitzhak (1887–1971) – b. Belorussia. A founder of *Po'alei-Zion*. a. 1912. Stressed agricultural labour and collective settlements. Member of *ha-Shomer* and the *G'dud ha-'Avoda*. Active in the founding of *ha-Kibbutz ha-Meuhad*, *Ahdut ha-'Avoda* (1919), the *Histadrut* (1920) and *Mapai* (1930). Following splits in labour ranks during the 1940s, founded *Mapam* (1948).

THON, Dr Ya'akov Yonathan (1880–1950) – b. Ukraine. a. 1907. Worked with Dr Ruppin in the Palestine Office, replacing him during his exile (1916–20). Organised the Jerusalem Jewish community after 1917, serving as its Chairman. Founding Chairman of the *Va'ad Zmani* and *Va'ad Leumi*, serving on its Praesidium (1920–25) and as Deputy-Chairman (1925–29). Member of *ha-Po'el ha-Tza'ir*. Managing Director of PLDC, 1921–50. A founder of *Brit-Shalom*, from which he later resigned.

TOLKOWSKY, Samuel (1886–1965) – b. Belgium. Agronomist. a. 1911. Took part in London negotiations for the Balfour Declaration, 1917. Secretary of the ZO Delegation to the Peace Conference, 1919. Active in public and economic affairs of Tel Aviv. Israeli Consul-General in Berne, 1949–56.

USSISHKIN, Menahem M. (1863–1941) – b. Russia. Prominent Zionist leader and publicist. Participated in Zst. Congs. from the first in 1897. Initiated pre-1914 efforts at organising the Yishuv. a. 1919, as head of the ZC. Organised the Hebrew school system and played an important rôle in establishing the Hebrew University. Chairman of the JNF, 1923–41.

UZIEL, Rabbi Bension Meir Hai (1880–1953) – b. Jerusalem. *Hakham Bashi* of Jaffa, 1911 *et seq*. Chief Rabbi of Tel Aviv, 1923–39. Sephardi Chief Rabbi of Palestine and Israel, 1939–53. Member of the *Va'ad Zmani* and *Va'ad Leumi*, and represented the Jewish community on various missions and before the authorities.

WILKANSKY, Yitzhak Avigdor (ELAZARI-VOLCANI) (1880–1955) – b. Lithuania. a. 1908. Agronomist, advocate of mixed farming. Member of *ha-Po'el ha-Tza'ir*. Adviser to Palestine Office, 1909–19. Founded Agricultural Experimental Station in Tel Aviv (later moved to Rehovot), 1921. Headed Faculty of Agriculture, Hebrew University, 1940–47.

YELLIN, Professor David (1864–1941) – b. Jerusalem. Distinguished writer, scholar and teacher. Founder and Principal of the Hebrew Teachers Seminary. Member of the *Va'ad ha-Lashon*. Deputy-Mayor of the Jerusalem Municipal Council, 1920–25. Founding member of *Va'ad Zmani* and *Va'ad Leumi*, serving as member of the Praesidium (1920–25) and Chairman (1925–29).

Notes

For full bibliographic references and an explanation of the archival references, see Bibliography.

Introduction

1. On the period before 1914, see: N. Mandel, 'Turks, Arabs and Jewish Immigration into Palestine, 1882–1914'; Y. Ro'i, 'The Zionist Attitude to the Arabs, 1908–1914'; N. Mandel, 'Attempts at an Arab-Zionist Entente, 1913–1914'; W. Laqueur, *A History of Zionism*, pp. 211–34.
2. E.g., Amos Elon, *The Israelis*, pp. 154, 158; Aharon Cohen, *Israel and the Arab World*, pp. 156f.
3. Quotation from Mandel, 'Turks . . .', p. 108; cf. other works cited in note 1.
4. On Kalvaryski's ideas and activities, see pages 36f., 40f., 98f., 128f., 200f., below.
5. Cf. Susan Lee Hattis, *The Bi-National Idea in Palestine during Mandatory Times*; Laqueur, *A History of Zionism*, pp. 251–5.
6. Yehoshua Porath, *The Emergence of the Palestinian-Arab National Movement*, p. 324, n. 67; Elon, *The Israelis*, pp. 172f.; Ro'i, 'The Zionist Attitude', pp. 203, 233; David Ben-Gurion, *Anahnu u-Shkhenenu* [We and our Neighbours], *passim*.
7. P. Alsberg, 'ha-She'ela ha-'Arevit bi-M'diniut ha-Hanhala ha-Tzionit lifne Milhemet ha-'Olam ha-Rishona' [The Arab Question in the Policy of the Zionist Executive before the First World War], p. 171; Ro'i, 'Zionist Attitude', pp. 230f.; Alex Bein, *The Return to the Soil*, pp. 238f., 424; Moshe Burstein, *Self-Government of the Jews in Palestine Since 1900*, p. 9. For later evidence, see: Blumenfeld remarks, VL meeting, 16.5.1921, J1/7224; Palestine Commission on the Disturbances of August 1929 [Shaw Commission], *Evidence Heard . . . in Open Sittings*, pp. 227f.
8. Figures are taken from ESCO Foundation, *Palestine: A Study of Jewish, Arab and British Policies* [cited hereafter as *ESCO*], Vol. I, 320–21; Bein, *Return to the Soil*, pp. 138f., 182; Burstein, *Self-Government of the Jews*, pp. 4–10; A. W. Money to CPO, 26.11.1918, CZA, Z4/16135. On the general composition and characteristics of the

Yishuv, see: *ESCO* I, 405f., 555f.; Burstein, *op. cit.*, *passim*; S. N. Eisenstadt, *Israeli Society*, chs. 2–4.

9. See, in particular, Haim Arlosoroff to Chaim Weizmann, 30.6.1932, WA (original in English). A Hebrew translation is given in Arlosoroff's *Yoman Yirushalayim* [Jerusalem Diary], pp. 333–42, and another English version (probably a re-translation from the Hebrew) appears in Walid Khalidi (ed.), *From Haven to Conquest*, pp. 245f. Cf. David Ben-Gurion, *My Talks with Arab Leaders*, pp. 12f.; W. Laqueur, *A History of Zionism*, p. 258.

10. Palestine Royal Commission, *Report* [cited hereafter as *Peel Report*], p. 121; cf. Burstein, *Self-Government of the Jews*, pp. 2f.

11. Eisenstadt, *Israeli Society*, pp. 14–24; Elon, *The Israelis*, ch. 6.

Chapter 1

1. See, e.g., Eisenstadt, *Israeli Society*, pp. 19–24.

2. Ruppin, *Three Decades of Palestine: Speeches and Papers on the Upbuilding of the Jewish National Home*, p. 62.

3. See, e.g., Mandel, 'Turks, Arabs and Jewish Immigration', pp. 95f., 98f.; Alsberg, 'ha-She'ela ha-'Arevit', p. 168; Ro'i, 'Zionist Attitude', p. 218.

4. 'Palestine: The Jewish Colonies', *Arab Bulletin* (64), 27.9.1917, pp. 389f.

5. See sources cited in note 1 of the Introduction, above, and also: M. Assaf, *ha-Yihasim ben 'Aravim ve-Yehudim be-Eretz-Israel, 1860– 1948* [Arab-Jewish Relations in Palestine], pp. 9–83; Cohen, *Israel and the Arab World*, chs. 2–3; N. Mandel, *The Arabs and Zionism before World War I*.

6. A detailed account of the latter activity is given in Y. Ro'i, 'Nissionotaihem shel ha-Mosdot ha-Tzioniyim le-Hashpi'a 'al ha-'Itonut ha-'Arevit be-Eretz-Israel ba-Shanim 1908–1914' [The Attempts of Zionist Institutions to Influence the Arabic Press in Palestine].

7. Burstein, *Self-Government of the Jews*, p. 79.

8. Clayton to Sykes (tgm.), 30.12.1917, PRO, FO 371/3061, file W44/ 245447/214354; cf. Moshe Medzini, '*Esser Shanim shel Mediniut Eretzyisraelit* [Ten Years of Palestine Politics], p. 45.

9. Note of conversation between S. Hoofien, Y. Thon & M. Georges-Picot, 24.1.1918, CZA, L3/310 (Heb.); cf. Bein, *The Return to the Soil*, pp. 176f.

10. *Political Report of the Executive to the XIIth Zionist Congress (1921)*, pp. 14f., (cited hereafter as *PRE XII ZC*); cf. Bein, *op. cit.*, pp. 179–82.

11. ZC notes of reception by Sir R. Wingate, 22.3.1918, CZA, L3/285; Report on Dr Weizmann's visit to Gen Allenby at GHQ, 3.4.1918, CZA, Z4/16051; K. Cornwallis, Memorandum to Symes on the Effect of the Weizmann Interviews on Syrian and Arab Opinion, 20.4.1918, PRO, FO 371/3394, file W44/85169/11053; Clayton to Balfour, 16.6.1918, FO 371/3395, file W44/130342/11053.

12. For some reactions to this paternalism, see: Y. Ben-Zvi, *The Hebrew Battalions* (Letters), p. 97; B. Katznelson, *Igrot, 1919–1922* [Letters], pp. 61, 77; *Kitvai Berl Katznelson* [Writings], vol. I, 236; cf. note 14, below.

13. For details, see N. Caplan, *Futile Diplomacy: A Study of Zionist-Arab Negotiation Attempts, 1913–1939*, ch. 2.

14. VZ meetings of 9.9.1918 (CZA, J1/8767) and 11.6.1919 (J1/8777); Medzini, *'Esser Shanim*, pp. 80–3; Eder to Weizmann, 13.7.1919 and 24.7.1919, Z4/16044; I. Sieff to J. Simon, 20.10.1919 (Z4/936) and 11.11.1919 (L3/289); Katznelson, *Writings* I, 187f. Cf. pages 32f. and 135f., below.

15. Weizmann to Balfour, 30.5.1918, *Letters and Papers of Chaim Weizmann*, Series A: Letters, vol. VIII [hereafter *LPCW*], p. 205; cf. same to same, 17.7.1918, *ibid.*, p. 229; Weizmann report, ZC meeting, 16.6.1918 (cancelled version of minutes), CZA, Z4/483.

16. Weizmann and Sieff to Sokolow, 18.4.1918, *LPCW* VIII, 137; 'The Work of the ZC.' (n.d.), L4/392/I; *Zionist Review*, Dec. 1918, p. 139; 'Notes on Zionism', 6.2.1919, PRO, FO 371/4171, file W44/77574/1051; Sieff to Simon, 20.10.1919, CZA, Z4/936.

17. Weizmann to Ormsby-Gore, 16.4.1918, *LPCW* VIII, 128; cf. ZC meeting, 13.4.1918, CZA, L3/285; Cohen, *Israel and the Arab World*, p. 138.

18. ZC minutes, 16.6.1918 (n. 15). Cf. Weizmann, *Trial and Error*, pp. 290–4 and *LPCW* VIII, 210.

19. ZC meeting, 16.6.1918 (n. 15); Weizmann to Balfour, 17.7.1918 (n. 15).

20. CZA, J1/8763; cf. Cohen, *Israel and the Arab World*, p. 140.

21. For details, see: ZC meeting, 5.4.1918, CZA, L3/285; Weizmann to Ormsby-Gore, 7.4.1918, *LPCW* VIII, 121–2; Ormsby-Gore to Sykes, 9.4.1918, Sledmere Paper No. 107; de Sola Pool, 'Preliminary Impressions on the Jerusalem Situation', 1.4.1919, CZA, A182/86(1).

22. Second Preparatory Assembly, 19.6.1918, CZA, J1/8763. Cf. Bein, *The Return to the Soil*, pp. 105f.; *Zionist Review,* Aug. 1919, pp. 55f.

23. VZ meeting, 14.8.1918, CZA, J1/8767; cf. meeting, 10.9.1919, J1/8781/I, and *Sefer Toldot ha-Hagana* [hereafter *STH*] I/2, p. 641.

24. Aims quoted in *STH* I/2, 879; cf. Bein, *Return to the Soil*, pp. 227f. Elias Gilner, *War and Hope: A History of the Jewish Legion*, ch. 23; *STH* I/2, 495–515; E. Golomb, *Hevion 'Oz* [Hidden Strength], I, pp. 145f., 158f., 171, 174f., 179f.

25. For an indication of this preoccupation, see, e.g.: *PRE XII ZC.*; Medzini, *Esser Shanim*; *STH* I/2, 538f., 549.

26. Thon to Weizmann, 10.7.1918, CZA, L4/426. For a fuller discussion of this point, see N. Caplan, 'The British Impact on Jewish-Arab Relations in Palestine'.

27. Jabotinsky, *Neumim, 1905–1926* [Speeches], pp. 89f., 141; Jabotinsky, draft tgm. [to Weizmann? – Nov. 1918], CZA, L4/255; same to same, 27.12.1918 (Z4/16135) and 7.10.1920 (Z4/16011); Medzini, *'Esser Shanim*, pp. 69–75, 110f.; *STH* I/2, 541f.

28. Weizmann to Eder, 28.11.1918, *LPCW* IX, 35. Cf. same to Brandeis, 29.10.1918, *Ibid.*, pp. 3f.; Sokolow to Husain, 7.10.1918, PRO, FO 371/3413, file W38/188461/173356.

29. On Weizmann-Faisal relations during this period, see: Caplan, *Futile Diplomacy*, ch. 2; Moshe Perlmann, 'Chapters of Arab-Jewish Diplomacy, 1918–1922', pp. 133f.; Walter Laqueur (ed.), *The Israel–Arab Reader*, pp. 36f.

30. See Porath, *Emergence*, ch. 2.

31. Yellin to Eder, 15.11.1918, CZA, L4/283 (Fr.). Cf. Eder to Weizmann (tgm.), 3.1.1919, L4/58/II; Y. Abadi to D. Yellin, 27.7.1919, A153/162 (Heb.); 'Arab Movement in Palestine' (secret memo), 19.3.1920, Z4/16078; Ben-Zvi, *Writings* IV, 250; Porath, *Emergence*, pp. 20, 22.

32. Lewin-Epstein to Sokolow, 22.1.1919, PRO, FO 371/4170, file W44/25158/1051; cf. full report by Lewis-Epstein to ZC meeting, 20.1.1919, CZA, L4/65/III.

33. See Porath, *Emergence*, pp. 31–2.

34. For details, see Yellin to Eder, 8.11.1918, CZA, L4/283 (Fr.). Storrs to HQ, 11.11.1918, ISA, 2/140.

35. Yellin to Eder, 15.11.1918 (n. 31); cf. ZC meeting, 24.11.1918, CZA, L4/65/I; Thon to Jabotinsky, 11.2.1919, Z4/255 (Heb.); Gad Frumkin, *Derekh Shofet bi-Irushalayim* [The Way of a Judge in Jerusalem], p. 219; Assaf, *Yihasim*, p. 89.

36. Jabotinsky, draft tgm. [Nov. 1918], CZA, L4/255; Jabotinsky to Weizmann, 28.11.1918, Z4/538.

37. Jabotinsky to Weizmann, 12.11.1918, CZA, Z4/16135.

38. Golomb, *Hevion 'Oz* I, 158, 168, 171; Gilner, *War and Hope*, pp. 238, 268f., 292f.; Ben-Gurion, *Igrot* I [Letters, 1904–1919], 399; R. Salaman, *Palestine Reclaimed*, p. 121; Jabotinsky to Weizmann, 28.11.1918 (n.36).

39. Jabotinsky to Weizmann, 12.11 (n. 27) and 28.11.1918 (n. 36).

40. ZC meeting, 24.11.1918, L4/65/I; Yellin to Eder, 15.11.1918 (n. 31); Eder to Sokolow, 27.11.1918, Z4/538; Frumkin, *Derekh Shofet*, p. 221.

41. The following account is based on the minutes of the conference (also known as the Third Preparatory Assembly) in CZA, J1/8766/I (18–22.12.1918). Cf. Burstein, *Self-Government of the Jews*, p. 93; Jabotinsky, *Neumim*, 82–121.

42. Original text and handwritten revisions reproduced in Appendix I.

Chapter 2

1. The following section is based largely on Eisenberg's report to VZE, 28.5.1919 (CZA, J1/8791) and Yellin's report to VZ, 9.6.1919 (J1/8777).

2. The points were: (1) insufficient stress on the right of the *entire* Jewish people to a decisive voice in the administration of Palestine; (2)

'Eretz-Israel' as the official name; (3) the Zionist flag as the official flag; (4) the position of an 'Under-Secretary of State for Palestine' at the FO; (5) ZO control over appointments to the Executive Council of Palestine; and (6) insufficient stress on the priority of Jews in the development of natural resources. The official ZO memorandum to the Peace Conference is reproduced in J. C. Hurewitz, *Diplomacy in the Near and Middle East* II, 45–50.

3. Ormsby-Gore to Weizmann, 22.2.1919, W.A.; Stein to Kisch, 12.6.1923, CZA, Z4/16061; Bein, *Return to the Soil*, p. 176; Medzini, *'Esser Shanim*, pp. 80, 84f., 90f.

4. Faisal was likely referring to Zangwill's article, 'Before the Peace Conference', *Asia*, Feb. 1919; cf. *ESCO* I, 158f.

5. Note of meeting, 20.4.1919, CZA, A153/149 (Fr.); Yellin to Dizengoff, 8.6.1919, *loc. cit.* (Heb.).

6. Yishuv Delegation to Inner Actions Committee, 28.4.1919, *loc. cit.* (Heb.).

7. Original letter from Faisal to Frankfurter, 1.3.1919, CZA, Z4/25001; reproduced in Laqueur (ed.), *Israel-Arab Reader*, pp. 38f. (incorrectly dated 3.3.1919). Cf. Perlmann, 'Chapters of Arab-Jewish Diplomacy', pp. 139f.; *ESCO* I, 142f.

8. See n. 6; also Yellin to Sokolow, 13.5.1919, *Kitvai David Yellin* [Writings], vol. V, p. 37.

9. For details, see VZ meetings, 4.2.(J1/8771) and 18.3.1919 (J1/8773); joint VZE–ZC meeting, 18.3.1919 (J1/8800); VZE meeting, 28.5.1919 (J1/8791); Porath, *Emergence*, pp. 34, 79f.; *ESCO* I, 473f.; Thon to Jabotinsky, 11.2.1919, Z4/255 (Heb.); Cohen, *Israel and the Arab World*, pp. 147f.

10. De Sola Pool, 'Preliminary Impressions on the Jerusalem Situation', 1.4.1919, CZA, A182/86(1).

11. Joint VZE–ZC meeting, 18.3.1919 (n. 9); report on 'Arab Movement', 20.3.1919, Z4/16004; ZC meeting, 20.3.1919, L4/65/IV; [Szold] to A. W. Money, ca. 20.3.1919, Z4/1366; Clayton to FO (tgm.), 26.3.1919, PRO, FO 371/4153, file 44A/49607/275; Gilner, *War and Hope*, pp. 322f.

12. Aaronsohn [unsigned letter] to 'Aaron and Felix', 8.5.1919, PRO, FO 371/4181, file W44/98082/2117. See also: Lewin-Epstein to Sh. Levin, 22.5.1919, CZA, Z4/16045 (Heb.); 'Actual Situation of the Arabic Question', [pre-8.1.1919], PRO, FO 371/4170, file W44/25158/1051; 'La situation actuelle de la question arabe', 20.1.1919, CZA, Z4/16004; ZC meeting, 12.3.1919, L4/65/III; J. B. Schechtman, *Rebel and Statesman*, pp. 296f.; *STH* I/2, 560f.

13. Y. Shohat, VZ meeting, 10.6.1919, CZA, J1/8777 (emphasis original).

14. VZ meeting, 10.6.1919, *loc. cit.*. Ettinger had spent the war years in London, where he had come to learn at first hand of Sykes' 'Arab-Armenian-Zionist Entente' scheme, which he described to the meeting with similar scepticism.

15. VZ meeting, 4.2.1919, J1/8771; joint VZE-ZC meetings, 8.3, 20.3 and 7.5.1919, J1/8800; VZ meeting 24.4.1919 (Friedenwald address,

in L4/65/IV); VZE meetings, 15.5 and 28.5.1919, J1/8791.

16. *Hevion 'Oz* I, 174f., also p. 179. See also: *STH* I/2, 500, 517f.; V. Jabotinsky, *The Story of the Jewish Legion*, pp. 146f., 166f.; London meeting, 17.5.1919, CZA, Z4/2333/I.

17. VZE meeting, 10.4.1919, CZA, J1/8791.

18. VZ meeting, 24.4.1919, J1/8775.

19. VZE meeting, 15.5.1919, J1/8791.

20. VZE meeting, 19.5.1919, *loc. cit.* It is difficult to understand why Dr Thon should have deliberately proposed a far-reaching 'bi-nationalist' formula at this time. Compare this, for example, with his distinctly 'uni-nationalist' statement to Brandeis, quoted below, page 46.

21. Members of the delegation were: Thon, Ettinger, Yellin, M. Glicken, M. Meirovitch, Kalvaryski. The following account is based on the reports given by Thon, Rabbi Uziel and Hoofien to the VZ meeting of 11.6.1919, J1/8777.

22. ZC meeting, 15–16.6.1919, L4/65/V; Weizmann to Friedenwald (tgm.), 18.6.1919, *LPCW* IX, 161; H. Howard, *The King-Crane Commission*, pp. 97f.

23. Friedenwald to ZE (London), 18.6.1919, CZA, Z4/16045.

24. See sources in note 32 to chapter 1; de Sola Pool report, 1.4.1919 (n. 10); Eder to Weizmann, 7.5.1919, Z4/16004; Friedenwald to ZO (Paris), [16].5.1919, PRO, FO 371/4180, file W44/81408/2117.

25. VZE–ZC joint meeting, 18.3.1919, CZA, J1/8800; VZE meeting, 13.4.1919, J1/8791.

26. ZC meeting, 30.5.1919, L4/65/IV.

27. ZC meeting, 15.6.1919, L4/65/V.

28. VZ meeting, 24.4.1919, J1/8775; cf. Medzini, *'Esser Shanim*, pp. 80f.

29. VZE meeting, 10.6.1919, J1/8791.

30. For details see: ZC meetings, 8.5 and 18.5.1919, L4/65/IV; Kalvaryski to Friedenwald, 3.6.1919, Z4/16045 (Heb.). One donation of £20 was returned with a note stating that 'political difficulties compel us to reject your kind contribution'.

31. ZC meeting, 8.5.1919, L4/65/IV. Nevertheless, the ZC did seem to have gone on to accept responsibility for at least £622.75 worth of Kalvaryski's activities surrounding the visit of the King-Crane Commission. See van Vriesland to Kisch, 12.7.1923, S25/10320.

32. VZE meetings, 13.5 and 10.6.1919, J1/8791.

33. The following account is based on the minutes of this meeting, J1/8777.

34. 'Beware, Zionists: governments come and go, but the people remain.' This dictum was much quoted in those days. Cf. Yellin remarks at the same meeting; Medzini, *'Esser Shanim*, p. 80; Laqueur, *History of Zionism*, p. 226.

35. W. Laqueur, (*op. cit.*, pp. 215f.) provides an interesting summary of a similar internal debate which took place during 1907–1908.

36. See page 47, below; also: D. Ben-Gurion, *Zikhronot* [Memoirs] I, 143 f.

37. The following section is based on the debates in J1/8777 and the original French text in A113/13; cf. *'Al Parshat Darkenu* [At the

Parting of our Ways], pp. 25f., 33; *ESCO* I, 562f.; Cohen, *Israel and the Arab World*, pp. 154f. For a fuller account of Zionist and *Arab* reactions to Kalvaryski's plan, see N. Caplan, 'Arab-Jewish Contacts in Palestine After the First World War', pp. 650f.

38. Weizmann to Mallett, 18.6.1919, *LPCW* IX, 161f.; Landman to Weizmann, 23.10.1919, CZA, Z4/16015; Ussishkin interview with Chief Administrator, 7.10.1919, Z4/16044; Weizmann to Meinertzhagen, 31.1.1920, *LPCW* IX, 289f.
39. See Eder to Weizmann, 2.7 and 13.7.1919, Z4/16044; Weizmann to Balfour, 23.7.1919, *LPCW* IX, 188; Jabotinsky to Scott, 7.10.1919, Z4/2333/I; *PRE XII ZC*, p. 52.
40. Statement to Brandeis, 14.7.1919, L4/65/V.

Chapter 3

1. On the 'southern Syria' campaign at this time, see Porath, *Emergence,* pp. 93f.
2. Despatch to Curzon, 26.9.1919, reproduced in his *Middle East Diary, 1917–1956*, p. 52.
3. Ussishkin, note of 'Visit to the Head of the Town Council of Jerusalem' 8.10.1919, CZA, Z4/1392/I-B. For similar Arab views at this time, see: 'Memorandum of Interview with Emir Faisal', 19.10.1919, *loc. cit.* (re: Auni Abd al-Hadi).
4. VZ meeting, 22.10.1919, J1/8782. Dr Weizmann's reply went on: 'We have only demanded conditions which would make a Jewish state possible *in the future*. It is a question of tactics.'
5. Weizmann to ZE (tgm.), 3.11.1919, *LPCW* IX, 235; cf. Weizmann to Samuel, 22.11.1919, *ibid.*, pp. 256f.; Porath, *Emergence*, p. 95.
6. Weizmann to Samuel, 22.11.1919 (n. 5); cf. Gilner, *War and Hope*, pp. 335f.; Katznelson, *Igrot* I, 77. The following section is based on *STH* I/2, chs. 31–2 and Ben-Gurion, *Zikhronot* I, ch. 16. Quotations are from these sources unless otherwise indicated.
7. The Anglo-French agreement of 13 September 1919, for the replacement of British by French forces in defined areas. See Jukka Nevakivi, *Britain, France and the Arab Middle East*, pp. 190f., 265f.
8. Katznelson, 'A Stand', [26.]2.1920, *Writings* I, 201.
9. Settlers' decisions reproduced in *STH* I/2, 905, 907. The following account of the VZ meeting is taken from CZA, J1/8785/I. Cf. extracts in *STH* I/2, 575f. and Ben-Gurion, *Zikhronot* I, 129f.
10. For more on Jabotinsky's views on this question, see his *Neumim*, pp. 148f. and his articles in *ha'Aretz*, 22.1. and 20.2.1920; also Schechtman, *Rebel and Statesman*, pp. 313f. The quotation earlier in the paragraph is from Y. Aharonovitch, who was supported by Tabenkin and Ben-Gurion.
11. Ussishkin to Chief of Staff, OETA(S), HQ, 15.2.1920, and EEF to War Office, 17.2.1920, in ISA 2/45. Cf. *STH* 1/2, 528f.
12. *Mirat ash-Sharq*, [23.]?2.1920, Eng. translation in CZA, Z4/1366.

13. M. Nurock to Polit. Dept., ZO, 29.2.1920, *loc. cit.*; *Suriyya al-Junubiyya*, 24 and 26.2.1920, translated extracts in Z4/16078; Report of the Court of Inquiry ... regarding the Riots in Jerusalem, 1.7.1920, PRO, FO 371/5121, file E9379/85/44 (cited hereafter as *Palin Report*), para. 49; Eder to Weizmann, 14.3.1920, CZA, Z4/16033; Porath, *Emergence*, pp. 34, 96.

14. Medzini, *'Esser Shanim*, pp. 76, 116; VZE meetings, 28 and 30.3.1920, CZA, J1/8791; *STH*, I/2, 558, 560; Gilner, *War and Hope*, pp. 322f.

15. Y. Meyuhas to M. Ussishkin, 25.2.1920, Z4/1366 (Heb.).

16. *Zionist Review*, Apr. 1920, p. 197; Nurock report, 29.2.1920 (n. 13); Eder to Weizmann, 29.2. (Z4/25085) and 14.3.1920 (Z4/16033); Gilner, *War and Hope*, pp. 347f.

17. Zionist Intelligence report, 7.3.1920, in *STH* I/2, 778; cf. *ibid.*, pp. 586, 605; Gilner, *op. cit.*, p. 348.

18. For details, see: *STH* I/2, 604, 607; Haifa MCA proclamation, 29.1.1920, ISA 2/140; Assaf, *Yihasim*, p. 86; Ben-Gurion, *Zikhronot* I, 137.

19. *Palin Report*, para. 49; Haifa Jewish Community deputation interview with Acting MG, 8.3.1920, ISA 2/30; *STH* I/2, 606; Medzini, *'Esser Shanim*, p. 116.

20. Meyuhas to Ussishkin, 25.2.1920 (n. 15); Nurock report, 29.2.1920 (n. 13); Felman report, 'Situation à Damas' [March 1920], CZA, Z4/16078 (Fr.).

21. Text as given in Sati al-Husri, *The Day of Maysalun*, p. 136.

22. *Palin Report*, para. 49. For other descriptions, see: Porath, *Emergence*, pp. 96f.; Medzini, *'Esser Shanim*, p. 113; Ben-Gurion, *Zikhronot* I, 138.

23. D. Yellin to Storrs, 10.3.1920, ISA 2/140; Haifa Jewish Community to Stanton, 10.3.1920, ISA 2/30; *Palin Report*, para. 49; Storrs' announcement, 11.3.1920, quoted in *Palestine Weekly*, 19.3.1920; Medzini, *'Esser Shanim*, p. 114.

24. 'Arab Movement in Palestine', 19.3.1920, CZA, Z4/16078; cf. *Palin Report*, para. 33.

25. Jabotinsky to Weizmann, 12.3.1920, in *STH* I/2, 913.

26. See Schechtman, *Rebel and Statesman*, ch. 16; *STH* I/2, 627, 660f.; Gilner, *War and Hope*, pp. 346f., 352f.; Ben-Zvi, *Hebrew Battalions*, p. 241.

27. VZE meetings, 11.3. and 17.3.1920, CZA, J1/140. The following section is based on these two meetings.

28. Text of the proclamation in *Sefer ha-Te'udot*, pp. 15f.; cf. *Zionist Bulletin*, 14.4.1920, p. 3, and *The Times*, 14.4.1920, p. 15.

29. Weizmann to ZE, 25.3.1920, *LPCW* IX, 326f.; minutes of meeting, 25.3.1920, CZA, Z4/25085; Weizmann report to VZE meeting, 28.3.1920, J1/8823; Weizmann to ZE (tgm.), 3.4.1920, Z4/1219; Weizmann, *Trial and Error*, p. 322.

30. E.g., Jabotinsky to Weizmann, 12.3.1920 (n. 25); Schechtman, *Rebel and Statesman*, pp. 321f.; Aharonovitch, at VZE meeting, 28.3.1920, J1/8823.

31. *Palin Report*, paras. 26, 44, 60; Gilner, *War and Hope*, pp. 348f., 352; *STH* I/2, 608, 627f. The following pages are based on Palin, Gilner, *STH*, Medzini and VZE debates. Quotations are from the *Palin Report*, unless otherwise indicated.

32. Storrs to Representatives of the Jewish Self-Defence League, 31.3.1920, as reported in 'The Anti-Jewish Riots in Jerusalem', CZA, Z4/16078.

33. Felman to Weizmann, 23.4.1920, CZA, Z4/16078; VZE meeting, 12.4.1920, J1/8799; *Palin Report*, para. 68.

34. Ben-Zvi, 5.4.1920, in *Writings* I, 185f. and *Hebrew Battalions*, p. 242. Cf. Ben-Gurion, *Zikhronot* I, 137f.; Weizmann and Yellin to Prime Minister, 12.4.1920, PRO, FO 371/5117, file E3259/85/44.

35. ZC to ZO (London), tgm. via Beirut, 10.4.1920, CZA, Z4/25085.

36. Jabotinsky to Weizmann, 28.11.1918, Z4/538.

37. VZ meeting, 6.4.1920, J1/8823. Storrs was also singled out. See: *STH* I/2, 612, 620, 784, 786 and cf. pp. 119f., below.

38. Gilner, *War and Hope*, pp. 357, 360; *STH* I/2, 610f., 613, 633, 635.

39. See, *inter alia*: Ben-Gurion, *Zikhronot* I, 139f. and 142f.; Weizmann and Yellin to PM, 12.4.1920 (n.34); Jerusalem Jews' Report on The Riots, CZA, Z4/1212/II; *Zionist Bulletin*, 14.4.1920, p. 1.

40. Petitions in PRO, FO 371/5120, file E6203/85/44; cf. *Sefer ha-Te'udot*, p. 17; Ben-Gurion, *op. cit.*, pp. 138f.

41. For details, see: Z4/1212/II; Stein memo to Polit. Ctee., ZO, 11.6.1920, Z4/1449; Stein to MacIndee (WO), 2.6.1920, *loc. cit.*; Stein to Ussishkin, 21.6.1920, Z4/25120; *Sefer ha-Te'udot*, pp. 19–29.

42. Proceedings of the trials are in Z4/1213 and in Jabotinsky, *Neumim*, pp. 152–77. Cf. Gilner, *War and Hope*, ch. 38.

43. Bols to GHQ, 21.4.1920, PRO, FO 371/5119, file E5237/85/44. Cf. Medzini, *'Esser Shanim*, pp. 117f. and W. F. Boustany, *The Palestine Mandate: Invalid and Impracticable*, p. 136.

44. Stein to Ussishkin, 20.5.1920, CZA, Z4/1219; *STH* I/2, 608, 665; Medzini, *op. cit.*, pp. 115f.

45. *PRE XII ZC*, Cf. *Palin Report*, p. 55, para. 60; Landman to Under-Secretary of State, FO. 16.4.1920, PRO, FO 371/5117, file E3360/85/44.

46. For details, see: *STH* I/2, 636f., 641, 655, 662f., 667f.; Ben-Gurion, *Zikhronot* I, 148; *Ben-Gurion Looks Back*, p. 55; Allon, *Shield of David*, p. 70.

47. ZE (London) to ZC, 19.4.1920, CZA, Z4/25083; VZ to Allenby, 12.6.1920, PRO, FO 371/5120, file E7221/85/44 (Heb. in *Sefer ha-Te'udot*, p. 29); Eder-Samuel interviews, 2.7. and 26.7.1920, CZA, L3/222.

48. See petitions in ISA 2/30; 'Confidential Statement', n.d., CZA, Z4/25083; *Zionist Bulletin*, 21.4. (p. 4), 2.6. (p. 3) and 6.8.1920 (p. 3); 'The General Situation', 7.4.1920, Z4/16084; *STH* I/2, 665.

49. The following account is based on the minutes of two meetings, a plan for a 'Society of Friends' (Muslim–Jewish), and an unpublished draft of G. Frumkin's memoirs in CZA, A199/45 (Heb.). Members of the

committee were Kalvaryski, Meyuhas, Frumkin, Thon, Hankin, Shabtai Levi, Dizengoff, Eisenberg and Meirovitch. Cf. Frumkin, *Derekh Shofet*, pp. 220f. and Cohen, *Israel and the Arab World*, pp. 159f. It would seem that the references in these two works to the operations of the committee in 1919 are mistaken.

50. The lands belonging to Omar al-Baitar were mentioned in this connection. Other proposals included the collection of pro-Zionist petitions; the employment of Hadassa doctors in the Lydda-Ramle region for the benefit of Arabs; and a loan fund for the use of Arab farmers.

51. 12.4.1920, J1/8799.

52. Frumkin, *Derekh Shofet*, pp. 222f.

53. ISA 2/141. Cf. Stein, *Balfour Declaration*, pp. 662f.

54. Eder to Weizmann, 27.5.1920, CZA, Z4/16033. For more details, see: same to same, 14.5., 9.6. and 21.6.1920, *loc. cit.*; Blumenfeld to Thon, 16.6.1920, J1/228; *STH* I/2, 599, 667; Ben-Gurion, *Zikhronot* I, 141.

55. Eder to Weizmann, 5.5.1920, Z4/16033. Cf. Gilner, *War and Hope*, p. 383; *ESCO* I, 259.

56. For details, see: Eder telegrams to ZE (London), 4.6. and 9.6.1920, Z4/1446; Gilner, *op. cit.*, pp. 390f.

57. Borochov, Schiller and Chelouche to Thon, 17.6.1920, J1/8812; Gilner, *op. cit.*, pp. 392f.

58. Weizmann to Eder, 8.6.1920, *LPCW* IX, 355.

59. Eder to Weizmann, 28.6.1920, Z4/16033. Cf. Landman report on visit to Palestine [Aug. 1920], PRO, FO 371/5122, file E11006/85/44.

Chapter 4

1. Hemda Ben-Yehuda, *Nosseh ha-Degel* ['The Standard-Bearer'], pp. 192f.; Samuel, *Memoirs*, pp. 168 and 176; I. Ben-Avi, *'Im Shahar 'Atzma'utenu* ['With the Dawning of Our Independence'], pp. 373f.; Ben-Gurion, *Zikhronot* I, 144f.; Frumkin, *Derekh Shofet*, pp. 233f.; Ruppin, *Memoirs*, p. 186; N. & H. Bentwich, *Mandate Memories*, pp. 59–62.

2. *Zionist Bulletin*, 6.8.1920, p. 1.

3. Creedy to Under-Secretary of State, FO, 14.8.1920, PRO, FO 371/5121, file E9379/85/44; Jabotinsky to ZE (London), 10.7.1920, CZA, Z4/1213; Jabotinsky *et al.*, petition to Samuel, n.d., PRO, FO 371/5122, file E10893/85/44; Ben-Gurion, *Zikhronot* I, 179; Katznelson, *Writings* I, 283.

4. *Zionist Bulletin*, 21.7.1920, p. 5; Jerusalem speech, in *Neumim*, p. 178; *ESCO* I, 260; VZ speech, quoted below, page 94; interview in *The Times*, 2.9.1920, p. 9. For Jabotinsky's less optimistic *private* views, see: Gilner, *War and Hope*, p. 383; his tgm. to ZE, 10.7.1920 (n. 3).

5. Thon speech, VLE meeting, 24.11.1920, CZA, J1/139; Landman report on visit to Palestine, [August 1920], PRO, FO 371/5122, file E11006/85/44; Stein to Lattes, 31.8.1920, CZA, L3/278.

6. See Porath, *Emergence*, pp. 103f.; Jabotinsky, *Neumim*, p. 188.

7. E.g., Jabotinsky interview, *The Times*, 2.9.1920, p. 9; Landman report
(n. 5) and interview with Scott, 3.8.1920, CZA, Z4/25004; Eder to
Weizmann, 21.7.1920, L3/289; Thon speech, 24.11.1920 (n. 5).

8. For details, see: *Zionist Review*, Aug. 1920, p. 69; *Zionist Bulletin*,
13.8. (p. 6), 17.9. (p. 3) and 15.10.1920 (p. 1); *The Times*, 29.12.1920,
p. 7; Assaf, *Yihasim*, p. 88; Ussishkin-Samuel interview, 15.11.1920,
CZA, L3/222; Sokolow to Weizmann, 25.2.1921, Z4/16055.

9. L. Stein, 'Situation in Palestine, August 1921', PRO, CO 733/16/
52260, para. 14; *STH* II/1, 55; *ESCO* I, 260; Porath, *Emergence*, p.
104. Cf. Bentwich, *Mandate Memories*, pp. 70–72.

10. *Igrot* I, 173 (30.11.1920).

11. *STH* II/1, 15, 57; Bein, *op. cit.*, pp. 241f.; *PRE XII ZC*, p. 56; Katznelson, *Igrot* I, 160, 169, 173, 175.

12. *ESCO* I, 262f.; Ben-Gurion, *Zikhronot* I, 145f.; Bowle, *Viscount
Samuel*, pp. 199f.; Samuel, *Memoirs*, p. 156.

13. Deedes to Weizmann, 7.11.1920, CZA, Z4/16073. Cf. Samuel,
Memoirs, pp. 151, 156, 167.

14. Ussishkin-Samuel interviews, 20.9., 19.10., 15.11. and 24.11.1920,
L3/222.

15. See n.10, above.

16. For details, see: Sacher to Weizmann, 25.10.1920, Z4/16151; Medzini,
'Esser Shanim, pp. 152, 154, 166, 174; Quigley to Deedes, 4.11.1920,
Luke to Deedes, 13.12.1920, and Brunton to GSI (HQ), 28.2.1921 –
all in ISA 2/163; VL meeting, 28.12.1920, CZA, J1/7224; ZO Polit.
Ctee. meeting, 10.3.1921, ISA 2/143; *STH* II/3, 1265; below, pages
169f.

17. Haifa Congress memorandum to Mr Churchill, 28.3.1921, enclosed in
Polit. Rpt. for March 1921, PRO, CO 733/2/21698, reproduced in
Klieman, *Foundations of British Policy*, pp. 259–67. Cf. pages 80f.,
below.

18. Weizmann report, VL meeting, 28.12.1920, CZA, J1/7224.

19. Porath, *Emergence*, pp. 108f., *ESCO* I, 283f., 474f.; Medzini, *'Esser
Shanim*, p. 154.

20. For details, see: Sokolow to Weizmann, 25.2.1921, Z4/16055; VLE –
HC interview, 24.1.1921, J1/138; VL memorandum, 7.2.1921, J1/
6282; *STH* II/1, 61; Muslim-Christian anti-immigration meeting,
Beisan, 18.2.1921, cited in Brunton report, 28.2.1921 (n. 16).

21. Samuel to Curzon, 19.12.1920, and Samuel to Baron Edmond de
Rothschild, 31.12.1920, both in ISA 100/7.

22. VLE meeting, 7.12.1920, CZA, J1/139; cf. Ruppin, *Memoirs*, p. 189.

23. S. Tolkowsky, H. M. Kalvaryski and M. Dizengoff to ZE (London),
4.3.1921, Z4/1366. This account is based on this letter and on the
following: Tolkowsky to Inner Executive, 7.7.1921, *loc. cit.*; Tolkowsky memorandum, Aug. 1921, discussed below, pages 103f.; Kalvaryski memorandum, 10.10.1923, WA (Fr.).

24. VL meeting, 16.5.1921, J1/7224.

25. For details, see: Ruppin to ZE, 11.3.1921, Z4/1366 (Ger.); Eder to
ZE, 22.4.1921, L3/222.

26. Meyuhas to Weizmann, 17.1.1921, CZA, Z4/16151 (Heb.); cf. *ha-'Olam*, 17.2.1921, pp. 6–9.
27. *STH* II/1, 72f. and II/3, 1263f. In the text, *'hagana'* will be used to denote the idea or concept of self-defence, while *'Hagana'* will denote the organisation which was later to become the Israel Defence Forces.
28. *Ibid.*, 66f., 95; Allon, *Shield of David*, p. 63.
29. Meeting, 27.7.1920, J1/8799; cf. *Neumim*, pp. 183–8.
30. *Hevion 'Oz* I, 205; cf. *STH* II/3, 1263f.
31. Cf. M. Breslavski, *Tnu'at ha-Po'alim ha-Eretzyisraelit* [The Palestinian Labor Movement] I, 199f.; Bein, *Return to the Soil*, pp. 258f.
32. See, e.g., *STH* II/1, 67 and II/3, 1265.
33. Quoted in *STH* II/3, 1265f.; cf. *ibid.*, 1269.
34. Letters of appointment addressed to Jabotinsky, B. Yaffe and Ben-Gurion, 2.6.1920, J1/8812; cf. VZ meeting, 25.5.1920, J1/8786.
35. Golomb, *Hevion 'Oz* I, 200f.; Ben-Gurion, *Zikhronot* I, 144, 148; Haifa mass meeting, 9.6.1920, resolutions transmitted in Kaiserman to ZE (tgm.), 20.6.1920, Z4/1446.
36. 'Memorandum on the proposals of the ZO Relating to the Defence of Palestine', [April 1921], in PRO, CO 733/17B/17879. Cf. Jabotinsky to Deedes, 22.10.1920, CZA, J1/72 (Eng.).
37. *The Times*, 2.9.1920, p. 9; 'Memorandum' (n. 36).
38. VZ speech, 27.7.1920, CZA, J1/8799. Cf. Schechtman, *Rebel and Statesman*, p. 377; *STH* II/1, 59.
39. War Office to EEF, 7.10.1920, ISA 2/45; *STH* II/1, 58f. and II/3,1100; *PRE XII ZC*, p. 56; undated memorandum in CZA, Z4/25044, referring to Ruppin-Deedes interview, 16.11.1920.
40. Allenby to WO (tgm.) 6.6.1919, *DBFP* I/IV, 300. Cf. Klieman, *Foundations of British Policy*, p. 118.
41. For details, see: VL to Samuel, 10.4.1921, in *Sefer ha-Te'udot*, pp. 52f.; Gilner, *War and Hope*, p. 399; *STH* II/1, 59 and II/3, 1266; Klieman, *Foundations of British Policy*, pp. 118, 173; Eliash to Weizmann, 28.4.1921, CZA, Z4/16151 (Heb.).
42. Golomb, in *STH* II/1, 73 and II/3, 1266.
43. This section is based largely on the Political Report for March 1921 (n. 17, above); Medzini, *'Esser Shanim*, pp. 170f.; *Zionist Review*, May 1921, pp. 4f.; Klieman, *op. cit.*, pp. 127f.
44. Polit. Rpt. (n. 17); D. Hoz to VL 1.4.1921, CZA, J1/300; Haifa Jewish Community Ctee. to Symes, 1.4.1921, *loc. cit.*; *STH* II/1, 63. In addition to the two deaths, ten Jews, one Christian and five policemen were injured.
45. ZO Polit. Ctee. meeting, 1.3.1921, ISA 2/143. The ZE sent Nahum Sokolow to Palestine to work for the success of Churchill's visit.
46. VLE secret circular, [5.4.1921?], CZA, J1/138; *Zionist Review* (n. 43).
47. Joint VLE–ZC meeting, 23.3.1921, J1/6282.
48. Petition, dated 29.3.1921, enclosed in Polit. Rpt. (n. 17); cf. Polit. Rpt. for May 1921 (Samuel to Churchill, 6.6.1921), PRO, CO 733/3/30264; Assaf, *Hit'orirut ha-'Aravim be-Eretz-Israel u-Vrihatam* [The Arab Awakening in Palestine, and their Flight Therefrom], p. 89.

49. See n. 17, above.
50. Following the Hebrew version in *Sefer ha-Te'udot*, pp. 47f.; government translation enclosed in Polit. Rpt. (n. 17), and full text reproduced in Klieman, *Foundations of British Policy*, pp. 275f.
51. Quoted in *Zionist Review* (n. 43); cf. Churchill speech quoted in Klieman, *op. cit.*, pp. 283f. and *ibid.*, p. 136.
52. Churchill reply to AE memorandum, 29.3.1921, enclosed in Polit. Rpt. (n. 17); full text reproduced in Klieman, *op. cit.*, pp. 269–73.
53. Churchill reply to VL memorandum, 29.3.1921, enclosed in Polit Rpt. (n. 17); full text reproduced in Klieman, *op. cit.*, pp. 279f. ('The fact that Palestine shall contain a National Home for the Jews does not mean that it will cease to be the National Home of other people, or that a Jewish government will be set up to dominate the Arab people.')
54. E. M. Epstein, *Zionist Review* (n. 43).
55. Minutes of meeting, 1.4.1921, CZA, J1/138.
56. Eder to ZE, 22.4.1921 (n. 25, above).

Chapter 5

1. Sprinzak, *Igrot* I, p. 216; Sprinzak and Radler-Feldman speeches, VL meeting, 16.5.1921, CZA, J1/7224; *Ha'aretz*, 4.4, 7.4 and 8.4.1921, following the Arabic press (cuttings in J1/300); Klieman, *Foundations of British Policy*, pp. 177f.; Porath, *Emergence*, pp. 128f.; Assaf, *Hit'orirut*, p. 98; Polit. Rpt. for April 1921, PRO, CO 733/3/24596.
2. D. Hoz, to VL, 1.4.1921, CZA, J1/300; cf. *STH* II/1, 63.
3. On the unexpectedness of the riots, see: VL meeting, 3.5.1921, CZA, J1/7224; *Palestine: Disturbances in May 1921*, Cmd. 1540 [cited hereafter as *Haycraft Report*], p. 47; Sprinzak, *op. cit.*, 214; Golomb, *Hevion 'Oz* I, 210f.; *STH* II/1, 95, 105.

  The following description of the riots is based on the *Haycraft Report*, pp. 7–16, 22–32, 35f.; *STH* II/1, 79–91, 107f.; and numerous situation reports in CZA, J1/300.
4. Minutes in ISA 2/144.
5. For accounts of this meeting, see: *STH* II/1, 83; Y. E. Chelouche, *Parshat Hayay* [Autobiography], pp. 382f.
6. E.g., VL meetings of 3.5 and 16.5.1921, CZA, J1/7224; Ben-Zvi, at Government's Advisory Council meeting, 3.5.1921, PRO, CO 733/3/24594; Ben-Zvi-HC interview, 5.5.1921, CZA, J1/138; Ben-Zvi to HC [letter of resignation from Advisory Council], 11.5.1921, in *Sefer ha-Te'udot*, pp. 58f.
7. 7.5.1921, J1/138. On the immigration question generally, see Moshe Mossek, *Palestine Immigration Policy Under Sir Herbert Samuel*, ch. 3.
8. Blumenfeld, quoted in *STH* II/1, 92. Cf. VLE meetings, 8 and 9.5.1921, J1/139; VLE interviews with the HC (5.5) and the CS (7.5.1921), in J1/138; Katznelson, *Writings* I, 273.
9. Katznelson, *Igrot* I, 246; Blumenfeld, at VL meeting, 16.5.1921, CZA, J1/7224.

10. VL, 'Statement' to HC (private), 8.6.1921, Eng. text in J1/7224. Cf. *Sefer ha-Te'udot*, pp. 63f., 66f.; VLE meetings, 21.5 (J1/139), 22.5 (J1/138) and 31.5.1921 (J1/300); Mibashan to VLE, 29.5.1921, J1/300; Golomb, *Hevion 'Oz* I, 215; Katznelson, *Igrot* I, 235f.

11. The following discussion of, and extracts from, Samuel's policy statement are based on the text forwarded to Churchill, 6.6.1921, PRO, CO 733/3/30263.

12. Eder to ZE, 4.6.1921, CZA, Z4/16151. Cf. Storrs, *Orientations*, p. 383; Bentwich, *Mandate Memories*, p. 81; Stein, 'Situation in Palestine, August 1921', para. 23; VL to ZE, 3.6.1921, CZA, Z4/16151; *Sefer ha-Te'udot*, p. 63.

13. *Memoirs*, p. 192.

14. Weizmann to Churchill, [July 1921, draft not sent], quoted in R. Crossman, *A Nation Reborn*, p. 127. Cf. VL 'Statement' (n. 10); Golomb, *Hevion 'Oz* I, 314.

15. *Zionist Review*, Aug. 1921, p. 69. Cf. *Sefer ha-Te'udot*, pp. 66f.

16. VL 'Statement' (n. 10). Cf. Eder to ZE, 4.6.1921 (n. 12); Katznelson, *Writings* I, 274; Crossman, *Nation Reborn*, pp. 127f.; Medzini, *'Esser Shanim*, pp. 189f.

17. *Hevion'Oz* I, 314.

18. VL to HC, 27.6.1921, CZA, J1/6282.

19. Sokolow, at VL meeting, 16.5.1921, J1/7224. Cf. *Report* of the XIIth Zionist Congress (1921), pp. 44, 65; Katznelson, *Writings* I, 273f.; Sprinzak, *Igrot* I, 214; *Sefer ha-Te'udot*, pp. 58, 61; Weizmann, *Trial and Error*, p. 343.

20. *STH* II/1, 81.

21. Golomb, *Hevion'Oz* I, 218; Katznelson, *op. cit.*, p. 275.

22. On this aspect, see Caplan, 'The Yishuv, Sir Herbert Samuel and the Arab Question'.

23. Dr Y. Levy, VLE meeting, 9.5.1921, CZA, J1/139; *Sefer ha-Te'udot*, p. 59; Golomb, *Hevion'Oz* I, 219, 313; Katznelson and Tabenkin speeches, VL meeting, 16.5.1921, J1/7224; joint VLE-ZC meeting, 23.3.1921, J1/6282.

24. For details, see: VLE meetings, 8.5 and 9.5.1921, J1/139; VL meetings, 16.5 and 6.6.1921, J1/7224; Eder to Cowen, 9.5.1921, Z4/16151; Golomb, *op. cit.*, pp. 216f.; Ruppin, *Memoirs*, p. 192; Samuel to Churchill, 12.5.1921 (tgm.), PRO, CO 733/3/23678. There is no evidence to support the claim in *ESCO* (I, 274) that any mass resignations in fact occurred.

25. For details, see: *Sefer ha-Te'udot*, pp. 57f. and 66f.; joint VLE-*Ahdut ha-'Avoda* meeting, 13.6.1921, CZA, J1/138; Eder to ZE, 13.6.1921, Z4/16151; VL meetings, 6.6 and 29.6.1921, J1/7224. On June 4th, Eder had also submitted his resignation, but was prevailed upon to withdraw it.

26. *Sefer ha-Te'udot*, pp. 54f.

27. *Haycraft Report*, p. 43. Cf. *Ahdut ha-'Avoda*, 'Memorandum ... on the Events in Jaffa ...', 26.5.1921, in *Palestine and Jewish Labour: Two Documents*; *ESCO* I, 273f.

28. *Haycraft Report*, p. 44. Cf. P. Graves, *Palestine: Land of Three Faiths*, pp. 102f., 173.
29. Yellin, VL meeting, 3.5.1921, J1/7224, and VLE meeting, 5.5.1921, J1/138; Ben-Zvi, at same meetings; Ruppin, *Memoirs*, p. 190; H. Arlosoroff, *Writings* I, 9.
30. E.g., Dr Y. Epstein, in *ha-Shiloah* (XVII), 1907, 196. Cf. Cohen, *Israel and the Arab World*, pp. 58f., 67f.; Laqueur, *History of Zionism*, pp. 215f.
31. 16.5.1921, J1/7224.
32. *Writings* I, 5–9.
33. *Hevion'Oz* I, 218 (letter dated 7.6.1921).
34. VL meeting, 16.5.1921, J1/7224. Cf. page 75, above.
35. Eisenberg, Schiller and Tabenkin speeches, *loc. cit.* Cf. Sokolow, VLE meeting, 8.5.1921, J1/139; *Zionist Review*, June 1921, pp. 26f. Sokolow also warned of the *tactical* danger of the Jews weakening their own arguments by admitting publicly that there existed an Arab national movement. VL meeting, 16.5.1921, J1/7224.
36. Sokolow, Meirovitch, Radler-Feldman and Kalvaryski speeches, *loc. cit.*
37. 'Situation in Palestine', para. 28.
38. For examples of local contacts, see: Y. Danin and Sufrasky (Jaffa) to VL, 15.5.1921, J1/78; Glickin (Migdal) to VL, 31.5, 21.6 and 8.7.1921, J1/300; Meirovitch (Rishon-le-Zion) to VLE, 14.6.1921, *loc. cit.*
39. ZC meeting, 11.5.1921, Z4/2701/V; Finance and Budget Commission, ZE London, meeting, 2.6.1921, Z4/16055. At the subsequent Zionist Congress in September 1921, a sum of £25,000 was budgeted for 'Special Expenses'. See *Report*, p. 140.
40. ZE meeting, 29.3.1921, ISA 2/143; H. Franck to Weizmann, 17.8.1921, CZA, Z4/1250 (Fr.).
41. Kalvaryski to Eder, 14.8.1921, Z4/16151 (Fr.). Cf. Porath, *Emergence*, pp. 215f.
42. Kalvaryski to Eder, 27.11.1921, CZA, Z4/2701/V (Fr.); cf. pages 121 and 128f., below. The MNA is also referred to as the 'National Islamic Society' and the 'National Muslim Society' in contemporary British and Zionist sources.
43. Weizmann to Stein, 21.7.1921, WA.
44. 'Situation in Palestine'. The following section is based on this report, paras. 10, 11, 28, and Conclusions, part C.
45. On Weizmann's views, see Caplan, 'Arab-Jewish Contacts in Palestine' p. 640; Weizmann to Samuel, 22.11.1919, *LPCW* IX, 257. Cf. Tiversky's comment at the VL meeting of 2.1.1923: 'Weizmann has always said that the representatives of the Arabs can be bribed and that we can acquire them with money.' CZA, J1/7226.
46. Castel to Weizmann, 16.8.1921, 'Re: The Solution of the Arab Question in Palestine: A Proposal', Eng. translation from the Heb., WA. A Hebrew version, dated 23.8.1921, is in CZA, Z4/1250.
47. Cf. his article in *ha-Aretz*, 25.7.1923. For the history of this idea in

later years, see Hattis, *The Bi-National Idea*.

48. Another individual who was advocating an equally non-conformist solution in those days was Ittamar Ben-Avi. On his cantonization proposals, see his *'Im Shahar 'Atzma'utenu*, pp. 414f. and Hattis, *op. cit.*, pp. 33, 89, 116f.

49. Tolkowsky to Weizmann, 24.8.1921, WA (apparently incomplete; pp. 1–6).

50. Dizengoff, Meirovitch, Schiller and Eisenberg remarks, VL meeting, 16.5.1921, CZA, J1/7224; Rutenberg emergency budget proposal, VLE meeting, 20.5.1921, J1/139; Aharonovitch to Thon, 27.5.1921, J1/300; Golomb, *Hevion 'Oz* I, 313.

51. For more detail on this aspect, see Caplan, 'The Yishuv, Sir Herbert Samuel and the Arab Question'.

52. VL delegation interview with HC, 10.6.1921, J1/138.

53. Golomb account of interview with HC, 5.6.1921, *Hevion'Oz* I, 217.

54. Ben-Zvi, during interview of 10.6.1921 (n. 52).

55. Compare, e.g., the VL definition given on page 91 with Dr Thon's statement to Justice Brandeis, quoted on page 46, above.

56. Stein, 'Situation in Palestine', para. 10. Cf. Tabenkin's remarks, VL meeting, 16.5.1921, CZA, J1/7224, and Ro'i, 'Zionist Attitude', pp. 211f.

Chapter 6

1. See, e.g.: *STH* II/1, 120; VLE meetings, 8.5, 19.5, 20.5, 21.5 and 23.5.1921, CZA, J1/139; Katznelson, *Igrot* I, 237; Stein, 'Situation in Palestine, August 1921', paras. 25, 26.

2. *STH* II/1, 119f.

3. See his *Igrot* I, 72, and 'Conversation concerning the creation of a new Hebrew Battalion in Palestine', 18.9.1919, Z4/2333/I; *STH* I/2, 530, 768.

4. VL meeting, 16.5.1921, J1/7224. Cf. *STH* II/1, 58, 157.

5. *STH* II/1, 105f., 110f., 119f. and II/3, 1269; Golomb, *Hevion'Oz* I, 211.

6. Golomb, *op. cit.*, p. 220; also *ibid.*, pp. 212, 215; Sprinzak, *Igrot* I, 216, 219; Stein, 'Situation in Palestine', para. 26.

7. *Sefer ha-Te'udot*, pp. 68f.; cf. *Haycraft Report*, pp. 17, 36; Golomb, *op. cit.*, p. 221; Eder to ZE, 13.6.1921, CZA, Z4/16151.

8. *Hevion'Oz* I, 213, 215, 220, 295f.; *STH* II/1, 122.

9. Golomb, *op. cit.*, pp. 215f., 229, 295f.; *STH* I/2, 664 and II/1, 75, 110, 128f.; Allon, *Shield of David*, pp. 72f.

10. Jabotinsky to Churchill, 8.5.1921, PRO, CO 733/17A/24068; same to VLE, 11.5.1921, CZA, J1/300; *The Times*, 14.5.1921, p. 6; Golomb, *Hevion'Oz* I, 314.

11. ZE to Samuel (tgm.), 6.5.1921, ISA 2/144; cf. Schechtman, *Rebel and Statesman*, p. 377.

12. For details, see: Samuel to Churchill, 12.5.1921 (tgm.), PRO, CO 733/3/23802; Eder to ZE, 22.5.1921, CZA, Z4/16151; *STH* II/1, 202f.; interviews with Deedes, 1.8 and 5.9.1921, L3/222; Deedes to Young, 11.7.1921, PRO, CO 537/848; same to same, 2.8.1921, CO 537/849.
13. For details, see: *STH* II/1, 163f., 208f.; D. Duff, *Sword for Hire*, pp. 157f.; Eder to ZE, 13.6.1921, CZA, Z4/16151; H of C Deb. (Vth Ser.), vol. 150, col. 1745 (21.2.1922).
14. Eder to ZE, 4.6.1921, Z4/16151. Cf. Katznelson, *Writings* I, 275; Golomb, *Hevion'Oz* I, 219f., 314; *Sefer ha-Te'udot*, pp. 70f.; *STH* II/1, 202f. and II/3, 1130.
15. 8.5.1921 (n. 10). This was a favourite argument of Jabotinsky. See: *The Times*, 14.5.1921, p. 6; *Story of the Jewish Legion*, pp. 147f., 166f.; Schechtman, *Rebel and Statesman*, p. 272; Medzini, *'Esser Shanim*, pp. 190f.; *STH* I/2, 642, 792f.
16. The following account is based on Jabotinsky, *Neumim*, pp. 191–207 and *STH* II/1, 155f. After the Prague meeting, Jabotinsky continued to press his argument in the strongest terms. See *STH* II/3, 1121, 1277, and his memorandum to the ZE, 5.11.1922, CZA, Z4/1396.
17. See, e.g., Golomb, *Hevion'Oz* I, 301; *STH* II/1, 611f.
18. See, e.g., Eder to ZE, 13.6.1921, Z4/16151; Churchill to Weizmann, 14.12.1921, PRO, CO 733/16/60086.
19. Samuel to Churchill, 8.5 (PRO, CO 733/3/24660), 13.6 (*loc. cit.*, 31760) and 14.10.1921 (CO 733/6/52954); Samuel to Weizmann, 1.7 and 10.8.1921, CZA, Z4/16151; VL-HC interview, 10.6.1921, J1/138; Klieman, *Foundations of British Policy*, pp. 191f.
20. Weizmann memo to Churchill, 'The Situation in Palestine', 21.7.1921, PRO, CO 733/16/38128; meeting at Mr Balfour's house, 22.7.1921, in Meinertzhagen, *Diary*, pp. 105f.; Klieman, *op. cit.*, pp. 188f.; Ben-Gurion, *Igrot* II, 74.
21. Samuel to Weizmann, 17.8.1921, CZA, Z4/16151.
22. *Report*, p. 150. The resolution was quoted in *ESCO* (I, 276f.) as evidence that Zionists were 'doing their utmost to conciliate the Arabs'. Cf. Hattis, *Bi-National Idea*, pp. 29f., n. 13 and 43f., n. 35.
23. See, e.g., Landman to Young, 19.8.1921, PRO, CO 733/16/41952; *ESCO* I, 414–7.
24. *Report*, pp. 15f.; cf. *ESCO* I, 415f.
25. *Sefer ha-Te'udot*, pp. 72f.
26. *Writings* I, 284.
27. *Report*, pp. 149f.
28. Weizmann to ZO of America, 22.10.1921, *LPCW* X, 265. Cf. Eder to Weizmann, 5.10.1921, CZA, Z4/16055; Meinertzhagen minute, 21.10.1921, PRO, CO 733/17B/53308; Weizmann to Under-Secretary of State, CO, 1.12.1921, *LPCW* X, 302f.
29. Jaffa CID report, 6.9.1921, ISA 2/168; Zionist Intelligence reports, enclosed in Weizmann to Shuckburgh, 11.12.1921, PRO, CO 733/17B/61530; Thon-Samuel interview, 14.10.1921, CZA, J1/6282; Porath, *Emergence*, pp. 133f.; *STH* II/1, 133.

30. Thon-Samuel interview (n. 29); Eder to Weizmann, 30.10.1921, Z4/16151.

31. Keith-Roach circular, 19.10.1921, and Samuel to Churchill, 11.11.1921, PRO, CO 733/7/59563.

32. For details, see: Samuel to Churchill, *loc. cit.*; Polit. Rpt. for Nov. 1921, CO 733/8/62765; Deedes to Shuckburgh, 23.12.1921, CO 537/854; Porath, *Emergence*, p. 132, n. 43.

33. Eder to Weizmann, 30.10.1921 (n. 30). Cf. *Palestine Weekly*, 2.12.1921, p. 777; *Zionist Review*, Jan. 1922, p. 142.

34. Eder to Weizmann, 30.10.1921 (n. 30). Cf. Sprinzak, *Igrot* I, 244; Porath, *Emergence*, pp. 133f., n. 53.

35. *STH* II/1, 133, 136.

36. *Ibid.*, pp. 133f.

37. The following account is based on *STH* II/1, 134–8.

38. Polit. Rpt. for Nov. 1921 (n. 32); cf. Porath, *Emergence*, pp. 133f.

39. Eder to Weizmann, 13.11.1921, CZA, Z4/2701/V.

40. See, e.g.: Ruppin, *Memoirs*, p. 194; Ben-Gurion, *Zikhronot* I, 179f.; *STH* II/3, 1272f.; VLE meeting, 20.10.1921, J1/139; VLE-HC interview, 21.10.1921, J1/6282; VL to HC, [3].11.1921 (not sent), J1/75.

41. There are reasons to suspect that the Yishuv's stubborn insistence on the dismissal of Storrs may have been more due to its grudge against him for the 1920 'pogrom' and to its growing self-assertion vis-à-vis London Zionists, who appeared all too ready to patch things up with the British, than to any factor immediately connected with the November 2nd disturbances. For details, see: *Sefer ha-Te'udot*, p. 74; Ben-Zvi, *Writings* I, 195; Ben-Gurion, *op. cit.*, p. 180; VL meeting, 14.11.1921, J1/7225; Storrs, *Orientations*, p. 363; Eder to Weizmann, 13.11.1921 (n. 39); Katznelson, *Writings* I, 374f. and *Igrot* I, 205.

42. *Zikhronot* I, 179f.

43. *STH* II/1, 138f., 162, 164, and II/3, 1272; Golomb, *Hevion'Oz* I, 315; Sprinzak, *Igrot* I, 244; Schiller remarks, VL meeting, 14.11.1921, J1/7225.

44. *Loc. cit.* Quotations in the following sentence are from this source. Cf. Kalvaryski to Eder, 27.11.1921, Z4/2701/V (Fr.).

45. For details, see: *STH* II/1, 107f., 128, 134; *Zionist Review*, Jan. 1922, p. 142; Remez speech, VL meeting, 9.5.1923, J1/7226; *ESCO* I, 561f.; Ben-Gurion, *Igrot* II, 71, 76, 94, 103; Bein, *Return to the Soil*, pp. 346, 349f.

46. *Zionist Review*, Feb. 1922, p. 167; press clippings, 13.1.1922 (ISA 2/145) and 25.3.1922 (CZA, Z4/1392/II-A).

47. Porath, *Emergence*, p. 134.

48. For details, see: Duff, *Sword for Hire*, pp. 111f.; *STH* II/1, 204, 214; Golomb, *Hevion'Oz* I, 254; VLE-CS interview, 1.2.1922, CZA, J1/6282; *Zionist Review*, Apr. 1922, pp. 192f.; Deedes to Young, 15.2.1922, PRO, CO 733/38/9616; Deedes to Weizmann, 17.2 (W.A.) and 30.3.1922 (CZA, Z4/16145); Eder to Stein, 2.4.1922, Z4/2701/V.

49. *STH* II/3, 1272, 1274 and II/1, 128f., 139, 141, 143f.; VL meeting, 14.11.1921, J1/7225; Golomb, *op. cit.*, pp. 248f.

50. *Op. cit.*, p. 242.
51. Deedes to Weizmann, 30.3.1922, CZA, Z4/16145; Eder-CS interview, 22.3.1922, Z4/2701/V; Eder to Stein, 2.4.1922. *loc. cit.*; Eder-HC-CS interviews, 3.4.1922, *loc. cit.*; Ben-Zvi and Yellin remarks, VL meeting, 5.4.1922, J1/7225.
52. VL meeting, 5.4.1922 (n. 51); meeting of Arabs at Dr Eder's house, 2.4.1922, Z4/16056.
53. On the peace initiative involving the Masonic Lodge, Ahmad Zaki Pasha and Zionist Jacques Hoefler, see: ISA, file 2/162; Polit. Rpt. for May 1922, PRO, CO 733/22/29590; Hoefler to Weizmann, 18.4.1922, W.A. (Fr.); *Israël* (Cairo), 22.11.1929, p. 1. On the Syrian nationalist committee, see Caplan, *Futile Diplomacy*, ch. 3.
54. *Zionist Review*, July–Aug. 1922, p. 266; [Girling?] to GSI (HQ), 1.6.1922, ISA 2/164; Polit. Rpt. for May 1922 (n. 53); Ruppin, *Memoirs*, p. 198; Golomb, *Hevion 'Oz* I, 265f.; *The Times*, 11.7.1922, p. 10; *STH* II/1, 149.
55. Polit. Rpt. for May 1922 (n. 53). Cf. Polit. Rpt. for June 1922, CO 733/23/34884; VL to Storrs, 18.4.1922, CZA, J1/75; VL to Luke, 3.5.1922, J1/75; Luke to Yellin, 5.5.1922, J1/75; VL-CS interview, 19.5.1922, J1/6282; VL meeting, 24.5.1922, J1/7225. On the 1928–9 situation, as well as this 1922 prelude, see Porath, *Emergence*, pp. 262f.
56. Porath, *op. cit.*, pp. 263f.; VL–HC interview, 6.10.1922, J1/76.
57. 'The Mandate for Palestine', ZO memorandum to the Council of the League of Nations, July 1922, p. 30. Cf. Weizmann to Eder, 4.7.1922, *LPCW* XI, 132f.; Eder to ZE, 10.7.1922, CZA, Z4/1392/II-A; Eder to Weizmann, 17.7.1922, WA; Eder-CS interview, 18.7.1922, CZA, Z4/1053.
58. VL meeting, 10.7.1922, J1/7225.
59. Eder to Stein, 5.7.1922, Z4/1053; cf. Eder to ZE, 10.7.1922, Z4/1392/II-A; Yellin, VL meeting, 10.7.1922 (n. 58).
60. Eder-Deedes interview, 1.5.1922, Z4/2701/V.
61. Duff, *Sword for Hire*, pp. 111f.; *STH* II/1, 149, 204; Yellin and Ben-Zvi remarks, VL meeting, 10.7.1922 (n. 58).
62. Meyuhas to Eder, 13.7.1922, S25/10295 (Fr.); Eder to Stein, 17.7.1922, Z4/1053; Eder-Deedes interview, 18.7.1922, *loc. cit.*
63. Avissar and Thon remarks, VL meeting, 10.7.1922 (n. 58); VL to HC, 11.7.1922, J1/75 (Eng.).
64. Eng. translation in PRO, CO 733/24/70732.
65. See Porath, *Emergence*, p. 148; *STH* II/1, 149, 204; Eder to Stein, 17.10.1922, Z4/1053.
66. *The Times*, 27.7.1922, p. 9. For the text of the Mandate, see Laqueur, *Israel–Arab Reader*, pp. 54f. Cf. *ESCO* I, 234–40; Ingrams, *Palestine Papers*, ch. 9.
67. For details, see: *STH* II/1, 149 and II/3, 1123f.; Golomb, *Hevion 'Oz* I, 274f.; VL to HC, 27.8.1922, J1/72 (Eng.); Jaffa Jewish Council to HC, 27.8.1922, *loc. cit.*; Zikhron Ya'akov Ctee. to VL, 24.8.1922, J1/78.
68. Interview with Deedes, 22.8.1922, J1/76; VL and Jaffa Jewish Council memoranda to HC, 27.8.1922 (n. 67).

69. See: sources cited in notes 67–8, above; *Doar ha-Yom*, 25.8.1922; Polit. Rpt. for Aug. 1922, PRO, CO 733/25/46820; van Vriesland to Stein, 3.9.1922, CZA, Z4/1053; Ahad ha-Am, *Igrot* VI, 202f.

70. See, e.g., Samuel to Devonshire, 8.12.1922, CO 733/28/62328; *Report of the Exec. to the XIIIth Zionist Congress (1923)*, p. 23; Kisch to Weizmann, 16.11.1923. CZA, Z4/16061; *Peel Report*, pp. 186, 189.

71. VL meeting, 14.11.1921, J1/7225.

Chapter 7

1. 'Proposed Plan for Political Work among the Arabs', Oct. 1922, CZA, J1/289.

2. For details, see: Eder to Kalvaryski, 12.1.1922, S25/10320; van Vriesland to Kisch, 12.7.1923, *loc. cit.*.

3. For details, see: Ben-Avi, *'Im Shahar 'Atzma'utenu*, pp. 416f.; Eder letters to Weizmann, 13.11. (CZA, Z4/2701/V), 27.11. (Z4/16151), 29.11. (Z4/2701/V), 11.12. (WA) and 14.12.1921 (WA).

4. On Weizmann, see: Almaliah remarks, VL meeting, 5.4.1922, CZA, J1/7225; Y. Katz to Weizmann, 8.12.1922, WA (Yiddish). Although Rutenberg's activities are not documented, we may gain an indication of them from the complaints against 'the separatist political activities among the Arabs of the representatives of P. [inhas] R.[utenberg]' by Jewish Agency official Bernard Joseph, 30.1.1939, CZA, S25/43. On the ICA, cf. above, page 99.

5. Eder to Weizmann, 13.11.1921, CZA, Z4/1250.

6. Stein to Kisch, 28.6.1923, S25/10320; Stein memorandum, 'The Kalvaryski Claim', 24.9.1923, S25/1180.

7. Kalvaryski to Polit. Dept., ZE, 2.7.1923, S25/4793 (Heb.).

8. Kisch memorandum, 13.12.1922, S25/518; cf. club budgets in S25/10302.

9. Eder to Weizmann, 29.11.1921 (n. 3). Cf. Stein to Kisch, 17.5.1923, S25/10320.

10. Eder to Weizmann, 29.11.1921 (n. 3). For the case of *Lissan al-Arab*, see: Kalvaryski to Kisch, 16.8.1923, S25/4379 (Fr.); Kisch to Kalvaryski, 31.8.1923, *loc. cit.*; Yellin remarks, VL meeting, 18.6.1924, J1/7227. Except where otherwise indicated, all Kalvaryski letters cited in subsequent notes to this chapter are in French.

11. Samuel to Churchill, 18.11.1921, PRO, CO 733/7/59565. Cf. Porath, *Emergence*, p. 220, and below, pages 143f., for the British attitude.

12. As reported in Zionist Intelligence report, 11.9.1921, CO 733/17B/61530. Cf. Porath, *op. cit.*, p. 68.

13. Samuel to Churchill, 18.11.1921 (n. 11); Eder-Deedes interview, 18.7.1922, CZA, Z4/1053; Porath, *op. cit.*, p. 220.

14. Memorandum, Aug. 1922 (for the Zionist Annual Conference), Z4/4112 (Fr.). Cf. E. Sasson, *Doar ha-Yom*, 13.2.1922, p. 2.
15. Polit. Rpt. for May 1922, PRO, CO 733/22/29590. Cf. Clayton to Devonshire, 24.8.1923, CO 733/48/43839; *Palestine*, 13–20.1.1923, p. 58; *Doar ha-Yom*, 9.3.1923; *Zionist Review*, June 1923, p. 28.
16. MNA telegrams to Churchill and to League of Nations, in CZA, Z4/1053. Other petitions and telegrams may be found in files J1/289, S25/10301, S25/10295 and S25/10321. Cf. Porath, *Emergence*, pp. 218f.
17. Eder to Weizmann, 17.7.1922, WA. Cf. Eder-Deedes interview, 18.7.1922 CZA, Z4/1053.
18. Kisch memo, 13.12.1922, S25/518; Kisch to Weizmann, 23.2.1923, WA; Polit. Rpt. for Feb. 1923, PRO, CO 733/43/14202; Porath, *Emergence*, pp. 219f.; F. H. Kisch, *Palestine Diary*, p. 34.
19. Castel to Jabotinsky, 25.10.1922, CZA, J1/289. On MNA internal problems, see: MNA representatives' meeting with Eder, 24.3.1922, S25/4380; N. Mallul, 'The Work of the Arab Secretariat of the *Va'ad Leumi*', [March 1923], S25/4384 (Heb.).
20. Kalvaryski to Weizmann, 17.2.1923, S25/10320. Cf. Kisch to Weizmann, 16.1. and 7.2.1923, Z4/16049; Weizmann to Wormser, [Feb. 1923] and Wormser to Weizmann, 17.2.1923, *loc. cit.*; Weizmann to Kaplansky, 23.2.1923, S25/10320; van Vriesland to Kaplansky, 19.3.1923, *loc. cit.*
21. Weizmann to Kalvaryski, 6.2.1923, *loc. cit.*
22. Stein to Kisch, 23.2.1923, *loc. cit.*; cf. same to same, 19.4.1923, *loc. cit.* ('He may now and then be useful for certain definite jobs, but generally speaking I regard his judgment as unsound, and his methods are open to serious objection.')
23. Kisch, 'Palestine Political Report: Internal Policy', 31.5.1923, Z4/16061.
24. Kisch to Weizmann, 5.12.1923, Z4/16060. Cf. same to same, 16.11.1923, *loc. cit.*; Kisch, *Diary*, p. 87; Porath, *Emergence*, p. 226.
25. For a more detailed exposition of Kisch's work, see Caplan, 'Arab-Jewish Contacts in Palestine', pp. 644f.
26. A more detailed discussion of Jewish labour activity on the Arab question is given in *ibid.*, pp. 647f.
27. Breslavski, *Tnu'at ha-Po'alim* II, 301; Haim Arlosoroff, *Kitvai Haim Arlosoroff* [Writings] III, 137; E. Sereni & R. E. Ashery, eds., *Jews and Arabs in Palestine*, pp. 11f.; Ben-Gurion, *Anahnu u-Shkhenenu*, pp. 67–71, 76f., 80 (n.); *ESCO* I, 573, 575f., 587–92.
28. Ben-Gurion, *Zikhronot* I, 210 and *Anahnu u-Shkrenenu*, pp. 63–6; Breslavski, *loc. cit.*; Arlosoroff, *op. cit.*, p. 136; *ESCO* I, 587f.
29. E.g., the joint chauffeurs' strike, summer 1924. See Kisch, *Diary*, p. 136; *New Judaea*, 26.9.1924, p. 8; Campbell to CS, Political résumé for period ended 4.7.1924, PRO, CO 733/71/35742. For other activities, see: *ESCO* I, 588–92; Breslavski, *op. cit.*, p. 302; Ben-Gurion, *Anahnu u-Shkhenenu*, pp. 99–109.
30. Wilkansky to Weizmann, 15.8.1922, WA (Heb.). Cf. Kisch to Tol-

kowsky, 26.12.1923, CZA, S25/651.

31. Minutes of meeting in CZA, J1/7225.
32. VLE meeting, 6.4.1922, J1/139.
33. Cf. Tolkowsky memorandum, discussed above, pp. 103f.
34. VL meeting, 14.11.1921, CZA, J1/7225. Cf. Ben-Gurion, *Zikhronot* I, 300.
35. Meyuhas, VL meeting, 5.4.1922 (n. 31). Cf. Mossinsohn, VL meeting, 2.1.1923, J1/7226; Ben-Zvi, VL meeting, 6.11.1923, J1/7227; Cohen, *Israel and the Arab World*, pp. 159–60.
36. Meyuhas, VL meeting, 5.4.1922 (n. 35). Cf. Ben-Gurion, VL meeting, 10.7.1922, J1/7225; Ben-Zvi, VL meetings, 28.11.1922 and 2.1.1923, J1/7226; Ben-Avi, diary entries, 20.10. and 6.11.1922, S25/905 (Heb.); Meyuhas, VL meeting, 18.6.1924, J1/7227.
37. The PZE insisted that Yishuv members sat in an advisory capacity only. See: Yellin, VL meetings, 10.7.1922 (J1/7225) and 2.1.1923 (J1/7226); Yellin, ZE (London) meeting, 20.10.1922, Z4/302/7; Ben-Zvi, VL meetings, 2.1. and 9.5.1923, J1/7226; Yellin to Kisch, 18.2.1924 and Kisch to Yellin, 29.2.1924, J1/78; Yellin, VL meeting, 18.6.1924, J1/7227.
38. VL meeting, 10.7.1922, J1/7225. Also Epstein to VL, 10.9.1924, J1/78.
39. On Mallul's pre-war activities, see: Ro'i, 'Nissionotaihem', pp. 215f.; Mandel, 'Attempts', pp. 254f.
40. VL meeting, 5.4.1922, J1/7225. Cf. p. 234, n. 30, above.
41. See: Mallul memoranda, 20.12.1922 (J1/289) and [March 1923] (S25/4384; Heb.); Ben-Zvi reports, VL meetings, 2.1. and 9.5.1923, J1/7226; Mallul to VLE, 11.2.1923, J1/289.
42. Details in file J1/8817.
43. Reports in files J1/289, J1/291 and S25/518. Cf. Ben-Zvi, VL meeting, 11.9.1922, J1/7225; Kisch to Stein, 13.3.1923, Z4/16035; Husni Abd al-Hadi [via Mallul] to HC, 25.8.1922, ISA 2/168; VLE–HC interview, 1.9.1922, J1/76; Porath, *Emergence*, p. 219.
44. See Porath, *op. cit.*, pp. 216, 220; below, pages 144f.
45. Hafiz al-Khawaja, Sept. 1922, J1/289.
46. Ibrahim 'Abdin to Mallul, 16.1.1923, J1/291; cf. 'Abdin to Kalvaryski, 15.4.1925, S25/10298.
47. Haidr Tuqan, n.d., J1/8817.
48. Mallul to S. Berger, 19.10.1922, J1/290.
49. Correspondence in files J1/289, J1/290 and J1/291.
50. *Zionist Review*, Jan. 1923, p. 354; 'ha-Hozeh' to Thon, 5.12.1922, J1/290; Thon, VL meeting, 2.1.1923, J1/7226; L. Lorenz to Mallul, 3.12.1922, J1/291.
51. PZE meeting, 26.3.1922, CZA (no file number). Cf. Stein to Eder, 7.7.1922, S25/4782.
52. For details, see: Golomb, *Hevion 'Oz* I, 286, 291f.; Jabotinsky to ZE, 5.11.1922, Z4/1396; van Vriesland to Weizmann, 22.11.1922, WA; Kisch to Weizmann, 16.1.1923, CZA, Z4/16049; Katznelson, *Writings* II, 37f.

53. See: Ro'i, 'Nissionotaihem', pp. 221f.; Cohen, *Israel and the Arab World*, pp. 88f. On an irregular basis, *as-Salam* would appear under the editorship of Mallul, while the *Doar ha-Yom* group would sometimes produce an Arabic bi-weekly *Barid al-Yawm*. But both these papers were too visibly Jewish to carry any real authority in the Arab world.

54. On *Halutzai ha-Mizrah*, see E. Eliachar, *Li-Hiyot 'Im Falastinaim* [Living with Palestinians], pp. 13f.

55. The following section is based mainly on Avissar's letter to VL, 12.3.1923, J1/78 and an undated circular, J1/72.

56. The Polit. Rpt. for Feb. 1923 (PRO, CO 733/43/14202) noted the appearance and contents of this pamphlet, but apparently did not regard it as dangerous enough to merit suppression.

57. For details about this group (involving Almaliah, Mallul, Moyal and others), see: Ro'i, 'Nissionotaihem', p. 204, n. 9; Chelouche, *Parshat Hayay*, pp. 167f.

58. Translation of an article entitled 'The Arab Fear of Zionism', *ha-Shiloah*, XLI, 99–108; cf. Klausner, *Darki Likrat ha-Tehia ve ha-Ge'ula* [My Path Toward Revival and Redemption], II, 161f.

59. Correspondence in J1/73 and J1/78. Cf. Storrs, Polit. résumé for period ended 31.8.1924, PRO, CO 733/73/45209.

60. Stein, 'Situation in Palestine, August 1921', para. 11.

61. For a fuller discussion of the British factor, see Caplan, 'The British Impact on Jewish-Arab Relations'.

62. E.g., Saphir, *Unity or Partition*; Cohen, *Israel and the Arab World*, esp. pp. 157, 165, 174.

63. E.g., Stein 'Situation in Palestine', esp. paras. 11, 17, 28; Stein to Kisch, 12.6.1923, CZA, Z4/16061; Kisch, 'Palestine Political Report', (n. 23); Kisch, *Diary*, pp. 19f., 46f., 75, 87, 112f., 126, 135, 142.

64. E.g., HC's private secretary to Meyuhas, 11.9.1922, CZA, J1/291 (Eng.); VL to HC, 22.9.1922, ISA 2/145; [Richmond?], for CS, to President, National Moslem Society, Jerusalem, 25.9.1922, J1/291 (Eng.); Kisch, *Diary*, p. 73.

65. See: VL meeting, 26.3.1923, J1/7226; Kisch, *Diary*, pp. 42f., 47, 59f., and unpublished diary, 22.3.1923, Z4/1392/II-B; VL to HC, 3.4.1923, J1/72; Stein to Kisch, 10.4.1923, and Kisch to Stein, 30.4.1923, Z4/16132.

66. E.g., Graves in *The Times*, 6.5.1921, p. 11; Samuel to Devonshire, 8.12.1922, PRO, CO 733/28/62328.

67. Deedes to Shuckburgh, 22.11.1921, PRO, CO 537/852. Cf. Samuel to Churchill (tgm.), 24.5.1921, CO 733/3/26134; Kedourie, 'Sir Herbert Samuel', in *Chatham House Version*, p. 71; *Haycraft Report*, pp. 52, 55.

68. Cmd. 1700, p. 18. This was endorsed dutifully in the *Report of the Executive to the XIIIth Zionist Congress (1923)*, p. 22.

69. Stein, 'Situation in Palestine', para. 28.

70. 'Memorandum to Members of the XIIIth Zionist Congress: Proposal for a Practical-Political Programme for a Solution to the Arab Question in Palestine', 25.7.1923, CZA, S25/4384 (Heb.).

71. VL meeting, 2–3.1.1923, J1/7226; Mallul to VLE, 11.2.1923, J1/289.

72. See, e.g., joint VLE–ZC meeting, 23.3.1921, J1/6282; Eder-Deedes interview, 4.1.1922, Z4/2701/V; Eder meetings with MNA representatives, 24.3., 30.3. and 2.4.1922, S25/4380; Miller to Eder, 13.6., 10.7. and 16.7.1922, *loc. cit.* (Heb.); Miller to VL, 14.3.1924, J1/78; Glickin to VL, 4.12.1922, J1/291; Kisch, *Diary*, pp. 126f.
73. Kalvaryski to Polit. Dept., ZE, 24.6.1923, S25/4793 (Heb.)

Chapter 8

1. Ormsby-Gore to Weizmann, 22.2.1919, WA. Cf pages 25 above, and 167 below.
2. See, e.g., Porath, *Emergence*, pp. 133f.
3. See: Porath, *op. cit.*, pp. 108, 224; above, pages 74, 81; Jamal al-Husaini to HC, 9.7.1921, ISA 2/244.
4. 'Palestine Political Report: Internal Policy', 31.5.1923, Z4/16061.
5. Churchill, *H of C Deb.* (Vth Ser.), vol. 143, col. 284 (14.6.1921); Samuel, quoted below, page 160; [Samuel]-Sulaiman Bey Nassif interview, 1.6.1924, ISA 2/142(2); Samuel, *Report (1925)*, p. 45 and *Memoirs*, p. 171.
6. Cf. Ch. 4, n. 52, above.
7. Samuel to Churchill, 8.5.1921, PRO, CO 733/3/24660. The remainder of this section is based on telegraphic correspondence in CO 733/3, files 23678, 25095, 25349 and 27792.
8. Weizmann to Money, 26.1.1919, *LPCW* IX, 105. Cf. his letters to Ormsby-Gore, 16.4.1918 (*ibid.* VIII, 130) and to Balfour, 30.5.1918 (*op. cit.*, pp. 201f.).
9. E.g., *Zionist Review*, Dec. 1919, p. 124.
10. Landman to Under-Secretary of State, CO, 1.6.1921, PRO, CO 733/16/27373. Cf. Weizmann to Samuel, 19.7.1921, *LPCW* X, 221; Medzini, *'Esser Shanim*, p. 197.
11. Jabotinsky, letter in *The Times*, 14.5.1921, p. 6. Cf. ZE to HC (tgm.), 6.5.1921, ISA 2/144.
12. Stein, 'Situation in Palestine,' para. 14. Cf. Caplan, 'The Yishuv, Sir Herbert Samuel, and the Arab Question'.
13. Stein, 'Situation in Palestine', para. 27. Cf. Ben-Zvi, VL meeting, 14.2.1923, J1/7226.
14. CZA, J1/8766/I (22.12.1918).
15. For Yishuv counter-proposals based on national-communal autonomy, see: Katznelson, *Writings* II, 47; Ben-Gurion, *Anahnu u-Shkhenenu*, pp. 72f.; Thon, notes for a speech [1926?], J1/76; Ben-Gurion, 'A Draft Constitution for Palestine', 23.11.1929, S25/6297; Burstein, *Self-Government of the Jews*, pp. 283f.
16. Report of interview, VLE meeting, 23.6.1921, J1/138.
17. VL meeting, 28–30.6.1921, J1/7224.
18. *Sefer ha-Te'udot*, p. 70.
19. Cmd. 1700.

20. *Palestine: Papers Relating to the Elections for the Palestine Legislative Council, 1923*, Cmd. 1889 (June 1923).
21. See Porath, *Emergence*, pp. 148f., and ISA file 2/168.
22. VLE-HC interview, 1.9.1922, CZA, J1/76. Cf. Ben-Zvi, VL meeting, 11.9.1922, J1/7225; van Vriesland to Stein, 3.9.1922, Z4/1053; Bentwich, *Mandate Memories*, pp. 68–9.
23. Kisch to Stein, 13.3.1923, Z4/16035. Cf. Kisch, *Diary*, p. 35; Porath, *Emergence*, pp. 152f.; Kedourie, *Chatham House Version*, pp. 74f.
24. CZA, J1/7226. Cf. Kisch to Stein, 18.2.1923, Z4/16035; Kisch, *Diary*, pp. 32f.
25. The major lines along which the Yishuv was split at this time were: (a) labour versus 'capitalists'; (b) Zionist (i.e., VL and PZE) versus anti-Zionist (mainly Jerusalem orthodox communities); and (c) Ashkenazi (or Jews of European origin) versus Sephardi (Jews of Mediterranean and Oriental origin).
26. Since early 1921, the VL had been active in presenting proposals for such an ordinance (which was to grant statutory authority for taxation, etc.), but this was not sanctioned by the British until late 1927. For details, see: Burstein, *Self-Government of the Jews*, pp. 157–70; *Sefer ha-Te'udot*, pp. 39, 75, 77–80, 81, 107–9; Kisch, *Diary*, pp. 126, 177f.
27. VL meeting, 2–3.1.1923, J1/7226. Cf. 'Declaration of the 3rd of June 1921: Its Consequences and Interpreters', 29.4.1922, J1/65 (Eng.).
28. VL meeting, 15.2.1923, J1/7226.
29. For details of the interview, see: Polit. Rpt. for Feb. 1923, PRO, CO 733/43/14202; Kisch to Stein, 18.2.1923, CZA, Z4/16035; Mossinsohn and Kisch reports, VL meeting, 18.2.1923, J1/7226.
30. Samuel to Devonshire, two letters dated 16.2.1923, PRO, CO 733/42/10140–1.
31. See Cmd. 1889, pp. 7–12.
32. Avissar and Kalvaryski, VL meetings, 26.3 and 9.5.1923, CZA, J1/7226.
33. Samuel comment, 18.7.1923, PRO, CO 733/47/35674.
34. Cmd. 1889, pp. 9f. The following account is based on Porath, *Emergence*, pp. 169f.
35. Kisch to Weizmann (tgm.), 3.6.1923, CZA, Z4/16035.
36. Details in: Kisch-Sulaiman Bey Nassif interview, 8.6.1923, WA; Kalvaryski to Polit. Dept., ZE, 11.6.1923, CZA, S25/10296 (Heb.); Kisch to Stein, 13.6.1923, Z4/16035.
37. Yellin-Thon-Kalvaryski interview with HC, 8.6.1923, J1/76.
38. On Kisch's efforts to win the cooperation of Raghib an-Nashashibi and 'Arif ad-Dajani, see Caplan, 'Arab-Jewish Contacts in Palestine', p. 655.
39. *The Times*, 17.7.1923, p. 11.
40. Weizmann to Churchill, 18.6.1921, in Cmd. 1700; reproduced in C. Sykes, *Crossroads to Israel*, pp. 69–70.
41. Stein to Mond, 19.7.1923, Z4/16050. Cf. Weizmann to Devonshire, 26.7.1923, *LPCW* XI, 348f.
42. Y. H. Castel, *ha-Aretz*, 25.7.1923.

43. *Ha-Tor*, 13.7.1923. Cf. *Zionist Review*, Aug. 1923, pp. 42f.

44. Kisch to Weizmann, 5.10.1923, CZA, Z4/16050. Cf. Weizmann to Kisch, 14.11.1923, *LPCW* XII, 26f.

45. Samuel to Churchill (tgm.), 24.5.1921, PRO, CO 733/3/26134. Cf. same to same, 31.5.1921, *ibid.*, file 27262; Churchill to Samuel (tgm.), 2.6.1921, *loc. cit.*

46. *Palestine: Proposed Formation of an Arab Agency*, Cmd. 1989 (Nov. 1923). Subsequent quotations are from this source.

47. *Official Gazette*, 1.12.1923, quoted in *The Times*, 4.12.1923, p. 12. Cf. *ibid.*, 24.12.1923, p. 9.

48. Cmd. 1989, p. 10. Cf. Kisch to Weizmann, 16.11.1923, CZA, Z4/16050; Kisch, *Diary*, p. 128.

49. Weizmann to Under-Sec. of State, CO, 15.11.1923, *LPCW* XII, 34f.; resolutions of VL meeting, 6–7.11.1923, *Sefer ha-Te'udot*, p. 91. Cf. press clippings in PRO, CO 733/51/57864; VL meeting, 6–7.11.1923, CZA, J1/7227; VLE-HC interview, 21.11.1923, J1/76.

50. See, e.g., Kalvaryski to James de Rothschild, 12.10.1923, S25/1180 (Fr.); Weizmann to Under-Secretary of State, CO, 15.11.1923 (n. 49); Kisch to Weizmann, 19.10 (Z4/16050) and 16.11.1923 (n. 48); Kisch, *Diary*, p. 75.

51. On the revival of discussions regarding a legislative council in the 1920s, see: Porath, *Emergence*, pp. 245–7, 254–7; Caplan, 'Arab–Jewish Contacts in Palestine', pp. 658f., 661.

Chapter 9

1. E.g., *Zionist Review*, Sept. 1917, pp. 70f., 82f.; *Zionist Bulletin*, 14.7.1920, p. 7; Ben-Gurion, *My Talks with Arab Leaders*, pp. 22f.

2. Censored extracts of ZC minutes, 16.6.1918, PRO, FO 371/3395, file W44/137853/11053; ZO Polit. Ctee. meeting, 16.8.1918, in *ibid.*, file W44/152266/11053. Cf. Kedourie, *England and the Middle East*, pp. 68 f. (on Mark Sykes).

3. Weizmann to Balfour, 30.5.1918, *LPCW* VIII, 202; *Zionist Review*, Dec. 1919, pp. 124f.; Ben-Gurion, *Anahnu u-Shkhenenu*, pp. 13–30, 55f.

4. Ro'i, 'Zionist Attitude', p. 220. Cf. Mandel, 'Attempts', p. 246, and *The Arabs and Zionism*, pp. 199, 206f.

5. 19.5.1936. *My Talks with Arab Leaders*, p. 68.

6. *Ibid.*, chs. 5, 7–9, 11–12.

7. On the history of Zionist-Faisal relations, see: Perlmann, 'Chapters of Arab–Jewish Diplomacy, 1918–1922'; Caplan, *Futile Diplomacy*, ch. 2.

8. E.g., Ben-Gurion, *My Talks with Arab Leaders*, pp. 4f.; I. M. Sieff, *Memoirs*, pp. 112f.; *ESCO* I, 562.

9. Jabotinsky, VZ meeting, 27.7.1920, CZA, J1/8799. Cf. pp. 18f., 32f., 48f., 58, above.

10. See sources in Ch. 4, n. 16, above; Stein, 'Situation in Palestine', para. 6; ISA, file 2/163.
11. *PRE XII ZC*, p. 52.
12. Nordau to Weizmann, 2.6.1920, Z4/16078. Cf. Eder memorandum, 18.6.1920, Z4/25118; E. Sasson to Ussishkin, 15.4.1920, L3/240 (Heb.); J. Caleb to Weizmann, 6.6.1920, Z4/16078 (Fr.); Felman, Damascus report, 20.6.1920, *loc. cit.* (Fr.).
13. E.g., Castel and Tolkowsky memoranda (above, pages 101f.); Stein, 'Situation in Palestine', paras. 6, 8.
14. Ruppin, *Memoirs*, p. 196. Cf. Eder to Weizmann, 13.11.1921, Z4/1250; same to same, 17.7.1922, WA; Kisch to Weizmann, 7.2.1923, CZA, Z4/16049.
15. Kisch, note of interview with Sa'id al-Bakri, 29.9.1923, Z4/16050; Kisch to Stein, 3.10.1923, *loc. cit*; Kisch to Weizmann, 21.3.1924, Z4/16028; Kisch, *Diary*, pp. 109f.; correspondence between Jacques Hoefler and Dr Weizmann, in CZA files Z4/1250, Z4/1392/II-A, S25/592 and S25/3548 and in WA; Cohen, *Israel and the Arab World*, pp. 245f.; p. 238, n. 53, above.
16. VL meeting, 5.4.1922, J1/7225. Cf. Cohen, *Israel and the Arab World*, p. 67; Castel, memorandum to XIIIth Zionist Congress (1923), 25.7.1923, S25/4384 (Heb.).
17. See, e.g., VLE-HC interview, 22.9.1922, ISA 2/145; Porath, *Emergence*, pp. 158f.; above, pages 123f.
18. 30.10.1922, CZA, S25/905 (Heb.).
19. Memorandum, [Oct. 1922], J1/289.
20. Stein 'Situation in Palestine', paras. 2, 12; Weizmann to Samuel, 19.7.1921, *LPCW* X, 221.
21. Eder to Weizmann, 30.10.1921, PRO, CO 733/16/57721. Cf. same to same, 27.11.1921, CZA, Z4/16151; Eder-Deedes interview, 27.12.1921, Z4/2701/V.
22. Stein to Eder, 2.12.1921, *loc. cit.*; Eder-Deedes interview, 27.12.1921 (n. 21).
23. Weizmann to Sokolow, 10.10.1922, *LPCW* XI, 185.
24. Actual records of these Weizmann-Abdallah talks do not seem to be available. For details, see Caplan, *Futile Diplomacy*, Ch. 3.
25. VL meeting, 28.11.1922, J1/7226. Cf. VL meeting, 2.1.1923, *loc. cit*.
26. Dr Weizmann did convene a closed meeting in Tel Aviv, but Ben-Zvi claimed that no VLE members had been present. Mossinsohn gave a coloured, anti-Weizmann account of the closed meeting to the VL meeting of 2.1.1923. As far as Weizmann was concerned, the Tel Aviv meeting was the 'Executive' meeting he had promised to inform, and he failed to understand the accusations brought against him. See Weizmann to Kisch, 7.2.1923, *LPCW* XI, 240f.
27. *Doar ha-Yom*, 31.12.1922. Cf. *Zionist Review*, Feb. 1923, p. 374.
28. *Ha-Aretz*, 1.1.1923; VL meetings, 2.1 and 9.5.1923, J1/7226; Katznelson, *Writings* II, 46f.; VL meeting, 6.11.1923, J1/7227; Kisch to Stein, 9.1.1923, Z4/16049.
29. Eder, *Palestine Weekly*, 19.5.1922, p. 345; Kisch to ZE, 12.12.1922,

Z4/4113; Jabotinsky memoranda, 10.12 and 29.12.1922, S25/2073; Weizmann report on Visit to Palestine, 15.2.1923, PRO, CO 733/62/9354; Samuel to Devonshire, 12.12.1922, CO 733/28/64281; Samuel to Curzon, 15.12.1922, ISA 2/128; [Deedes] to Shuckburgh, memorandum on Confederation of Arab States (n.d.), *loc. cit.*; Samuel interviews with Arabs, 11.2 and 15.2.1923, PRO, CO 733/42/10145.

30. Weizmann to Halpern, 13.6.1923, *LPCW*, XI, 332.
31. VL closed session, 2–3.1.1923, CZA, J1/7226.
32. See sources cited in n. 28, above; Kisch to Weizmann, 9.1, 10.1 and 16.1.1923, Z4/16049; *Doar ha-Yom*, 9.1.1923.
33. Kisch to Weizmann and to Stein, both 9.1.1923, Z4/16049; Kisch to ZE, 12.12.1922 (n. 29).
34. Kisch to Weizmann, 9.1.1923 (n. 33). Cf. same to same, 10.1.1923, *loc. cit.*; Kisch, VL meeting, 9.5.1923, J1/7226.
35. Weizmann to Kisch, 7.2.1923 (n. 26); Weizmann to Halpern, 13.6.1923, *LPCW* XI, 331f.
36. Report on Visit to Palestine, 15.2.1923 (n. 29). Cf. Stein to Philby, 26.3.1923, CZA, Z4/16135.
37. *Doar ha-Yom*, 23.4.1923; Kisch to Stein, 23.4.1923, Z4/16049. Neither Shuckburgh at the CO nor Samuel in Jerusalem were, in fact, ever sympathetic to the idea of 'Abdallah ruling over a re-united Palestine. See: Weizmann-Shuckburgh interview, 9.11.1922, Z4/16135; Stein-Shuckburgh interview, 19.1.1923, *loc. cit.*, Samuel conversations with Arabs, 11.2 and 15.2.1923 (n. 29).
38. For details, see: Kisch to Clayton, 25.4.1923, ISA 2/146; Kisch to Samuel, 25.4.1923, *loc. cit.*; Kalvaryski to Polit. Dept., ZE, 27.4.1923, CZA, S25/10296 (Heb.); Kisch, VL meeting, 9.5.1923, J1/7226; *ha-Aretz*, 6.5.1923; Polit. Rpt. for May 1923, PRO, CO 733/46/31975; Stein interviews with Meinertzhagen and Shuckburgh, 14–15.5.1923, CZA, Z4/16135.
39. Kisch to Stein 7.5.1923, Z4/16050. Cf. Kisch, *Diary*, pp. 55f.; Porath, 'The Palestinians and the Negotiations for the British-Hijazi Treaty, 1920–1925', pp. 20–35.
40. VL meeting, 9.5.1923, J1/7226.
41. Polit. Rpt. for May 1923 (n. 38); Kisch, *Diary*, pp. 56f.
42. Yellin-Thon-Samuel interview, 22.5.1923, CZA, J1/76; Porath, 'Palestinians and Negotiations', p. 35; sources cited below, n. 44.
43. Kisch, 'External Arab Situation', 21.5.1923, Z4/16061; Kisch to Stein, 22.5.1923, Z4/2421; Yellin-Thon-Samuel interview, 22.5.1923 (n. 42); *The Times*, 27.6.1923, p. 12; Kisch, *Diary*, pp. 57f.; *Report of Executive to XIIIth Zionist Congress (1923)*, p. 13.
44. Eisenberg remarks, VL meeting, 30.5.1923, J1/7228; Kisch to Stein, 30.5.1923, Z4/16050; Katznelson, *Writings* II, 46f.; Ahad ha-Am, *Essays, Letters, Memoirs*, p. 296; Yellin-Thon-Samuel interview, 22.5.1923 (n. 42).
45. Kisch to Stein, 27.5.1923, Z4/16050. Cf. his 'External Arab Situation', 21.5.1923, and his letter to Stein, 22.5.1923 (n. 43), which are more optimistic.

46. Kisch to Stein, 30.5.1923 (n. 44). Cf. Kisch, *Diary*, p. 60. The follow-ing account of the VL meeting is based on the minutes, 30.5.1923, in J1/7228.
47. Official communiqué, quoted in *Rpt. of Exec. to XIIIth Zionist Con-gress (1923)*, pp. 13f. Cf. *ESCO* I, 481f.
48. See: Porath, 'Palestinians and Negotiations', pp. 36f. and *Emergence*, pp. 111, 178f., 225f.; *Zionist Review*, July 1923, p. 38; Kisch to Stein, 24.6.1923, Z4/16061; Kisch, Report on VIth Palestine Arab Congress, 25.6.1923, PRO, CO 733/46/34366.
49. Stein to Under-Secretary of State, CO, 27.6.1923, CO 733/59/32588. Cf. *Rpt. of Exec. to XIIIth Zionist Congress (1923)*, pp. 13f., 61; Stein interviews with Ormsby-Gore and Shuckburgh, 31.5.1923, CZA, Z4/16060; Weizmann to Stein, 18.6.1923, *LPCW* XI, 335; Weizmann to Vansittart, 27.6.1923, *loc. cit.*
50. Porath, 'Palestinians and Negotiations', pp. 44f., and *Emergence*, p. 226; Kisch to Weizmann, 21.1.1924, Z4/16028; *The Times*, 24.1.1924, p. 9; *ESCO* I, 484.
51. Kisch-Samuel interview, 4.1.1924, Z4/16071; Kalvaryski to Riad as-Sulh, 11.1.1924, S25/10297 (Fr.).
52. VLE–HC interview, 13.1.1924, J1/76. Cf. Kisch to Weizmann, 21.1.1924 (n. 50); Kisch-Samuel interview, 23.1.1924, Z4/16071; Kisch, *Diary*, pp. 92f.
53. Kisch to Weizmann, 21.1.1924 (n. 52); cf. Kisch-Samuel interview, 4.1.1924 (n. 51); Kisch, *Diary*, p. 93.
54. Kisch-Samuel interview, 23.1.1924 (n. 52).
55. The following account is based on the report (31.1.1924) by Yellin in J1/3487. Cf. Kisch, *Diary*, pp. 94f.; Cohen, *Israel and the Arab World*, pp. 191f.; *Zionist Review*, March 1924, p. 111.
56. Kisch, *Diary*, pp. 95f.
57. Avissar, Radler-Feldman, VL meeting, 3.3.1924, J1/7227; PZE to Weizmann (tgm.), 16.2.1924, Z4/16028; Kisch to Sokolow, 21.2.1924, *loc. cit.*; *ESCO* I, 420.
58. *al-Muqattam*, 27.2.1924, Eng. translation in Z4/2421; Weizmann statement to Jewish Telegraphic Agency, 5.2.1924, *loc. cit.*; Weizmann to Marshall, 13.2.1924, *LPCW* XII, 129f.
59. Kisch, unpublished diary, 4.2.1924, CZA, Z4/2421 and *Diary*, pp. 97f.; Kisch to ZE, 6.2.1924, Z4/2421; Kisch to Stein, 16.3.1924, *loc. cit.*; Kisch to Weizmann, 21.3.1924, Z4/16028.
60. Kisch, VL meeting, 3.3.1924, CZA, J1/7227; Kisch to Sokolow, 21.2.1924 (n. 57).
61. E.g., *New Judaea*, 10.10.1924, p. 20; Kisch to Landau, 27.10.1924, CZA, Z4/16071.
62. Zionist attention soon turned to Ibn Saud and Arabia. See: Kisch, *Diary*, p. 210; ZAC meeting, 4.6.1926, A137/93.
63. See, inter alia, Arlosoroff, *Yoman Yirushalayim*; Kisch, *Diary*, p. 374; Ben-Gurion, *My Talks with Arab Leaders*; M. Sharett, *Yoman Medini* [Political Diary]; E. Elath, *Shivat Zion ve-'Arav* [Zionism and the Arabs].

Conclusion

1. E.g., Katznelson, *Writings* II, 46f.; *New Judaea*, 3.7.1925, p. 337; Assaf, *Hit'orirut*, pp. 102f.
2. See, e.g., *Zionist Review*, July 1924, pp. 33f. and Jan. 1926, p. 104; Weizmann to Samuel, 14.11.1923, WA; Kisch, *Diary*, p. 144; Samuel, *Report (1925)* p. 5, 40f.
3. E.g.: 'The great mass of Arabs are realising, first that Zionism will never be abandoned; and, secondly, that its implications, as now being worked out, far from menacing them, enable them to live happily side by side with the Jews, and even to profit from their economic progress.' *New Judaea*, 19.12.1924, p. 112. Cf. Kisch, *Diary*, p. 194.
4. *Ha-'Olam*, 12.12.1924, copy in CZA, A113/13 (Heb.). Cf. Ruppin, *Memoirs*, pp. 215f.
5. *New Judaea*, 21.11.1924, pp. 78f.; Kisch to Landau, 27.10.1924, Z4/16071.
6. Symes report, 6.12.1923, PRO, CO 733/63/3301; Symes report, 28.4.1924, CO 733/68/26359; Samuel to Thomas, 25.1.1924, CO 733/63/5508; Storrs, Polit. Résumé for Jaffa/Jerusalem, period 9.4. to 15.5.1925, CO 733/93/2583.
7. Cf. pages 100, 114 and 142, above; Ruppin, *Memoirs*, p. 191; Kisch, *Diary*, p. 137; *PRE XII ZC*, p. 57; VL memorandum to HC, 27.6.1921, CZA, J1/6282; Bein, *Return to the Soil*, p. 282.
8. Kisch to Cowen, 16.12.1923, CZA, Z4/16104. Cf. Kisch, *Diary*, pp. 27, 137, 150.
9. See: Above, page 132; Kisch, *Diary*, p. 161; Kalvaryski to Kisch, 15.9.1925, S25/10327 (Fr.); file S25/10298; *ESCO* I, 345, 586; Ben-Gurion, *Igrot* II, 351; Jacobson to Weizmann, 3.7.1925, WA (Fr.).
10. *New Judaea*, 26.9.1924, p. 8; Kalvaryski, *ha-'Olam*, 12.12.1924 (n. 4); *Zionist Review*, June 1925 (p. 17) and Jan. 1926 (p. 104).
11. Symes report, Nov. 1924, PRO, CO 733/76/59814; Storrs, résumé, 9.4.–15.5.1925 (n. 6); Samuel, *Report (1925)*, pp. 11, 40f., 43.
12. For details, see: Jacobs to Kisch, 20.7.1924, CZA, S25/751; Ruppin-Thon-Clayton interview, 1.9.1924, Z4/16028; Kisch to Weizmann, 24.9.1924, *loc. cit.*; Kalvaryski to Rothschild, 8.9.1924, A113/25/1 (Fr.).
13. See *ESCO* I, 370, 584f. and II, ch. 10.
14. *My Talks with Arab Leaders*, p. 80 (9.6.1936). Cf. *ESCO* I, 584f.; Storrs, *Orientations*, pp. 357, 377; *Peel Report*, p. 131; Laqueur, *History of Zionism*, p. 259.
15. On the Muslim-Christian alliance, see: Porath, *Emergence*, pp. 276f., 293f.; Kedourie, *Chatham House Version*, pp. 317f., 340f.; Storrs, *op. cit.*, p. 371, n. 1.
16. E.g., Frumkin, *Derekh Shofet*, pp. 219f.; Cohen, *Israel and the Arab World*, pp. 158f.; A. S. Yahuda to Weizmann, 7.3.1920, CZA, Z4/16033 (Heb.); Kalvaryski, memorandum (n.d.) on the Muslim-Christian alliance, S25/10295 (Fr.).
17. Yessod ha-Ma'aleh Ctee. to Kalvaryski, 29.6.1923, *loc. cit.* (Heb.). Cf.

D. Miller (Nablus) to Eder, 13.6. and 16.7.1922, S25/4380 (Heb.); Miller to Kisch, 9.8.1924, S25/518 (Heb.).

18. Kalvaryski to James de Rothschild, 4.2.1925, A113/25/1 (Fr.).

19. See, e.g., Porath, *Emergence*, pp. 208f., 242; Samuel, *Report (1925)*, p. 43; Medzini, *'Esser Shanim*, pp. 245f.

20. Ben-Zvi, VL meeting, 5.4.1922, J1/7225, and VLE meeting, 6.4.1922, J1/139. Examples of such islands were non-Sunni Muslim minorities (Mutawwali, Druse, Circassians, Samaritans). See: Golomb, *Hevion 'Oz* I, 313; Kalvaryski to Szold, 19.7.1919, Z4/16044 (Fr.); B. 'Ibri to Weizmann, 30.9.1919, *loc. cit.*; Glickin to VL, 21.6.1921, J1/300.

21. *New Judaea*, 3.7.1925, p. 338.

22. Kisch to Stein, 14.3.1923, Z4/16049. Cf. Kisch, *Diary*, pp. 27, 34, 56.

23. VL meeting, 14.2.1923, J1/7226.

24. *Loc. cit.* Cf. Caplan, 'Arab-Jewish Contacts in Palestine', pp. 656f.

25. See, e.g., Moshe Smilansky's attempt to break the 1936 general strike by a 'bridge of silver' as described in Ben-Gurion, *My Talks with Arab Leaders*, pp. 77f.

26. For details, see: Assaf, *Yihasim*, p. 92; Duff, *Sword for Hire*, pp. 112, 128; VL to Storrs, 15.3. and 22.3.1923, ISA 2/169; Levin to Kisch, 1.5.1924, CZA, Z4/4112; Kisch, *Diary*, pp. 111, 113; VL correspondence with outlying colonies, files J1/72, J1/73 and J1/78.

27. *STH* II/1, 207; Kisch to Weizmann, 5.12.1923, Z4/16050; Kisch to Stein, 22.4.1924, Z4/4112; *Zionist Review*, June 1924, p. 19, and June 1925, p. 17; Porath, *Emergence*, p. 134; Samuel, *Report (1925)*, p. 5.

28. *Hevion 'Oz* I, 301. Cf. *ibid*., pp. 280, 282, 286; *STH* II/1, 164, 242f. and II/3, 1140f.

29. Samuel to Devonshire, 12.12.1922, PRO, CO 733/28/64281. Cf. same to same, 8.12.1922, *ibid.*, file 62328.

30. Deedes to Young, 15.2.1922, CO 733/38/9616; Deedes to Shuckburgh, 22.12.1922, ISA 2/128.

31. E.g., Symes reports, 6.12.1923 (n. 6) and Nov. 1924 (n. 11); Cox to ACS (Pol.) 24.12.1923, PRO, CO 733/63/3301; Clayton to Devonshire, 6.7.1923, CO 733/47/35674; Samuel to Thomas, 25.1.1924 (n. 6).

32. *My Talks with Arab Leaders*, p. 12.

33. Interview with Sulaiman Bey Nassif, 25.1.1923, WA.

34. Conversation with Philby, 4.12.1922, CZA, Z4/1392/II-B. Cf. above, pages 175f.

35. Kisch to Weizmann, 21.3.1924, Z4/16028.

36. *PRE XII ZC*, p. 52. It is likely that V. Jabotinsky was the author of this report.

37. Kisch to Tolkowsky, 26.12.1923, S25/751; *Zionist Review*, Aug. 1923, p. 42; Kisch, VL meeting, 3.3.1924, J1/7227; Kisch, *Diary*, pp. 132, 178.

38. Levin to Kisch, 1.5.1924, Z4/4112. Cf. Kisch, *Diary*, p. 177; B. Jacobs to Under-Secretary of State, CO, 29.4.1924, PRO, CO 733/84/20555. Ben-Gurion, *Anahnu u-Shkhenenu*, p. 91; Katznelson, *Writings* II, 159.

39. VLE meeting, 16.4.1925, CZA, A153/152(A) (Heb.). Cf. Ben-Gurion, *loc. cit.*
40. VL meeting, 13.5.1925, J1/7228. Cf. *New Judaea*, 8.5.1925, pp. 279f.
41. *Report (1925)*, pp. 24–40; extracts quoted here are from pp. 32, 40.
42. E.g., Ruppin, *Memoirs*, p. 218; Kisch, *Diary*, p. 190; Dizengoff farewell speech for Samuel, n.d., CZA, J1/76; Bentwich, *Mandate Memories*, pp. 104f.
43. Two exhaustive critiques were Ben-Gurion, in *Anahnu u-Shkhenenu*, pp. 84–94 and Katznelson, in *Writings* II, 153–61. The former was the 'milder' of the two, but still invoked comparisons between Samuel's administration and the previous military régime (1917–20). The latter is discussed below.
44. E.g., Rabbi B. Uziel to VL, 2.12.1924, J1/73; Epstein to VL, 10.9.1924, J1/78; Kalvaryski, 'Situation politique', 9.10.1924, S25/10297 (Fr.).
45. See: Kisch, *New Judaea*, 26.9.1924, p. 8; sources cited in n. 2, above; Kisch, *Diary*, pp. 50f., 73, 75, 86, 136f., 141, 147f.
46. Kalvaryski to Rosenheck, 2.12.1923, S25/10296 (Fr.); Kalvaryski to Shvueli, 13.7.1924, S25/10297 (Heb.); Kisch to Franck, 12.1.1928, S25/10320; VL meeting, 18.6.1924, J1/7227.
47. VL meeting, 13.5.1925, J1/7228. Cf. Radler-Feldman, VL meeting, 18.6.1924 (n. 46); Assaf, *Yihasim*, pp. 92f.; Ruppin, *Memoirs*, pp. 215f.
48. Jabotinsky to Kisch, 4.7.1925, S25/2073. Cf. Laqueur, *History of Zionism*, pp. 256f.
49. VL meeting, 13.5.1925, J1/7228. Cf. *ha-Aretz*, 26.8.1925; Kisch, *Diary*, pp. 89f., 199f.
50. Berligne and Schiller spoke most forcefully in this sense. Cf. Aaronsohn's outspoken condemnation of Kalvaryski's mixed school near Rosh Pina. *Arab Bulletin*, 27.9.1917, pp. 389f.
51. See: Ruppin, *Memoirs*, pp. 216–20 and *passim*; Hattis, *Bi-National Idea*, pp. 38f.; circular letter, 24.11.1925, in CZA, A113/25/1 (Heb.); Laqueur, *History of Zionism*, pp. 251f.; Elon, *The Israelis*, pp. 183f.
52. Ben-Gurion, *My Talks with Arab Leaders*, p. 22.

Bibliography

I. Unpublished Sources

A. ARCHIVES

Note on Archival Sources. Some of the material cited in the footnotes may be found in more than one archive. For brevity, I have cited only one source (the original, wherever possible). I have also cited PRO sources and have omitted the Israeli location of documents which are available in both places. Scholars in Europe and in North America may find this more useful, as CO and FO files are available in several libraries on microfilm.

The language of the original documents cited in the notes is *English*, *except*:

(a) all files in the CZA, J1 series, which are *Hebrew* in the original, and
(b) where otherwise indicated (French, German, Yiddish).
  Translations from the Hebrew and the French are my own.

Crown copyright records appear by permission of the Controller, Her Majesty's Stationery Office.

1. *The Central Zionist Archives, Jerusalem* (CZA)
  Series J1 : *Va'ad Zmani, Va'ad Leumi*
  Z4 : Zionist Organisation, Central Office, London (ZO)
  L3 : Zionist Commission, Jerusalem (ZC)
  L4 : Zionist Commission, Jaffa (ZC)
  S25 : Political Department, Palestine Zionist Executive (PZE), Jerusalem
  Private Archives: A113: Haim Margaliut Kalvaryski
  A153: David Yellin
  plus: occasional sources in A199 (Gad Frumkin), A18 (Nahum Sokolow), A182 (Harry Friedenwald), A226 (Samuel Landman), A137 (Shlomo Kaplansky), L2 (Palestine Office, Jaffa).

2. *The Israel State Archives, Jerusalem* (ISA)

Series 2: Chief Secretary, Palestine Government (including Civil Secretary, OETA (S))
Series 100: Herbert Samuel Papers
Series 103: Edwin Samuel Papers
3. *Weizmann Archive, Rehovot* (WA)
    Chronologically arranged.
4. *Public Record Office, London* (PRO)
    Series CO 733 : Colonial Office – Palestine
            CO 537 : CO – Palestine (Supplementary)
            FO 371 : Foreign Office – General Correspondence, Political
5. Private Papers Collection, Middle East Centre, St. Antony's College, Oxford
    Sledmere Papers (Mark Sykes)
    Humphrey Bowman, Diary
B. OTHER
Arab Bulletin, Cairo, 1917–1918 (PRO).
'Report of the Court of Inquiry ... regarding the Riots in Jerusalem', 1.7.1920, PRO, FO 371/5121, file E9379/85/44. (Cited as *Palin Rpt*.)
Stein, Leonard, 'Situation in Palestine, August 1921', PRO, CO 733/16/52260. (Cited as Stein, 'Situation in Palestine')

II. Published Sources

A. GREAT BRITAIN: OFFICIAL PUBLICATIONS

1. *Command Papers*: Colonial Office: Palestine (in chronological order)
    Disturbances in May, 1921: Reports of the Commission of Inquiry with Correspondence Relating Thereto, Cmd. 1540, October 1921. (Cited as *Haycraft Rpt*.)
    Correspondence with the Palestine Arab Delegation and the Zionist Organisation, Cmd. 1700, June 1922.
    Mandate for Palestine, together with a Note by the Secretary General Relating to its Application to the Territory Known as Trans-Jordan ... , Cmd. 1785, July 1922.
    Papers Relating to the Elections for the Palestine Legislative Council, 1923, Cmd. 1889, June 1923.
    Proposed Formation of an Arab Agency: Correspondence with the High Commissioner for Palestine, Cmd. 1989, November 1923.
    Palestine Royal Commission, *Report*, Cmd. 5479, July 1937. (Cited as *Peel Rpt*.)
2. *Other*:
    Colonial Office, Palestine: *Report of the High Commissioner on the Administration of Palestine, 1920–1925*, Colonial No. 15, 1925. (Cited as Samuel, *Report (1925)*.)
    ———, Palestine Commission on the Disturbances of August 1929, *Evidence Heard ... in Open Sittings*, Colonial No. 48, 1930.

Documents on British Foreign Policy, First Series, vol. IV ed. E. L. Woodward and R. Butler, London 1952.
————, vol. XIII, ed. R. Butler and J. P. T. Bury, London 1963.
Parliamentary Debates, House of Commons, Fifth Series – occasional references, 1921–1923.

B. PRESS AND PERIODICALS

New Judaea, Zionist Organisation, London.
The Times, London.
Zionist Bulletin, Zionist Organisation, London.
Zionist Review, English Zionist Federation, London.
ha-Aretz, Tel Aviv.
Doar ha-Yom, Jerusalem.
Kuntres, Tel Aviv.
ha-'Olam, Zionist Organisation, London.
ha-Po'el ha-Tza'ir, Tel Aviv.
ha-Shiloah, Odessa and Tel Aviv.

C. OTHER PUBLISHED WORKS

Aaronsohn, Aaron, *Yoman, 1916–1919* [Diary], Tel Aviv 1970.
Ahad ha-Am, *Igrot* [Letters], Jerusalem/Berlin 1925 (vol. VI, 1918–1921).
————, *Essays, Letters, Memoirs*, ed. & tr., Sir Leon Simon, London 1946.
Ahdut ha-'Avoda, *Palestine and Jewish Labour: Two Documents*, London 1921.
Allon, Yigal, *Shield of David: The Story of Israel's Armed Forces*, London 1970.
Almaliah – See: Elmaleh.
Alsberg, P. A., 'ha-She'ela ha-'Arevit bi-M'diniut ha-Hanhala ha-Tzionit lifne Milhemet ha-'Olam ha-Rishona' [The Arab Question in the Policy of the Zionist Executive before the First World War], *Shivat Zion*, IV (1956–7), 161–209.
Antonius, George, *The Arab Awakening*, London 1938.
Arlosoroff, Haim, *Kitvai Haim Arlosoroff* [Writings], Tel Aviv 1934 (vols. I and III).
————, *Yoman Yirushalayim* [Jerusalem Diary], 2nd ed., Tel Aviv 1949.
Assaf, Michael, *Hit'orirut ha-'Aravim be-Eretz-Israel u-Vrihatam* [The Arab Awakening in and Flight from Palestine], Tel Aviv 1967.
————, *ha-Yihasim ben 'Aravim ve-Yehudim be-Eretz-Israel, 1860–1948* [Arab-Jewish Relations in Palestine], Tel Aviv 1970.
Bardin, Shlomo, *Pioneer Youth*, New York 1932.
Bein, Alex, *The Return to the Soil*, Jerusalem 1952.
Ben-Avi, Ittamar, *'Im Shahar 'Atzma'utenu* [With the Dawning of our Independence], Tel Aviv (?) 1961 (posthumous autobiography).
Ben-Gurion, David, *Anahnu u-Shkhenenu* [We and our Neighbours] Tel Aviv 1931 (articles and speeches).

———, *Igrot* [Letters], ed. & annotated, Y. Erez, Tel Aviv 1971 and 1972 (vol. I – 1904–1919; vol. II – 1920–1928).

———, *Ben-Gurion Looks Back in Talks with Moshe Pearlman*, London 1965.

———, *My Talks with Arab Leaders*, Jerusalem/New York 1972.

———, *Zikhronot* [Memoirs], Tel Aviv 1971 (vol. I).

Bentwich, Norman and Helen, *Mandate Memories, 1918–1948: From the Balfour Declaration to the Establishment of Israel,* New York 1965.

———, and Michael Kisch, *Brigadier Frederick Kisch: Soldier and Zionist,* Vallentine, Mitchell & Co., London 1966.

Ben-Yehuda, Hemda, *Nosseh ha-Degel: Hayai Ittamar Ben-Avi* [The Standard Bearer: The Life of Ittamar Ben-Avi], Jerusalem 1944.

Ben-Zvi, Yitzhak, *The Hebrew Battalions*, tr. T. Baker & M. Benaya, Jerusalem 1969 (letters and articles).

———, *Kitvai Yitzhak Ben-Zvi* [Writings], Tel Aviv 1936 (vols. I and IV).

Boustany, W. F., *The Palestine Mandate: Invalid and Impracticable,* Beirut 1936.

Bowle, John, *Viscount Samuel*, London 1957.

Breslavski, Moshe, *Tnu'at ha-Po'alim ha-Eretzyisraelit* [The Palestinian Labour Movement], Tel Aviv (?) 1956 and 1966 (vols. I and II)

Burstein, Moshe, *Self-Government of the Jews in Palestine Since 1900*, Tel Aviv 1934.

Caplan, Neil, 'Arab-Jewish Contacts in Palestine After the First World War', *Journal of Contemporary History* XII (1977), pp. 635–68.

———, 'The British Impact on Jewish-Arab Relations in Palestine', *Wiener Library Bulletin*, XXXI (1978), new series nos. 45.

———, *Futile Diplomacy: A Study of Zionist-Arab Negotiation Attempts, 1913–1939* (forthcoming).

———, 'The Yishuv, Sir Herbert Samuel, and the Arab Question in Palestine', *Middle Eastern Studies* (forthcoming).

Chelouche, Yosef Eliahu, *Parshat Hayay,* 1870–1930 [Autobiography], Tel Aviv 1930/1.

Cohen, Aharon, *Israel and the Arab World*, New York 1970.

Crossman, Richard, *A Nation Reborn*, London/Rehovot 1960.

Duff, Douglas V., *Sword for Hire*, London 1934.

Eisenstadt, S. N., *Israeli Society*, London 1967.

Elath, Eliahu, *Shivat Zion ve-'Arav* [Zionism and the Arabs], Tel Aviv 1974.

Eliachar, Elie, *Li-Hiyot 'Im Falastina'im* [Living with Palestinians], Jerusalem 1975.

Elon, Amos, *The Israelis: Founders and Sons*, London 1972 (paperback ed.).

Epstein, Elias M., *Jerusalem Correspondent, 1919–1958*, ed. M. Medzini, Jerusalem 1964.

Epstein, Yitzhak, 'She'ela Ne'elma' [An 'Unapparent' Question], *ha-Shiloah*, XVII (1907), 193–206.

ESCO Foundation for Palestine, Inc., *Palestine: A Study of Jewish, Arab, and British Policies*, New Haven 1947 (vol. I.)

Frumkin, Gad, *Derekh Shofet bi-Irushalayim* [The Way of a Judge in Jerusalem], Tel Aviv 1954.

Gilner, Elias [Eliahu Ginzburg], *War and Hope: A History of the Jewish Legion*, New York 1969.

Golomb, Eliahu, *Hevion 'Oz* [Hidden Strength], Tel Aviv 1950 (vol. I; collected letters and articles).

Graves, Philip, *Palestine, The Land of Three Faiths*, London 1923.

Hattis, Susan Lee, *The Bi-National Idea in Palestine During Mandatory Times*, Haifa 1970.

Haycraft – See: II. A. 1, above, 'Disturbances in May . . .'

Hobman, J. B. (ed.), *David Eder: Memoirs of a Modern Pioneer*, London 1945.

Howard, Harry N., *The King-Crane Commission: An American Inquiry in the Middle East*, Beirut 1963.

Hurewitz, J. C., *Diplomacy in the Near and Middle East: A Documentary Record*, 1914–1956, Princeton, N. J. 1956 (vol. II).

al-Husri, Abu Khaldun Sati, *The Day of Maysalun: A Page from the Modern History of the Arabs*, tr. S. Glazer, Washington 1966.

Ingrams, Doreen (ed.), *Palestine Papers 1917–1922: Seeds of Conflict*, London 1972.

Jabotinsky, Vladimir [Ze'ev], *Neumim, 1905–1926* [Speeches], Tel Aviv 1940.

———, *The Story of the Jewish Legion*, tr. S. Katz [from the Russian, 1928], New York 1945.

Kalvaryski, Haim Margaliut, 'Programmes and Speeches', in *'Al Parshat Darkainu* [At the Parting of Our Ways], Jerusalem 1939.

Katznelson, Berl, *Igrot, 1919–1922* [Letters; really 1919–1921], Tel Aviv 1970 (vol. I).

———, *Kitvai Berl Katznelson* [Writings], Tel Aviv 1946 and 1950 (vols. I (3rd ed.) and II).

Kedourie, Elie, *The Chatham House Version and other Middle Eastern Studies*, Cass, London 1970.

———, *England and the Middle East: The Destruction of the Ottoman Empire*, London 1956.

Khalidi, Walid (ed.), *From Haven to Conquest: Readings in Zionism and the Palestine Problem until 1948,* Beirut 1971.

Kisch, Frederick H., *Letter to the Chairman, Political Commission, XVIIth Zionist Congress* . . . (1931), Jerusalem, June 1931.

———, *Palestine Diary*, London 1938.

Klausner, Yosef, *Darki Likrat ha-Tehia ve-ha-Ge'ula* [My Path towards the Revival and the Redemption], 2nd ed., expanded and corrected, Tel Aviv 1955 (part B; autobiography).

———, 'Pahad ha-'Aravim mipne ha-Tzionut' [The Arab Fear of Zionism], *ha-Shiloah*, XLI (1923–4), 99–108.

Klieman, Aaron S., *Foundations of British Policy in the Arab World: The Cairo Conference of 1921*, Baltimore/London 1970.

Laqueur, Walter, *A History of Zionism*, London 1972.

———, (ed.), *The Israel-Arab Reader: A Documentary History of the*

Middle East Conflict, rev. ed., London 1970.

Mandel, Neville J., *The Arabs and Zionism Before World War I*, London/Berkeley 1976.

———, 'Attempts at an Arab-Zionist Entente: 1913–1914', *Middle Eastern Studies*, (1964–5), 238–267.

———, 'Turks, Arabs and Jewish Immigration into Palestine, 1882–1914', in *St Antony's Papers*, no. 17 (Middle Eastern Affairs, no. 4; ed. A. Hourani), Oxford 1965, pp. 77–108.

Medzini, Moshe, *'Esser Shanim shel Mediniut Eretzyisraelit* [Ten Years of Palestine Politics], Tel Aviv 1928 (a highly original historical study, from which it appears that the author had free access to confidential Zionist and VL sources).

Meinertzhagen, Richard, *Middle East Diary, 1917–1956*, London 1959.

Miller, David Hunter, *My Diary of the Peace Conference*, New York 1924 (vols. IV and XIV).

Mossek, Moshe, *Palestine Immigration Policy under Sir Herbert Samuel: British, Zionist and Arab Attitudes*, Cass, London 1978.

Nevakivi, Jukka, *Britain, France and the Arab Middle East: 1914–1920*, London 1969.

Palin – See: I. B., above, 'Report of the Court . . .'

Patterson, John Henry, *With the Judaeans in the Palestine Campaign*, London 1922.

Peel – See: II.A.1, above, 'Palestine Royal Commission'.

Perlmann, Moshe, 'Chapters of Arab-Jewish Diplomacy, 1918–1922', *Jewish Social Studies*, VI (1944), 123–154.

Porath, Yehoshua, 'The Palestinians and the Negotiations for the British-Hijazi Treaty, 1920–1925', *Asian and African Studies*, VIII, 2 (1972), 20–48.

———, *The Emergence of the Palestinian-Arab National Movement, 1918–1929*, Cass, London 1974.

Ro'i, Yaacov, 'Nissionotaihem shel ha-Mosdot ha-Tzioniyim le-Hashpi'a 'al ha-'Itonut ha-'Arevit be-Eretz-Israel ba-Shanim 1908–1914' [The Attempts of the Zionist Institutions to Influence the Arabic Press in Palestine], *Zion*, XXXII, 3–4 (1967), 200–27.

———, 'The Zionist Attitude to the Arabs, 1908–1914', *Middle Eastern Studies*, IV (1968), 198–242.

Ruppin, Arthur, *Memoirs, Diaries, Letters*, ed. A. Bein, tr. from the German, K. Gershon, London/Jerusalem 1970.

———, *Pirkai Hayay* [Chapters of My Life], ed. & tr. from German, A. Bein, Tel Aviv 1968 (vol. III).

———, *Three Decades of Palestine: Speeches and Papers on the Upbuilding of the Jewish National Home*, Jerusalem 1936.

Salaman, Redcliffe N., *Palestine Reclaimed: Letters from a Jewish Officer in Palestine*, London 1920.

Samuel, Edwin, *A Lifetime in Jerusalem*, Vallentine, Mitchell & Co., Jerusalem 1970.

Samuel, Herbert L., *Memoirs*, London 1945.

————, *Report (1925)* – See: II.A.2, above, 'Colonial Office, Palestine: *Report . . .* '

Saphir, Ascher, *Unity or Partition?*, Jerusalem 1937.

Schechtman, Joseph B., *Rebel and Statesman: The Early Years*, The Jabotinsky Story, vol. I, New York 1956.

Sefer ha-Te'udot shel ha-Va'ad ha-Leumi le-Knesset Israel be-Eretz-Israel, 1918–1948 [Documents of the VL], ed. M. Attias, 2nd enlarged ed., Jerusalem 1963 (valuable source-book of resolutions, memoranda and correspondence of the VL).

Sefer Toldot ha-Hagana [History of the Hagana], ed. B. Dinur *et al.*, 2nd ed., Tel Aviv 1964 (vol. I, pt. 2; vol. II, pt. 1; vol. II, pt. 3 – notes and appendices. Authoritative history of the Hagana in the broader framework of an original social and political history of the Yishuv as a whole; deals with and reproduces material from the CZA, WA, Labour Archive and its own private archives).

Sereni, Enzo and R. E. Ashery (eds.), *Jews and Arabs in Palestine: Studies in a National and Colonial Problem*, New York 1936.

Sharett [Shertok], Moshe, *Yoman Medini* [Political Diary], eds. A. Malkin, A. Sela, E Shaaltiel, 4 vols., Tel Aviv 1968–74.

Sieff, Israel, *Memoirs*, London 1970.

Simon, Leon, and Leonard Stein (eds.), *Awakening Palestine*, London 1923.

Sprinzak, Yosef, *Igrot* [Letters], Tel Aviv 1965 (vol. I – 1910–1929).

Stein, Leonard, *The Balfour Declaration*, Vallentine, Mitchell & Co., London 1961.

Storrs, Ronald, *Orientations*, definitive ed., London 1943.

Sykes, Christopher, *Crossroads to Israel, 1917–1948*, Bloomington/London 1973.

Tidhar, David (ed.), *Entziklopedia le-Halutzai ha-Yishuv u-Vonav* [Encyclopaedia of the Pioneers and Builders of the Yishuv], Tel Aviv 1947–1971 (19 vols.).

Trager, Hanna, *Pioneers in Palestine*, London 1923.

Weizmann, Chaim, *The Letters and Papers of Chaim Weizmann*, Series A. Letters, vols. VIII–XII [November 1917 – March 1926], General Editor: Meyer W. Weisgal, New Brunswick, N.J./Jerusalem 1977.

————, *Trial and Error*, London 1949 (autobiography).

————, 'Zionist Policy', speech to EZF, London, 21.9.1919.

Ya'ari-Poleskin, Y., *Pinhas Rutenberg: ha-Ish u-Fe'alo* [The Man and his Work], Tel Aviv 1939.

Yana'it (Ben-Zvi), Rahel, *Coming Home* [Anu 'Olim], tr. D. Harris & J. Meltzer, Tel Aviv 1963.

Yellin, David, *Kitvai David Yellin* [Writings], vol. V (*Igrot* [Letters], vol. ii), Jerusalem 1976.

Zeine, Zeine N., *The Struggle for Arab Independence*, Beirut 1960.

Zionist Organisation, *Political Report of the Executive . . . to the XIIth Zionist Congress*, Carlsbad, September 1921 ('Zionism During the War: A Record of Political Activity, 1914–1921'), London 1921.

————, *Report of the XIIth Zionist Congress*, Carlsbad, September 1st-14th 1921: Addresses, Reports, Resolutions, London 1922 (drastic abridgement of full German 'Protokoll').

————, *Stenographische Protokoll des Verhandlungen des XII Zionisten-Kongresses in Karlsbad . . .*, Berlin 1922.

————, *The Mandate for Palestine*, memo to the Council of the League of Nations, July 1922. London 1922.

————, *Report of the Executive to the XIIIth Zionist Congress*, Carlsbad, August 6th–18th 1923, London 1923.

Index

NOTE: * indicates biographical note (Appendix II).